R. D. LAING

R. D. LAING

A Personal View

BOB MULLAN

Duckworth

First published in 1999 by
Gerald Duckworth & Co. Ltd.
61 Frith Street, London W1V 5TA
Tel: 0171 434 4242
Fax: 0171 434 4420
Email: enquiries@duckworth-publishers.co.uk

A catalogue record for this book is available
from the British Library

ISBN 0 7156 2889 5

Typeset by Ray Davies
Printed in Great Britain by
Biddles Limited, Guildford and King's Lynn

Contents

For Jessica and Alex

Nothing is worth more than this day.
Goethe.

A look filled with understanding, an accepting smile, a loving word, a meal shared in warmth and awareness create happiness toward the Other.
Thich Nhat Hahn

It is easier to write ten volumes of philosophy than to put a single precept into practice.
Leo Tolstoy

Plates

The author would like to thank the following people for the use of their photographs.

1. R.D. Laing, Torquay, 1947. (Marcelle Vincent)
2. R.D. Laing, conference in Leuven, 1965. (Ross Speck)
3. Marcelle Vincent, Loch Lomond, 1949. (Marcelle Vincent)
4. John Bowlby. (Sir Richard Bowlby)
5. Charles Rycroft. (The Institute of Psychoanalysis)
6. D.W. Winnicott. (The Institute of Psychoanalysis)
7. Mary Barnes, Summer 1971.
8. Leon Redler, Kingsley Hall, 1967. (Leon Redler)
9. R.D. Laing and Victoria Crowe, London 1974. (M.K. Walton)
10. Victoria Crowe painting R.D. Laing for the Scottish National Gallery, London 1974 (M.K. Walton)
11. Portrait for the record sleeve, *Life before Death*, 1978. (Hag, aka Ian Hargreaves)
12. Jutta Laing, R.D. Laing, Jill Purce and Fritjof Capra, Zaragoza, Spain, 1980. (Fritjof Capra)
13. R.D. Laing and others, Zaragoza, 1980. (Fritjof Capra)
14. R.D. Laing, Zaragoza, 1980. (Theo Itten)
15. R.D. Laing, Zaragoza, 1980. (Theo Itten)
16. R.D. Laing and Allen Ginsberg, Hampstead, 1985. Photo by Tom Pickard. (The late Allen Ginsberg)
17. Thomas Szasz, Elly Jansen, R.D. Laing and Bernard Posner, London, 1984. (Elly Jansen)
18. R.D. Laing in his study, Hampstead 1985. (The late Allen Ginsberg)
19. Johnny Duffy and R.D. Laing, Glasgow, 1987. (Johnny Duffy)
20. R.D. Laing, Naropa Institute, Boulder Colorado, July 7th, 1987. Photo by Allen Ginsberg. (The late Allen Ginsberg)
21. R.D. Laing and Marguerita – 'two days after Charles's conception' – Boulder, Colorado, 1987. (M. R-K)
22. Charles, Marguerita, and R.D. Laing, 1988. (M. R-K)
23. Charles and R.D. Laing, 1988. (M. R-K)
24. R.D. Laing with son, Benjamin, early 1989. (Sue Sünkel)
25. R.D. Laing, the day before he died, St Tropez, 22nd August 1989. (M. R-K)

Preface

Austria, 1989.

Ronnie Laing, Marguerita Romayne-Kendon – his companion and mother of his tenth child – and I were enjoying dinner at my hotel in Kitzbühel. I was on one of my regular visits to Ronnie, tape-recording lengthy conversations with him for my book on his life and work. It had been a good day and Ronnie was on form. Despite having been teetotal for some time, he still had the capacity – and the desire – to shock, to be charming, funny, amusing – in other words to be his usual inimitable self. In full view of the other diners – and in fact with their eyes on him – he removed a dental plate from his mouth. He inspected it, and then laid it with some reverence beside his plate of broccoli. Even Marguerita, though his intimate for a number of years, was surprised by his audacious behaviour. He laughed loudly and raucously at her mild disapproval. I raised my eyebrows and commented that it was just as well he wasn't drinking, otherwise everyone in the hotel would hear him, not just our fellow diners. Marguerita concurred. At this point, Ronnie decided that everyone would indeed experience the pleasure of his voice. He proceeded to sing a few notes of some indecipherable song. A waiter *en route* to the kitchen threw him a disapproving glance, and this only served to fuel Ronnie's desire to express himself. Marguerita smiled at him indulgently and I waited for us to be thrown out.

Introduction

On a particularly wet Swansea morning at the University of Wales, I met an experimental psychologist called Pearl Parker. After the initial pleasantries, we somehow began to discuss the relationship between psychology and spirituality. Pearl let me into her secret: that whilst attempting to measure accurately the immeasurable, she was in addition an accomplished clairvoyant. Her penchant was shared by other members of her family, and especially her mother. She could see that, despite my good-natured response, I was not overly impressed with her alleged psychic skills. I *am* open-minded about the mysteries of the universe but still find it difficult to take seriously the claims of clairvoyants and stories of the 'other side'. But Pearl is one of life's charmers, and so I agreed to submit myself to a reading.

At about eleven o'clock, with the rain now lashing the walls of the University buildings, she asked if she could keep my watch for a couple of hours. I agreed, of course, despite a sudden increase in my scepticism. We agreed to meet at one o'clock for the actual session, where she would do whatever she believed she actually did.

Swansea is famous for its rain. As a new arrival in January of that year I asked a newsagent when he thought it might stop raining. 'April', was his measured reply. I was soaked to the skin within minutes by the relentless rain as I crossed the campus to meet Pearl. The overwhelming feeling that I was wasting my time was merely increased by my unpleasant journey and now my sodden clothing.

Pearl wore her pitch-black hair in the fashion that Cher favoured when she first performed with her now deceased and ex-husband, Sonny. Witch-like, one might say, somewhat uncharitably. When I arrived she was gently but purposefully rubbing my watch between her slender fingers. Wide-eyed she asked me to be seated. Then the reading unfolded.

I had become increasingly sceptical due to a previous experience at the hands of an alleged clairvoyant whom, whilst in 'contact' with the spirit world, felt the need to speak to me entirely in Spanish. Apparently, some Spaniard, dead for several centuries, had felt the need to communicate with me, despite my not knowing a word of his mother tongue.

My experience with Pearl was much less exotic. Instead I found it profoundly disturbing.

Pearl returned my watch to me as soon as we began. I never did ask her why she needed it. She closed her eyes but did not emit any bizarre sounds or shake her head in any involuntary manner. Rather she took on the appearance of someone puzzled, inquisitive. Perhaps this was a natural consequence of her hybrid nature. Within minutes she told me that a man wanted to talk with me, and asked me if I knew who he might be. Because she appeared so genuine about her endeavours and was herself so endearing, I offered a considered guess, namely that it was bound to be my late father. However, Pearl continued to repeat some of the comments this man was supposedly making about me and, by virtue of their exceedingly perceptive nature, I realised that this could not be my father. At that moment I imagined, not in a spirit of hostility but of amusement, that this was Pearl's own intuition at work not William Mullan's.

Fifteen minutes or so into our encounter I experienced something I can only describe as deeply disturbing. Following a knowing smile, Pearl informed me that the voice was becoming clearer. It, or should I say he, told her that every night he would see me 'in checks, looking in a mirror in the large white building'. Despite my misgivings, this appeared to describe quite accurately – without any leap of imagination on my part – my nightly teeth-cleaning ritual in my tartan pyjamas standing in front of the bathroom mirror in my flat, itself part of a large white Little Venice house*. I could not imagine how Pearl could have possibly known about this, and I felt somewhat uneasy at this moment. Literally, the hairs running along my spine moved their position, and I felt very cold. Again Pearl offered me another smile and told me that he was definitely a Scotsman.

I knew it was Ronnie.

* I was later to discover that Laing himself had briefly lived in the same house with Marguerita Romayne-Kendon, his final female companion.

I was once told by a Sufi sheykh in Cairo that he could astrally project himself anywhere in the world at that very moment. I suggested London. He refused: my scepticism remained. And so, although I desperately wished to believe I was experiencing a conversation with a dead man, I remained convinced that I wasn't, and I felt very sad about it.

Another fifteen minutes passed. Pearl began to look exhausted and appeared to be suffering terribly from her role as psychic conduit. She repeated some of the voice's observations on my state of mind and emotional state which, at that particular time of my life, were somewhat variable. I felt I needed some sort of 'proof', which was to me a surprising reaction, given that my major response to the reading was a mixture of playfulness and healthy, congenial scepticism. I was discomforted and required a route out of the impasse.

Pearl suggested that I asked him to repeat something about which only he and I knew. Accordingly I asked her to get the voice to talk about our last evening together. Once more Pearl gave one of her smiles, followed by a tired laugh. She then recounted an evening I had spent with Ronnie and Marguerita in Kitzbühel, close to where he was exiled in Going, Austria. Over dinner he had exhibited the roundness and uniqueness of his person. This exhibition included some peculiar eating habits, involving the removal of a dental plate, much laughing and considerable warmth. She also repeated how Marguerita and I had gently suggested between ourselves that the entire restaurant might well be treated to the pleasure of his raucous voice. Ronnie was of course Ronnie, and heroically made certain they did indeed hear the singing voice of R. D. Laing.

Pearl remained calm and dignified when I began to cry. After all, she hardly knew me. She was simply a colleague. I muttered something about him being like a father to me, not that my own father had *not* been a father to me, but rather he was around when I needed someone wise, and wise he was. Pearl's final smile was almost maternal, despite her tender years, when she warmly reported that Ronnie had told her to tell me he was looking out for me. He was keeping an eye on me. That I was not to worry.

Since that momentous time I have remained open-minded about the mysteries of life, if only a little less sceptical. I still cannot make sense of it, but somehow I have come to believe the truth of it. And is this surprising? I still cannot fathom the exact process whereby the Internet can almost instantaneously put me in contact with someone in Texas who, like me, is interested in Lithuanian art. Neither can I fully understand the precise mechanisms of memory whereby, for example, I can recall episodes from over thirty years previously after a serendipitous thought.

The story does not end with Pearl helping me leave the room, eyes sore with tears and heavy heart. Since that time I have seen 'Ronnie' on two occasions. Each time the circumstances and the locations were different, but unmistakably I encountered him. Both times the moment I had left the situation – once at a London Underground station, the other at a newsagent – I recognised him and then he was gone. The two faces did not particularly resemble his, but there was no mistake. It was him. Yet I am neither mad nor am I an incurable romantic.

As he is looking after me, I feel I ought to look after R. D. Laing. He certainly needs it. Since his death a number of biographies have appeared, all of which emphasise the undoubted truth: he was an imperfect human being. Less has been written about the fact that he *remains* the inspiration for thousands of us who are professionally or personally concerned with issues of mental distress. Nevertheless, despite the numerous biographies, there are many who know next to nothing about the profound ideas and the powerful writing of R. D. Laing. It is my aim in this biography to rectify that. The Laing within these pages is Laing, pure and simple; unreconstructed and unmitigated.

When R. D. Laing died in 1989 I was engaged in writing his authorised biography, of course with his full co-operation. Had he not died at that time, this book would already have appeared and would have much more resembled a conventional biography: a narrative formed out of hundreds of interviews with those who knew or claimed to know him. However his death resulted in a number of the Laing family deciding, for their own reasons, that it was inappropriate for me to continue. Following ten years of silence I have now decided to attempt to write about the individual who has influenced me philosophically more than anyone else. Ronnie enabled me to make sense of my life.

R. D. Laing was an unconventional man, and I have written an unconventional biography. In parts I have made much use of my own personal experience, for two reasons: firstly, I want to make the point that the damaging patterns of family behaviour which Laing identified and illustrated can occur, unrecognised and unquestioned, in any family. The patterns of mystification and confusion, double binds, no-win situations, seething resentment and dangerous secrets may not result in psychologically damaging a family member to the point of 'schizophrenia'. And of course, neither parents nor siblings deliberately set out to psychologically maim anyone. The process is often the result of unconscious motivation. However, this does not alleviate the victim's plight: life in a psychic no-man's land, with pain the only ally, and retreat into a private world the only salvation. This is the family life that Laing described and I want to make the point that one doesn't have to be diagnosed as a schizophrenic to have suffered from it. Secondly, my experiences in psychiatry and psychotherapy have taught me that Laing's critique of both was salient and urgent. At first hand, I have witnessed the degradation of patients in so-called asylums and other places of purported sanctuary. I have seen it inflicted on others, and I have had it inflicted on me. And the harmful and anti-human tendencies within psychiatry still flourish, with no R. D. Laing to speak out against them. So, in a very real sense, I include aspects of my own life experience as *evidence,* as proof that his ideas have true validity and relevance, and also in hope that he is listened to with more understanding and sympathy. Because the suffering he so vividly described goes on. But there is no new R. D. Laing to speak out against current psychiatric practice, no new R. D. Laing to write books which make people think about their own lives, and their effect on others. Above all, I want to show that Laing's ideas were more than mere froth and bubble. They were powerful enough to change people's lives, and I can prove this assertion, because they changed my life.

If this book results in readers turning to Laing's own works, my aim will have been realised. Duncan Double, Steven Gans, Tracy Mullan and Leon Redler have all helped me enormously but, of course, the opinions and errors remain mine alone.

London, March 1999

1

Disturbed and Disturbing Families

In the present state of society, it was impossible to say anything serious which would have a wide or deep effect ... (and) ... the conflict between Left and Right, particularly since the collapse of Marxism, now seemed one of ridiculous pettiness. The quality of the men and women entering politics, the puerile level of political debate in the newspapers, the fatuity of religious leaders and the absolute void left by the diminishing popularity of religion meant that it was almost impossible to imagine that the human race would ever again hear those tones of grave and interesting ethical discussion which had characterised the last century.

A. N. Wilson *Dream Children.*

Oliver Gold, the central character of Wilson's novel, is a failed academic or, more correctly, a conventional academic and therefore a poor scholar. Reflecting on his career he recognises that it is absurd to have thought of himself as a potentially great philosopher, yet such is the 'parochialism of the university, and the power of personal vanity', that he has entertained such a conceited belief for a number of years. He had fantasised that perhaps, given time and comfort, he would produce an epic work, one that would halt the decline of the West. Instead, after a summer reading and studying Hegel, he discovered that he was 'little more than a pygmy'. But Oliver, nevertheless, feels pain at the human condition as he presently observes it in the 1990s. The families he encounters are the sort which switch on their radio at breakfast and talk to each other simultaneously. He doubts that their hearing systems are more sophisticated than his, so he can only conclude that they are listening neither to the broadcast nor to each other. For Oliver, this becomes a paradigm of the human condition in the late twentieth century. 'No serious person could be heard above the din'. He imagines Hegel, or Tolstoy, being forced to squeeze their reflections into three-minute sound-bites, interrupted by jingles and traffic news, and then talked over by families munching their way through their breakfast.

In the September of 1969 I had never heard of R. D. Laing. One month later, after reading *The Politics of Experience and The Bird of Paradise*, he had changed my life – my view of life, my recollection of life and in fact my *experience* of life. From that moment I began to view the world in what I believed was a Laingian way.

I was a social work student studying at the less than salubrious Stevenage College of Further Education, a collection of small buildings found on the edge of a myriad of cycleways and footpaths, themselves situated just off the centre of this (in)famous new town. It was the only educational establishment that had accepted me, on account of its own need to recruit as many students as possible. The dismal fact that I had failed *all* of my school exams was, graciously, dismissed or at least ignored. The course formally began in the September, though it had been a requirement for us all to undertake beforehand an 'observation fortnight' in a children's department or a mental health office.

My two weeks were spent in Nuneaton, where I had been raised and was looking forward to leaving. Unlike the present time, social work in 1969 was conventionally carried out by the kind and the bureaucratic. It was more of a vocation, less of a career. Much of the work of the children's department was indeed bureaucratic and legally-bound, and very little involved seemingly pointless attempts at keeping families together in the face of relentless poverty and deprivation. Divorce was less common, sexual child abuse was seldom spoken about, and large children's homes still existed.

The majority of those social workers with whom I rubbed shoulders in the autumn of 1969 were middle-aged and well-spoken. They were probably merely in their thirties but, of course, they seemed old to me at that time of my youth. Many seemed religiously-motivated and indeed the phrase 'social work is the moral equivalent of war' was one which was often shared in the office. No one seemed to have too much difficulty with concepts such as *right and wrong*, and everyone appeared to believe that their role was totally justified and legitimate.

As is the way with these matters of coincidence, I was supervised by the one unconventional man in the office. Always smelling lightly of alcohol, I discovered, some months later, that he was the one and only social worker to have been dismissed by the council, his misfeasance being that of theft. Money which should have found its way into the pockets of foster parents was diverted into his own pocket, and paid for his alcoholism instead. At the time of being supervised by this man I was never certain what his accent signified: I realise now that it was the accent of a drunk. He disguised the full impact of his consumption exceedingly well.

Most of the time we would simply talk. Occasionally, we visited children in homes or met prospective foster parents. His talk was, not surprisingly, fulsome and at times exotic. I always left a conversation with him certain that I would never know as much as he about human nature, or deal with people in the way in which he appeared to be able, or understand the complex laws pertaining to social work. It was all so new to me. His *pièce de résistance* occurred following the one occasion in which he asked me to interview a young boy. This fifteen year old had begun to deviate from the straight and narrow. As a favour to his mother who was one of my supervisor's clients, I was to 'understand' him, and then 'dress him down'. This was something I had never previously attempted, having only recently emerged from my own troubled adolescence. Possessing only a stripped-down version of Freudian theory, my supervisor suggested I manoeuvred the discussion around to the subject of masturbation. *My* understanding of Freud was zero, and in fact I'd never previously heard his name.

As arranged the boy came to see me after school. He appeared almost as nervous as I certainly felt. We were polite and exchanged pleasantries. After a gruelling thirty minutes of such verbal shadow-boxing I came out with it: 'do you masturbate?' His denial was gentle yet decisive. We shook hands, he left.

The following day I described the encounter and again asked why it was a question of such relevance. I was treated to what I now realise was another cod-like account of Freudian theory, and my supervisor's less-than-clear and certainly bizarre beliefs as to the importance of masturbatory habits in the formation of juvenile delinquency. He said he would personally demonstrate the technique required to elicit the necessary information and arranged for the victim to return. 'How many times do you wank a night?', he asked. 'About twice', came the reply. My supervisor smirked at me, the boy left, and I never did learn what it was that I was supposed to have gleaned from the lesson.

The journey to Stevenage entailed my finally leaving home, my severance from my parents. Their immediate concern was where I would live, given that Stevenage College was in no position to provide accommodation. My father was a devout Catholic and so it was the parish priest from whom he sought guidance. And accordingly, two weeks later, I was on a southbound train heading towards a Catholic family who had agreed to provide me with lodgings.

My first impression of my Stevenage hosts centred around *size*. They were an Irish couple and extremely short in height: both approximately five feet tall. As they opened the door to me, together, they were further dwarfed by the size of the statue which was so prominent it could not help catch my eye. St Theresa holding roses.

I'd arrived late on Sunday evening. After the obligatory handshakes there was a knock at the door. In stepped the local parish priest, with a head as shiny as anything I had ever seen. Further handshakes, and then we all got down onto our knees, following his suggestion that we prayed together. We asked the Lord to make my stay in Stevenage a fruitful and happy one.

My hosts were so mean, they epitomised and possibly gave a new emphasis to the definition of the word. Despite their being practising Christians, they apparently knew little of the concept of Charity, even if they did know the theory. I was allowed one bath a week, and even then I was requested to keep the water to a minimum level. They encouraged me to stay late at the college, not for the benefit of my education, but to save electricity in my bedroom. I am sure they would have liked, if they were able, to police my use of electricity totally, but they had to leave the house at 5 a.m. to begin their jobs as shelf-stackers at a local supermarket. And this absence led to their greatest act of meanness. So frightened were they that I would have a blitz with the electrical supply, that they cooked my breakfast at 4.45 a.m. and left it on the table with a tea towel on top. As a result most mornings, at about 8.30, I would sit in silence attempting to devour cold rubbery eggs and limp toast, swilled down with equally cold tea. In the four months that I endured life there I never did ask them 'why?', nor did they voluntarily proffer an explanation.

My leaving was somewhat spectacular. My hosts had made it more than obvious that they disapproved of my staying at weekends, so often I would trek back to Nuneaton or stay locally with fellow students. On the one or two occasions that I did stay, they felt it incumbent upon themselves to try to improve my spiritual state. Invariably this would involve them regaling me with lengthy accounts of the many pilgrimages they had undertaken including photographic testimonies of Lourdes miracles. This particular Saturday there was a student party and I tentatively arranged to remain in the house over the weekend. It was around 4 a.m. when I arrived home, completely and utterly drunk. I tip-toed up the stairs as best I could and fell into bed, fully-clothed. I awoke within the hour desperately thirsty. I did not trust myself to get back downstairs to the kitchen and I did not dare use the bathroom. Suddenly I remembered that my hosts kept half a dozen bottles of 'holy water' in my wardrobe. I quickly consumed the contents of all six.

At 7.30 a.m. there was a knock on the bedroom door. It was my landlady. I said I couldn't possibly attend holy mass that morning as I had the flu. Then I saw her go to the wardrobe. Her one look spoke a thousand words. I was packed and out the house before midday.

Before Stevenage College I had never read a book cover-to-cover except Robert Louis Stevenson's *Kidnapped*. It was therefore hardly surprising that I found the books on the required reading list incomprehensible. Both Goffman's *Stigma* and *Asylums* were, to me, impenetrable, and the recommended social work texts seemed short on common sense and overloaded with jargon. I would sit in the library and stare at the pages whilst everyone around me *read*. My tutors made the right noises and assured me that it would all make sense in time. Despite such assurances I was convinced that my student career would be very short lived. Then I came across R. D. Laing's *The Politics of Experience and The Bird of Paradise*.

Given my interest in Laing, it is not surprising that I jumped at the opportunity to see him at a conference in London, organised by the Association of Social Psychiatry. It was March 1971, and I was on the eve of completing my social work course. The speakers were Laing, his colleague David Cooper, a relatively unknown Soviet psychiatrist, and Doris Lessing, who was plugging her psycho-novel *Briefing for a Descent into Hell* – opening lines, 'Category: Inner-space fiction. For there is never anywhere to go but in'. A packed audience was informed that Laing would be speaking after lunch.

Prior to this we were treated to Doris Lessing's description of her literary *modus operandi*. By denying herself food and sleep for a few days she was able to induce in herself an artificial state which she termed 'psychosis'. Amazingly, this state would disappear immediately after-wards once the keyboards had completed the literary task. Her delivery was monotonous yet pleasingly, somewhat hypnotic. She would begin almost every sentence with the words, 'It seems to me ...' This was followed by a pointless discussion on the precise nature of the 'psychosis' she claimed she had induced. Shortly afterwards the Soviet doctor spoke at length about the 'special hospitals' in his country. Meantime, David Cooper, who had been constantly swigging from bottles of red wine was finding it difficult to pay attention, or to stay in his seat. Much of the time he carried on a discussion with a member of the audience. It was his contribution which was to follow.

Cooper was introduced courtesy of a song performed by a young American psychiatrist, the lyrics of which castigated the psychiatric system and pleaded for freedom for all. Then it was clear that Cooper himself was unable to speak at all, and he merely laughed and slumped. Many of the audience were disgusted and aired their discontent. I found it somewhat reassuring that not everyone followed convention.

It was difficult to concentrate on lunch with the expectation that soon I would be listening to Laing. After we all resumed our seats the Chairman broke the news: 'R. D. Laing is preparing to leave the country to undertake some spiritual education in Ceylon'. I was just one of many who left the hall somewhat bewildered and disappointed at the news that my hero had left the stage.

By that time I had seen at first hand the insanity of much of what passes for *therapy*. At that particular time my own experience of therapy was limited, though varied in scope. Following a particularly unpleasant sexual experience at the tender age of fifteen, an occasion that could best be described as rape of an underage male by a woman, I found the physical attentions of women frightening and bewildering. So in 1970 I was persuaded by someone who claimed to know about these things to consult a psychoanalyst about my problem.

It was a particularly sultry day, and London seemed bleached out. I squinted my way around Holland Park, the address of the analyst who allegedly *specialised* in the matter I was about to disclose. It was the first time I had ever encountered an entry phone – such items being scarce on the ground in Nuneaton – and I was standing there a good five minutes with voices and noises carrying on around me. Eventually I was admitted. The creature who met me at the top of the stairs appeared bloodless: pale, almost motionless and emotionally distant. Despite the sun outside, his consulting room was dark and cavernous, lit only by an old-fashioned standard lamp. Velvet curtains adorned the room.

In the kind of voice that *still* renders me deferential, he explained how I was to pay him. He told me nothing of the treatment or the process. Anyone completely unfamiliar with psychoanalysis might find the following account of what transpired between myself and Dr Z surreal or at least bizarre. But believe me, it is an honest empirical account of the proceedings.

He indicated to me that I was to lie down on an unfamiliar piece of furniture, which I now know to be a *chaise-longue*. He had offered me the more easily recognisable alternative of a chair, but I felt so tired and confused that I welcomed the possibility of rest. For what must have been a good ten minutes neither of us uttered a word. Of course I cannot know what Dr Z was thinking about during those deeply unsettling minutes – perhaps weighing up his new patient, or dreaming of a white Christmas – but I just kept thinking 'thirty five pounds for fifty minutes, and he's not saying anything!'

It was I who broke the silence: 'should I be saying something?' 'Do you *want* to say something?' 'Perhaps I should tell you why I am here – when my problems began. That kind of thing?' Again silence. So I nervously and clumsily recited the script I had mentally rehearsed on the journey to see my saviour. Only once did he interrupt, in order to clarify what seemed to me an insignificant remark. After forty minutes of this *charade* I was already of the opinion that I was wasting my time and that Dr Z was a fraud. 'Sometimes I feel so *dirty* ...' – his ears pricked up. 'I go home and have to take a shower, to make myself really *clean* ...' The good doctor drew in his breath, which at least confirmed that he *was* alive, and uttered a sentence from the authority of his years' training and experience: 'I see. You have a water fetish'. 'Pardon?' 'You are, in my opinion, sexually attracted to hot water'. Not knowing whether to laugh or cry I made my way home, determined that his was one invoice which would remain unpaid.

At around the same time I underwent another kind of therapeutic experience when I attended an encounter group. At Stevenage College I

met a remarkable man named Jim Stringer. He had given a guest lecture
at the college and had spoken of the works of Carl Rogers, William
Schutz and others of the so-called human potential movement in psychology. Noting our collective enthusiasm, he suggested we formed our
own small encounter group. Membership totalled some nine students
with Jim acting as the 'facilitator'.

One of the exercises involved was that of the 'empty chair', a procedure which involved someone sitting in the middle of the circle. I
volunteered, in the belief that this would grant me preferential therapeutic attention. I was wrong. Instead I suffered a sense of humiliation. I was
asked to present to the group my 'self': so I smiled openly, somewhat
smugly. Within moments the smile had receded, and was replaced by the
downward turn of my mouth. Followed by tearfulness. The revelation of
my truer self was painful, like peeling layers off an onion, and I could
feel a general sadness in the room, in addition to my own keen pain.
Despite the empathy and the physical comforting which followed, I felt
damaged. I was a confused, melancholic and possibly depressed person
inhabiting a convivial skin. I felt unfit and ill-equipped to cope in the
world.

This group lasted eight weeks, and the finale of each weekly session
would involve all ten of us, Jim included, lying on the floor hugging each
other tight. Some would cry, some would kiss. Being puritanical and
innocent I would lie there imagining what my parents would say were
they to see me writhing on the floor with strangers. Indeed, similar
thoughts crossed my mind when we shared our sense of psychological
pain and injustice: that we felt shy, that we suffered jealousy, that we
experienced low self-esteem. My parents had no time for such sentiments
and were far too busy trying to feed their children and just survive. Who
is to say who was the better off?

My obvious vulnerability and apparent intelligence appealed to Jim
Stringer. After one particularly open encounter, during which an older
student colleague confided to us her husband's sexual impotence – an
admission followed by much mutual stroking and cuddling – I was left
emotionally drained and discomforted. Jim suggested I visited his home
that weekend to talk.

Reaching *chez* Stringer involved a drive along an off-road path, deep
into the woods of Hertfordshire. His cottage was a home for numerous

children, small animals and his wife, a dreamy astrologer. We ate mung beans and talked. At midnight we sat outside while he explained our smallness in the face of greater things: like the stars above. *But*, he added, at the same time each of us are nonetheless such unique and precious creatures. He had a profound effect upon me, and was one of my first mentors. Jim looked like Carl Gustav Jung, one of *his* mentors, and I intuitively felt that I was in the presence of a wise man. Unfortunately, we drifted apart.

Memory is selective. It would perhaps be impossible to remember everything which we experienced when young – moments of terror, experiences of joy, sensations of uncertainty. Yet of course we *do* remember bizarre events and often at the most unexpected of moments. This ability to retrieve coded messages and transmit them to us as memory, on an apparently *ad hoc* autonomous basis, is persuasive and cohesive evidence of the incredible power of the mind. It may well be that we are capable of what George Orwell termed 'double-think': whilst storing and retrieving events and information which are significant to us, simultaneously we are able to suppress – and forget the act of suppressing – events which are truly significant. Motivated forgetting, as it is sometimes called. And of course we sometimes simply forget, more so as we age. However true such propositions may be, they are largely beside the point. What we *act* on are those memories which we have decided, for one reason or another, should stay. By and large these are the memories that help to construct, reconstruct and deconstruct our chameleon-like image of 'self'.

I can remember absolutely nothing before the age of seven years. I certainly remember nothing of my birth, let alone any pre-birth intra-uterine experience. But what comes clearly to mind is a memory of playfully running up a hill, in the company of my father, thinking to myself 'I'm seven'. Simply that.

I was born into a respectable working-class family. My father was a proud Scotsman, exiled to the Midlands and working on the night shift at one of the many car factories which dotted the local map at that time, most of which have since disappeared. His exile was precipitated by the death of his brother who had perished in a pit accident. Unable to face the loss of another child to the pits, my grandmother sent her other son away from the coal fields of Scotland and down to Coventry. My mother was already with him, so she came too. Not having any recognisable employment skills, she took the only work which women in her situation could easily obtain – cleaning floors and washing dishes. This was, of course, in addition to her own domestic chores which included taking care of two children, my sister and I.

As young, un-socialised, naïve creatures my sister and I were friends. Once independent and more wily, we chose not to like each other. We shared an ordinary house, small, functional, unprepossessing, replete with flying ducks. Its yellow nicotine walls were the only irregular feature.

In my formative years my sister and I became particularly close after she almost died of pneumonia. I really thought she would die. She would squeal with pain when the doctor inflicted the daily dose of penicillin, through a needle the size of a baseball bat. The dingy bedroom, the fearful smell, the doctor's nonchalance and my own distress all remain in my memory. Not surprisingly I developed a 'respect' for doctors which could more accurately be described as fear.

My memories of early family life are less visual and more olfactory. I can smell the house and the people who inhabited it. For far too many years my mother suffered from rheumatoid arthritis. The sight of her in excruciating pain saddened and secretly angered me: why does my mother have to suffer? And: why can't I have an ordinary mother? I also felt that somehow, for some particular unspecified reason, it was my fault that she suffered. I can still remember the smell of the various creams she applied to her wrists and fingers, and which I rubbed into her neck and shoulders. Her pain was treated with the ubiquitous steroid Brufen, which actually appeared to do very little to ease her suffering. What it did achieve, however, was the distortion of my mother's face and the additional pain of gastric bleeding. In her sixties, what should have been little less than the prime of her life, she had to resort to the indignity of baby food. That smell lingers, alongside the taste of my anger.

On schooldays, my father would wake me with a cup of tea. As my schoolday was about to begin, his workday had already ended. I can still recall the reassuring aroma of mechanical oil which surrounded him on these early mornings. Unfortunately a kiss from either my mother or my father necessitated intimate contact with their heavily-nicotined breath. Both of them smoked enormous quantities of cigarettes daily and like the walls in the house, their fingers were stained yellow by nicotine. Later, they paid the price. My father in particular implored me never to take up the 'dirty habit' from which he appeared to take such pleasure. Today, the more I look into the mirror, the more I see him. I look increasingly like him and, if I stare long enough and with sufficient concentration, I can turn my face into his. He appears, so to speak.

'God gives and God takes away': whenever I asked any particularly complex question about God, this would be my father's reply. He was a fervent Roman Catholic, passionate and committed, yet in no way a proselytiser. I attended weekly church services, but with mixed feelings. The hymns and the untranslated Latin touched my soul and awakened in me a sense of mystery, yet I was also bored. Up and down, up and down, up and down: the standing and the kneeling and the standing and the kneeling seemed to have no apparent purpose apart from being painful to the body. But my father was a proud man when he was at church. This is surely what Marx meant when he talked of religion being the 'sob of the oppressed creature, the heart of a heartless world'*. It wasn't the 'opium of the people' in the sense of blinding them to the reality of their exploitation, but rather it was an analgesic, an anaesthesia. It eased the suffering caused by the knowledge that life was unpleasant and unjust. I have no doubt that my father's religious beliefs enabled him to cope with the numerous disappointments he suffered in his short life. Undoubtedly he truly believed that his reward would be in the 'next world'.

Another smell. Another recollection. I have returned home from church, cheerful and ravenous from fasting for communion, and I am looking forward to listening to Family Favourites on the radio. At a very young age I am already aware that there must surely be many different and invariably superior ways of living family life. Not that I was terribly unhappy. Indeed, those memories of listening to those songs and messages of love, and especially the roast beef lunches – these memories I hold dear.

Despite a house devoid of books and, on my part, no high expectations of scholarly success, I passed the eleven-plus exam and entered grammar school. The immediate consequence of this surprising develop-

---

* Karl Marx (1844) *Critique of Hegel's Philosophy of Right.*

ment was merely to increase my mother's snobbery. She, I am sad to say, always believed herself to be superior to her peers and indeed to her husband, my father. According to my mother, the only thing that prevented her from becoming a teacher, becoming in her eyes and in her terms a 'somebody', was her own mother's death. Unexpected, tragic – and inconvenient. My mother had to shoulder the burden of domestic responsibility and forsake more selfish enterprises. This and only this. Or so she told me. But through my unanticipated success she could happily, proudly, live her life through mine. Of course, she was also simply supportive of me in the ways in which mothers invariably are, through sheer love.

Up until that time I was not what one might call the life and soul of the party. Rather, I was a quiet, fearful and fragile child. I did not choose a solitary life and actively sought companionship and playmates the best I could. However, once I had made the friends I wanted and needed, I found it difficult to cope with the rough and tumble of childhood friendships. Consequently, much of my time was spent in solitary play. I constructed vast networks of complex road systems for the benefit of my friends, Dinky cars. At least I could control them.

Using the term shorn of any Freudian or psychiatric connotations it seems to me that a state of melancholia set in to my personality when I was quite young, certainly before I took the bold step of entering grammar school. This sense of sadness, of incompleteness, was never far away. It was lurking behind my shoulder waiting to make itself present. It was less a reaction against *loss*, more a sense that something was *missing* – but what exactly, escaped me.

I suffered throughout my childhood with earache. Invariably seasonal in onset, it was so painful that I constantly lived in fear of it. But there was another side to the matter. Administering glycerine into the ear was one cure, yet my mother's lap and soft hands were far more of a comfort. I would lay my head on her lap, and she would pour in the medicine, shushing and soothing me and I would feel engulfed by her love. It was always to her that I turned in moments of distress. It appeared self-evident that it was her job, not my father's. He always let her do the 'mothering', though he was neither a distant nor an unemotional man. There simply appeared to be a natural order of things.

The *melancholia* that drifted in and out of my consciousness was related to a sense I had of almost constantly being in a state of *waiting*. As I progressed in years this sense became less and less tied to an object, an event, person or decision, and more existential and non-specific in nature. But as a young child it was almost always connected with my mother.

Either alone in the house, or with my sister, or with my father asleep upstairs, I would anxiously wait for my mother to return home from work. In our front room – a 'special' place, reserved for special events of which there were none – I would wait for her quietly and with baited breath. The windows were paned, sculpted with lead which gave them an ugly and cage-like appearance. I would stare out of them and up to the corner of the street where, at any moment, I hoped I would see my mother emerge from around the corner. It always took longer than I had hoped, or expected. Sometimes the later post-school afternoon would turn into early evening and darkness. On such occasions the melancholic sensation would be enhanced by a tinge of excited anticipation. There was no substitute for the buzz.

Mothers cast something akin to a spell over their young children, though I can only speak from my own perspective as a boy. Certainly when I eventually caught sight of her my heart would lurch forward and almost leave my body. I could not wait to be reunited, though our separation might have been but a matter of hours. She was home: she was mine, I was hers. Yet as much as she would fill me with her love, she also brought with her a sense of despondency which soon settled like dust. My melancholia was never really lifted by her presence. An embittered and unfulfilled woman who loved her children, she had ways of making us grateful for what she saw as the sacrifices she had made on our behalf. These were extremely subtle messages, some linguistic, others paralinguistic – movements of her body, her facial muscles, a look of the eye.

Unlike *Oedipus* I did not hate my father. I loved them both equally, though my feelings for my mother were more intense, partly due to the strength of her feelings for me. Reciprocity was inevitable. My father was my hero, as fathers tend to be in the eyes of their impressionable sons. Of course, I grew out of the phase. I bitterly regret that I never told him how much I admired and respected him when such praise might have helped him. In fact, it is perhaps only since his death that I have come to see him clearly at all. I cannot recall a single incident of him comforting me in an unembarrassed manner, but neither was he insensitive. I imagine he came to see fatherhood shaped by the context of my mother's behaviour towards me; he saw it as a marginal activity. Considering that I was the apple of my mother's eye, it surprises me that he was so reasonable to me. I certainly represented competition, should he have still been seeking the same prize.

It is not at all unusual for parents to live their lives through their children, indeed it is almost surprising that they don't do it more. But taken to an extreme, it may become pathological. I certainly 'enjoyed' those educational opportunities which had been denied my mother, and by encouraging me she was able to partially satisfy her own thwarted ambitions. However I became the central feature of my mother's exist-ence. Somehow, even at a young age I became aware of this sad, but grisly fact. It was a responsibility for which I felt unprepared and was unwilling to bear. I felt more and more as belonging to her, and less to myself. As far back as I can recall I have always felt engulfed by my mother's love (and good intentions) and attention, and my sense of an independent self has always been a fragile and somewhat ambiguous one.

It is perhaps common sense, possibly mostly inevitable that fathers prefer their daughters, whilst mothers overdose on their sons. Of course, the scenario is much more varied and complex. In my own case, through myriad psychological and psychosexual processes originating in my own parents' family histories, it came to pass that I, unwittingly, became the family favourite. Sibling rivalry followed, and ruined any chance that my sister and I would become friends. Once I was *their* favourite, I was not hers: and a mild yet well-established sense of persecution set in to my sister's psyche.

It sounds extreme. But we were *at risk* of the extreme because of the absence of any kind of extended kith and kin. By the time I was approaching my teenage years we had become a troubled quartet. My sister and I shared the same territory yet we lived in different mental worlds. If I said A, she would say B, so I would say B. But she knew that I was only pretending, so she would say A knowing that it was I who really wanted to say A, and so on and so forth. On a few occasions I would protest my innocence to her, that it was not my fault that I was the favoured child, that I tried hard to avoid any preferential treatment.

She would see my protestations as deceitful and manipulative, which merely reinforced her dislike of me.

Discipline was meted out through an unusual and at times bewildering process. For example: if my mother believed that I had been naughty or, as it tended to be termed, disobedient, she would punish me by asking me, how could I hurt my father? Conversely, in a similar situation, my father would ask me how could I hurt my mother by behaving so badly. Never was I *directly* chastised or punished by them, just through my own feelings of guilt which they carefully inculcated in me.

My memory tells me that when I was under ten years of age I was separated from my mother for a somewhat lengthy period of time. I retain a vision of waving her goodbye, accompanied by an aunt and uncle, who were my guardians during her absence. My later under-standing of the situation and the odd stray cryptic comment from relatives has led me to believe that she was incarcerated in a psychiatric hospital for depression – or, as she tended to put it, her 'nerves'. She certainly was an anxious person. It was a mutual joke between us that she would worry that there was nothing for her to worry about. She deserved better. Perhaps she died a contented and happy woman. Though it didn't appear to be the case, how do I or anyone else know what was going on in her mind as she reflected over her lifetime before expiration and death?

*

Ronald David Laing was born in Glasgow on Friday October 7th, 1927. That much seems clear and somewhat indisputable. However, the rest of his biography is a matter of interpretation, an issue of reconstructing subjective experiences and points of view. His own version of events, expressed in his books, especially *Wisdom, Madness and Folly,* and *The Facts of Life,* and in his interviews with myself (published as *Mad to Be Normal*), invariably do not always coincide with those of others.

His ancestral line consisted of Scottish lower-middle-class lowland Presbyterians, none of whom were either distinguished or notorious. With his parents, David and Amelia, he lived at 21 Ardbeg Street, a three-room tenement flat in Govanhill. Ronald was their only child born nine years after their marriage. His mother's pregnancy was shrouded in mystery: Amelia disguised the impending event by wearing a large overcoat. The thought that people would realise she had been sexually active with her husband appalled her. If the baby had been stillborn no one other than the two of them would ever have been the wiser. After Ronald was born, David too colluded in the concealment, reluctantly announcing the birth only after several days had passed. 'Denial was intrinsic to the family'[1]. So strenuous was their denial that they had indeed performed the necessary sexual intercourse that their son was tempted to believe his birth had been the result of an immaculate conception. Years later both son and father compared birthmarks on their knees to reassure each other of their family ties.

It was after the British film star Ronald Colman that Amelia named her son. Colman had established himself as Hollywood's archetypal English gentleman in a series of films made between the wars, including *The White Sister*, *Beau Geste* and, perhaps significantly for Amelia, *The Dark Angel*.

Amelia Kirkwood was born in 1891, the fifth child of a local family. David Park McNair Laing, two years her junior, was also a local. Their respective families both felt that their child had married 'beneath them'. It appears that from her earliest years Amelia had harboured a sense of resentment against her family and indeed others. Therefore, marriage to David meant two things: an acceptable route away from her family, and secondly, a sense of freedom, of personal liberation. Little is known of David's own family, apart from its reputation of potential aggression. Indeed, Ronald was to witness occasional fights between his own father and his paternal grandfather, John.

Unlike Amelia, David was known to be an extrovert, easy-going and good-natured. But Amelia was a determined woman who was emotionally stronger than her husband. Once married, it was she who ran the Laing household. It appears that Amelia dominated both son and husband, and anyone else who cared to trespass into her territory. Caring for a young child, coupled with the inevitable pressures of domestic life was clearly a pressure on Mrs Laing. She came to be seen by the neighbours and later her son's friends, as somewhat odd, if not actually psychiatrically ill. Her apparent inability to be at ease with other people and express any positive feelings toward them, must have been as painful to her as it was to those in her company. Two months after her son's birth, Amelia's father died, followed less than a year later by the death of her husband's mother. Amelia also felt an additional dissatisfaction at living in Govanhill, an overspill of the Gorbals. She was rarely seen outdoors. She burned her own rubbish in case someone might pick at it and discover its secrets.

While Ronald was quite young his mother became increasingly possessive of him, reluctant to share her son with anyone else. Their house welcomed very few visitors, and neither did they venture outside as a family. Not surprisingly, such a claustrophobic environment led to Ronald delighting in the company of others, especially fresh faces. Indoors, Amelia's relationship with David was cool, though in their early years together they would share time at the piano, he singing, she playing. David was the principal baritone for the Glasgow University chapel choir, and he would rehearse at home, singing light Italian opera and Victorian ballads.

Like most mothers Amelia had high hopes for her one and only son. It is, of course, impossible to know whether Ronald felt painfully burdened by his mother's expectations of him. It is difficult to accept, or even imagine, that he was unaware of the extent to which his mother lived her life vicariously, through him. Even when he was still a young child. On the other hand, one can imagine that he enjoyed all the consequent attention from his mother, especially given that she appeared to be less tactile than her contemporaries, even for the 1930s. She rarely cuddled or even touched him. *Love or its absence* were later to become the central motifs of both the personal and professional life of R. D. Laing.

Ronald's was not a childhood of exuberant play. There were very few toys, even fewer playmates, and almost no laughter. One of his toys, a small wooden horse, came to symbolise to him the terrible emotional pain inflicted on him by his mother. Amelia had destroyed the toy when, in her view, Ronald had become too attached to it.

At the Ardbeg Street apartment, there was a piano, sufficient basic furniture and plenty of food. In his early years nearly all of his emotional life was tied up with his mother. Indeed, he shared a bedroom with this intense and determined woman, she sleeping alone in a double bed while his father was exiled to a room at the rear of the apartment. It appears that his mother protected him from seeing her naked, though she undressed and dressed in the same room in which they slept. Neither would he ever be allowed to leave his own small bed and climb into hers, whatever the circumstance. David Laing, his father, was as strict a parent as most men of his class and generation. The punishments he meted out to his son were usually a consequence of Ronald eating sweets and, thereby, disobeying his mother's strict instructions. David enjoyed almost no emotional, sexual and social life with his wife. They merely shared the same living space. As the years progressed, so did Amelia's tendency to speak badly of her husband, and to tell stories designed to create ill-feeling between David and his friends.

On Christmas Day 1932, the five-year-old Ronald was cold-heartedly told that Santa Claus didn't exist. It was a significant milestone in his young life. From that moment onwards, he never knew whether to believe his parents ever again. He wondered what else they had lied to him about.

Later, when Ronald was fourteen, he locked the bathroom door when bathing, not allowing his mother to scrub his back as she was accustomed. She protested. David supported his son, which, in turn, created a row resulting in Amelia being dragged away by her angry husband. Ronald was grateful. Amelia believed that her son had turned against her.

There is no doubt that much of Ronald's early years were spent at the mercy of his parents, particularly his mother who herself was the victim of her own self-created emotional turmoil. There was no extended family for variety or support, and not a great deal of warmth and happiness, although there was undoubtedly some. Added to these factors were, of course, those of economic hardship and the beginnings of the war, both of which helped create a less than congenial family atmosphere. This has led some to argue, especially given Amelia's odd behaviour, that a 'weaker or less self-possessed child' would have been tipped over the edge or suffered some sort of developmental retardation.[2] This, perhaps, overstates the case. Family life for Amelia, David and Ronald was far from perfect. Yet, for its time, and notwithstanding his mother's possessiveness and devious tendencies, Ronald's life was not as painful as might be imagined. And the discipline he suffered was, no doubt, in part due to Ronald's own abilities to create discord between his two warring parents. He was not a child without imagination or ingenuity. On top of this was David's tendency to feel that his son received more attention from Amelia than he, her husband, ever received. Perhaps the worst aspect was the confusion the young Ronald might well have felt when his mother told him that she loved and cared for him, yet behaved – in his view – as if she didn't.

Ronald was, however, both sensitive and reflective from a very young age. Like many children who had the luxury of being born before the advent of central heating, he would watch the coals burn in the fireplace, the embers glowing, and his imagination racing. In this trance-like state he could transport himself to worlds anew and also into himself.

As he himself recalled in later reminiscences, the young Laing excelled in music, and in particular at the piano. Earlier, at the age of ten, he was thought to possess perfect pitch. His ability as a pianist was encouraged by both parents, to the extent that on several occasions they disagreed with the techniques his teacher employed and insisted instead that he learned his father's.

As can perhaps be appreciated, the young Ronald found school an enjoyable, pleasant escape from home and family life. The solace he received through music was a bonus.

Ronald attended Sir John Neilson Cuthbertsons primary school from August 23rd, 1932. On this first, historic day, Amelia waved her small four year-old son goodbye, and cautioned him against the dangers of eating unusual or unhealthy food. She also warned him not to mix with the wrong sort of child. It is unlikely that she welcomed him sharing his time and affections with anyone else, and therefore also unlikely that she approved of Helen, to whom Ronnie was devoted. They carried on their courtship at school, and 'got married' in the playground. She and Ronald were inseparable for months before she left him. Of this, no doubt, Amelia would have approved.

Ronald was of course a bright child. Within a month, he was learning about the life and work of Sir Walter Scott. He compiled a personal lexicon, listing words in terms of their meaning, ambiguity and etymological origins.

Although the school was physically merely five streets away from his home, it enabled Ronald to realise that there was a world 'outside', other than the one he inhabited with his parents. Perhaps it also enabled Amelia, a participator of life through vicarious means, to enter the realms of a world other than her close domestic sphere. When her child returned from school, she would sit with him whilst he completed his homework, and then together they would gaze out at the world below, like the Lady of Shallot and a secret son.

The Govanhill Library was visible from the rear of the apartment, a building adorned by the statue of an angel poised to fly, a fitting symbol for this sensitive and imaginative boy. Years later he would spend hours there, either alone or accompanied by his mother, mesmerised by its contents.

The shadow of the Second World War hung over Ronald's education at Hutchesons Grammar School, which he attended from 1936 up until 1945, when he was seventeen. He was taught how to wear a gas mask should the unthinkable happen and the Germans bomb civilian targets in Glasgow. It is not surprising, therefore, that such matters of war, death and destruction preoccupied him from time to time. His life outside school was strictly disciplined: he would typically be home by 4.30 p.m., practise the piano or play outside, then back in at 6 p.m. for homework, tea and ablutions. Sometimes he would quietly listen to the radio. Then prayers and sleep. In later years he reflected positively on such moments: '... provided I looked all right, smelt all right and sounded all right, as long as my thoughts were good and my heart was pure, I was as free as a bird'.[3]

Ronald won a scholarship to Hutchesons. Upon entry, he was placed in the A stream. Later, he recalled that his intellectual development was profoundly influenced by his study of the classics, including Sophocles and Euripides, and at which he was found to be particularly talented. He was introduced to a wealth of writings and ideas generated by the minds of classical giants, and the sheer range is impressive: Homer, Ovid, Aeschylus, Plato, Aristotle, the cynics and sceptics, the fathers of Catholic and Protestant thought. He read *Oedipus Rex* in Greek. Compared to his excellence in the classics, he was weak in mathematics. Although interested in the philosophical aspects of mathematics, he was less interested and able in the more mundane, routine and formal aspects of the discipline.

He later joined the school's debating society, and as one might expect excelled at argument, but also at listening, a much rarer art. It was at this time he developed a voracious appetite for jazz. He also indulged in the activities which adolescent boys tend to see as pleasurable, for example, jokes based on sexual innuendo and lavatorial humour, masturbating and

morning', the woman expelled her baby into the world: 'grey, slimy, cold', a 'large human frog', an 'anencephalic monster, no neck, no head, with eyes, nose, froggy mouth, long arms'. Laing continues to recall that although the child may well have been still alive 'we didn't want to know'. Instead, with others, they wrapped her in newspaper so that she could be taken to the pathology laboratory. Laing, with this pitiful bundle under his arm, walked, two hours later, along streets feeling that the event 'seemed to cry out for all the unanswerable answers that I ever asked'. He concludes:

> I needed a drink. I went into a pub, put the bundle on the bar. Suddenly the desire, to unwrap it, hold it up for all to see, a ghastly Gorgon's head, to turn the world to stone.[5]

Just prior to his death in 1989, Laing talked more with me about this female monster, as well as the pain and anguish that her mother endured. And forty years after the incident, it left him sobbing with tears.

These incidents were merely two from a catalogue of many in which he saw human suffering and, at times, cold professional detachment from such misery. Perhaps like many inquisitive and sensitive souls he began to wonder afresh about matters such as the meaning of existence, the presence or absence of God, and whether this work was truly for him.

Laing's time spent at Glasgow University was by no means all work and no play. Neither did he neglect his intellectual horizons. He continued to read widely – Nietzsche, Husserl, Merleau-Ponty, Heidegger, *et al.* – and in particular was attracted to journals like *Horizon*, edited by Cyril Connolly, which he found in the University's bookshop and which kept him abreast of intellectual trends and fashions. Indeed, reading issue 97, January 1948, he stumbled across an article by Antonin Artaud titled 'Van Gogh, the Suicide Provoked by Society'. Questioning the definitions of both madness and sanity, this article was an early yet seminal influence on his own later views on the matter. Artaud had been a lifelong sufferer of both physical and psychological illness, having spent the last decade of his life incarcerated in a French asylum. He believed that his fellow artist Van Gogh was the victim of a society unable to cope with creativity.

... medical science, by asserting Van Gogh's madness, shows itself to be an unserviceable, irresponsible corpse. Psychiatry, challenged by Van Gogh's lucidity at work, is no more than an outpost of gorillas, themselves obsessed and persecuted, who have only a ridiculous terminology to alleviate the most appalling states of anguish and human suffocation.[6]

Artaud adds that through the asylum, society has managed to silence all those unconventional individuals who refused to conform, and that the 'lunatic' is actually the man whom it has prevented from 'uttering unbearable truths'. Such an argument was poetry to the ears of Laing who, through both love of existentialist literature and sensitivity to his patients, knew already that there were questions of human difference, the answers to which escaped him.

Despite the Cold War and the race towards potential Armageddon, neither parliamentary nor revolutionary politics were particularly of as much interest to Laing as many people believed they should have been. Although he once addressed a Communist Party meeting in Glasgow, on the contribution of Marx, Engels and Trotsky, he was more interested in the kind of work engaged in by the Iona Community Centre in Clyde Street, theological politics. However, he did not neglect his debating skills and founded the Socratic Club, a University debating society aimed at non-dogmatically discussing issues of politics, philosophy and theology. Following one particularly lengthy debate between Communists and Catholics, he dismissed them both and wished a plague on both their houses. Neither were Laing's musical interests and abilities allowed to lapse. Because he could turn his fingers to both the sublime and the ridiculous, his piano playing was much in demand. Parties, weddings, social events; Chopin, jazz or filth. They were all part of his repertoire.

Sport still played a minor role in his life and he managed to find time for leisure activities, including swimming, tennis, hitch-hiking and mountaineering. He joined the Glasgow University Mountaineering Club and met the man who was destined to be his best and long-standing friend, John 'Johnny' Duffy. He also met Marcelle Vincent, destined to be the woman whom perhaps he should have married, but didn't. She was an eighteen-year-old French student from the Sorbonne, teaching French on an exchange scheme in Glasgow schools. They were *au fait* with the same intellectual traditions and fashions; Camus, Sartre, Kafka and Marx. Subsequently he visited her in Paris, she him in Glasgow and, later, London. She became acutely aware of his mercurial nature and wondered whether his moods might not mix well with her own depressive tendencies. They found each other physically attractive, but it was their intellectual compatibility that lit the fuse. Sexual love came later.

Years later she recalled how the youthful Laing would 'often consider how little he attended to the voice of God, how careless he was about the true authentic possibilities of his own being, how little he had care for the things of God, how little trust in Him', and that he would ask the question, 'why do so many people go on living?'[7] Immersed in the French sensibility that Marcelle brought to their relationship, he briefly adopted Camus as his mentor. He flirted momentarily with Camus's sense of life as absurdity, and with his proclamation that the most important thing in life was the elusive state of love, both of which sensibilities appealed to him. For the time being at least, Laing had to really discipline himself to give the requisite attention to his work.

Although Laing had tended to his father when he had suffered his breakdown, his first introduction to other mental distress, and the psychiatric profession in particular, came when he attended Saturday morning sessions at the Psychiatric Unit in Duke Street Hospital as a volunteer, where Dr Isaac Sclare lectured on psychiatry. At the Unit he met individuals in considerable distress including catatonic patients. Stimulated by what he observed, he empathetically 'lived out' different psychoses. He imagined what it might be like to be a paranoid schizophrenic, and then ventured out onto the streets wearing that mask. His other early encounter with psychiatry was a University visit to Gartnavel Mental Hospital, where he genuinely confused the professor giving the lecture with the psychiatric patient sharing the platform with him.

After failing his examinations, the University requested him to resit them six months later. In the meantime he was allowed to work as a houseman in the psychiatric unit at Stobhill Hospital in Glasgow where he was employed on a full-time half-salary basis. He was of course required to live in, the first time that Laing had lived away from his home for any significant period of time, and this must have been an enjoyable release. He also met his future co-researcher and author, Aaron Esterson.

The Psychiatric Unit was led by Dr Hunter Gillis, a conventional psychiatrist who believed in the genetic and biological origins of mental distress and disease. But it was another physician, Dr Mackenzie, who left an impression on Laing. This unusual psychiatrist was able to develop a rapport with, and consequently proffer a somewhat unconventional treatment to his deeply depressed elderly male patients, most of whom held strong traditional Calvinist beliefs. Admitted by their exhausted relatives, these men approached death in the belief that they were destined for hell, by virtue of their less than perfect lives. Reason did not work with these men, so instead Dr Mackenzie injected turpentine into their buttocks, which resulted in a fever and swollen and painful buttocks. The technique had the consequence of forcing the patients to 'shut up and count their blessings' and a maximum discharge rate with no re-admissions.

In addition to learning the value of unusual and unconventional therapeutic interventions, at Stobhill Laing also witnessed at first hand the plight of patients suffering from *encephalitis lethargica,* the condition about which Oliver Sacks wrote in *Awakenings.* The Unit had eighty men and women who were initially thought to be victims of the influenza epidemic of 1927. In fact they were victims of an epidemic which swept Europe, and whose symptoms started off just like flu. It was in fact an inflammation of the brain that either killed its victims or caused them to linger on for years, demented, drooling, contorted and paralysed. At Stobhill Laing saw these patients treated with artane, the precursor of the drug L-dopa, whose effects were described by Sacks so vividly. Laing was staggered by the transformation he witnessed with his own eyes. Rip Van Winkles, as he termed them, coming back to life. Even in these early days of his career he was absolutely convinced of the human factors involved in the treatment of neuro-psychologically sick patients, especially in terms of encouraging them back to consciousness and life.

These were some of the experiences, turning points, which convinced Laing that psychiatry was not merely a matter of science, technique and medication, but rather one that centrally involved the presence of another human being, essentially, of a relationship between physician and patient. On Valentine's Day 1951, Laing eventually graduated from Glasgow University, and celebrated modestly with a drink with his friend Johnny Duffy. He also made his mandatory declaration of the Hippocratic Oath in which he solemnly vowed not to 'knowingly or intentionally do anything or administer anything to them to their hurt or prejudice for any consideration or from any motive whatsoever'. In other words, it was his duty not to inflict any treatment on an individual should he or she not wish to receive it. Laing personally believed that the point was to avoid doing harm, not necessarily to do good.

2

Just Listening

... a widow of seventy, who thinks she has a machine inside her breast. It is, she maintains, a structure injected into her at the last hospital she attended. She gyrates in her chair, winding herself up to a high-pitched whine. 'Now stop it,' remonstrates the consultant, more amused than annoyed. 'I want to be rid of it, Holy Mother of God. I'll kill myself if I'm not rid of it. Put it out of me'. The nurse intervenes: 'Doctor won't help you if you don't behave yourself.' The doctor turns to his colleague and asks them – again in her presence: 'Isn't she interesting? We haven't met one like this before.'

Barbara Robb (1967) *Sans Everything*

On November 10th, 1965, *The Times* published a letter from Barbara Robb protesting against the evil practice in certain psychiatric hospitals of stripping geriatric patients of their spectacles, dentures, hearing aids and other necessities, and of leaving them to vegetate in utter loneliness and idleness. Following publication, reams of letters poured in for her, cataloguing additional acts of barbarism, including outright violence against so-called 'troublesome' patients.

Working in such hospitals prepared me for the writings of R. D. Laing. However, my career started somewhat earlier in more congenial surroundings. After several short-lived and unsuccessful attempts at tolerating various kinds of clerical work, I landed a job as a hospital porter. This environment changed my life: for the first time ever, I felt publicly *useful*. This was the first step in a three-stage development which took me from the Manor General Hospital in Nuneaton, then on to a small so-called 'cottage' hospital nearby, for children suffering from *hydrocephalus,* and finally to a large psychiatric hospital in Warwick, a 'bin' by any other name.

Working at the general hospital simply made me aware of my early calling: to serve people. I had experience of this at home, tending to my mother when her arthritic pain became so acute that she could hardly raise her cup of tea to her mouth. But at home my apparent kindness masked if not resentment, then certainly ambivalence. Merely the sight of my mother's creased face, racked with pain, made me feel guilty and subsequently angry. But at the hospital it was much easier to care for those I could then leave behind, a kind of power without emotional responsibility, as I weaved my path away from the oxygen canisters down to the pub.

Moving huge and heavy oxygen canisters was only one of many jobs I had as a trainee porter. Delivering bottles of blood, which seemed to my untrained eye thicker and darker than that which ran through my veins, incinerating discarded limbs, moving beds – usually with their occupants still resident – and, most significantly, talking with patients. This was the bread and butter of my work. Of course, there were more dramatic and memorable moments: my first visit to the morgue where I suffered the terrifying sight of a yellow cadaver on the slab, emaciated by its prolonged illness, yet groaning and moving when the mortician touched it. It was only later that I discovered the ghoulish spasm was caused by air trapped inside the corpse. Of course, this scenario has become a cliché, but for the unprepared and uninitiated it was awful, in the true meaning of that word. Other bodies, shrivelled, gaunt, yellow: the mortician putting a dead man's brains into his stomach following examination: he explained to me that there was no longer any room inside the skull. The whole event was, of course, staged and part of my initiation process. And there was another occasion when I was working with one of my father's old friends – he on his way down the occupational ladder, coming to the end of his working life, me just starting mine. Both of us on low pay. Our task was to remove a dead body – a person, a middle-aged man, who had just died of heart failure – from the ward out through the hospital and into the morgue. This unpleasant task was made that much more onerous by the fact that the body had to be taken out in what can only be described as a large sardine tin. We tried and tried but couldn't fit him in. It was about 10 in the morning and, only protected by a thin screen, all the other patients could see and hear us struggling with what was rapidly becoming like a Rubik's Cube. We tried him all ways, but his body was a most irregular shape. The man had been a metallurgist which, when I was seventeen, was the equivalent of my knowing he was a nuclear physicist looking at the relationship between protons and pi-mesons. All I knew was that *I* was sweating and feeling distinctly criminal, and *he* had enormous feet and broad shoulders. The ward sister, whose name I could never pronounce, was from Polish stock, large and matter-of-fact in her approach to all matters, including life and death. She joined us and after much pushing and shoving – I, with my eyes firmly closed – we were able to put the lid on. It was only when we were wheeling him out of the ward that I noticed the trickle of blood down the side of the can. One patient looked aghast at us as we sped by. I merely attempted a smile, but offered no explanation.

But what left its impression on me was the plight of those who were still alive, especially the many people who struggled courageously in the face of pain and, invariably, the inevitable. One man of whom I had grown fond had a hole in his shin which refused to heal. The smell which emanated from the sore was indescribably foul. I would assist the nurses from time to time, when they were short staffed, and I was one of the few people there who did not flinch at the sight and odour of this hole. Its owner was, on the face of it, physically non-descript: small, bald, with a very shiny head, about forty years of age. But his personality was a mixture of black humour – he would tell terrible jokes about his shin – and deep sadness, visible by the look in his eyes. He knew, as I also learned, that he was dying. His way of telling me that he was aware of his imminent death was to tell me about his wife and his children. As I got to know him better over the weeks I spent bending over this putrid ulcer, almost gagging over the smell, the nature of his conversations about his family changed. At first his descriptions were bland and predictable – that his wife spent all his money when she went shopping, that his son showed promise as a footballer, that he didn't really understand his daughter's obsession with the Beatles. Later, when I knew him better and felt privileged to do so, he asked me, persistently and urgently, what I thought would happen to them should he not be there. When he first began in this vein, I behaved in the way in which one is subtly socialised by hospital environments – 'what are you talking about! You'll outlive me!' [said with much joviality]. But ultimately he squeezed out of me a promise that, upon his death, I would tell his widow the things he couldn't bring himself to say during his life. Yet another kind of power without responsibility. But the inherently intimate nature of these things prevented me, as a naïve seventeen year old, from ever repeating them even to the rightful recipient and as a man I am now ashamed that I broke my promise.

I also remember a young woman aged about twenty five who had the face of what I imagined to be an angel, and who was dying with Crohn's disease. It was not the smell of her demise that upset me, simply the sheer injustice of it. It seemed almost *incomprehensible* to me that someone so beautiful, so young, so apparently innocent, should be dying at the same time as I was running along the corridors full of life and vitality. She never, ever, complained of her pain and discomfort. She never mentioned death or dying, in case she embarrassed or upset any of her carers, including me. She broke all of our hearts when she slipped away quietly one Saturday morning. I was not on duty but lying in bed, feeling sick after drinking myself unconscious.

Despite the crash course in physical distress of various kinds which I took at the general hospital, I was still unprepared for what I encountered at my next job. Bramcote is a village near Nuneaton where, in addition to an army base, there used to be a small cottage hospital devoted, almost exclusively, to the care of hydrocephalic children.

When I left Bramcote Hospital for home each day, I could not leave the children behind me. On many occasions I would remember bizarre dreams about them, heads with laughing faces falling off shoulders and onto the ground where the facial expression would turn to terror. I was troubled, even haunted by them, especially Katy.

Strangely enough, when I met this eight year old, the first thing I noticed about her was the clicking noises she made with her shoes on the ward's shiny and hard linoleum floor. When I lifted my eyes, I noticed her wicked grin, and only then her enormous head. Before I could adjust to this unusual and slightly disturbing sight I saw another child, Peter who, like Katy, wobbled slightly when he walked due to the weight he was carrying above his less than broad shoulders.

I never *ever* talked with either child about their heads – the size of them, and whether or not they hurt – even though their conversational skills would, I believe, have allowed it. I simply spent time with them, especially when they were in the middle of their regular tantrums. I never did learn whether such behaviour was symptomatic of the disease, but Katy and Peter indulged in it daily. From time to time the excess fluid in the brain would be drained off to relieve pressure, through what I think was a Spitz-Holter valve. When this procedure was carried out the children were quiet for a day or two. But then the giggling and playfulness would restart.

It was not that they were exceptionally charming or clever, and they were not my own children of course, but nevertheless I felt deep affection for them both. Peter would lie on his bed while I changed him and it was like bathing Humpty Dumpty. His head seemed to cover the whole bed. Sometimes the weight appeared to give him pain, but he didn't speak of it. But occasionally I could see fear in his eyes. Like Katy he never seemed to want for anything *but* company. I was fortunate enough to work for a rare regime which believed it more important that I spent time with these children, rather than ensuring that the floor was clean and the linen cupboard full.

Katy was my 'girlfriend' and I, her 'boyfriend'. When she died, suddenly with little advance warning, I felt a sadness that I truly could not express in words. The nursing staff, in defiance of stereotype, wept with me. Katy was gone. A beautiful and courageous little girl with a big head had left us all behind.

It was the Central Hospital, Hatton, near Warwick, which was *the* turning point in my life, at least in terms of that part of me who was someone-interested-in-the-understanding-of-and-care-of-the-mentally-distressed. The hospital was established in 1852 to implement the terms of the Lunacy Act of 1845 which provided that by 'moral management' and supervised work, people could 'return to sanity'. Of course, one of the consequences of the so-called 'moral treatment' was that those who were considered morally inadequate were certified insane, by those who considered themselves to be wholly morally irreproachable. Those incarcerated included unmarried mothers, whom as it has since been well documented, were frequently released only by death.

This was no 'lunatic *asylum*', despite official claims to the contrary. It was neither a place of sanctuary, nor was much protection offered inmates. Rather, it was a hell hole. It was severely overcrowded with, in some wards – especially the female ones – bed touching bed. It stank of urine and polish. It was, in fact, a converted Victorian workhouse. Buildings were spread all over the grounds, dreary to look at and dreary to be in, rarely maintained. I recall meeting the Medical Superintendent after I had been there three months, and he over twenty years. He asked me which ward I worked on. 'Oh, I've never been to that side of the hospital', was his honest reply.

Not surprising perhaps, given its geographical location, that the largest male chronic ward was named after the Bard. And his tragedies were certainly enacted. My work was divided: a nursing auxiliary on Shakespeare Ward, and 'rehabilitation instructor' working with 'long-term schizophrenics'. A considerable number of the nursing staff I worked alongside were sadistic in behaviour and personality. Back in the late nineteenth century, the hospital's male nurses, or 'attendants' as they tended to be called, were recruited from the armed services where they were used to long hours and strict discipline. Unfortunately when they transferred to the Hospital it was *they* who meted out the discipline to mentally distressed paupers, under the name of treatment. When I worked there my senior nurse was an ex-serviceman and equally as sadistic as his predecessors. His approach to the job was neither scientific nor compassionate. He spent a considerable amount of his day talking on the telephone to other members of the North Warwickshire Hunt of which he was a prominent member. Indeed, many of the Hospital's visiting committee were Hunt members, and there was a close association with the Hospital through Lord Leigh and the Arkwright family, all enthusiastic predators of foxes.

My superior, to whom I was directly answerable, thought I was somewhat peculiar, sporting long hair as I did, and having no interest in his equine hobby. He was simultaneously surprised and disinterested that I took my job seriously and had expressed concern at the condition and fate of the patients whom I encountered. Before I really settled in to the job, patients would say nothing in response to my question – 'what's he like as a charge nurse?' They knew better than to express an opinion. Everyone on Shakespeare was on largactil (chlorpromazine), the so-called antipsychotic 'wonder drug'. Despite the precise dosage written down on their notes and without the benefit of any but the most rudimentary medical training, my superior would take a look at these poor defenceless creatures and pour out either less or more. Of course, he would feign surprise when their agitation, deep slumber or paranoia returned. After either working in the hospital or aimlessly trudging around the corridors, these patients would partake of lunch (i.e., school dinners) and then receive their medication. Then, through long-term usage of largactil, they would flop down into chairs, dribble from the mouth, and exhibit all the signs of madness. My superior merely repeated the mantra I was to hear for many subsequent years, that the use of such drugs meant that there was less need for closed wards. It was pointless trying to tell him that these people were now locked inside their bodies, minds and perhaps souls.

I witnessed too many acts of cruelty and violence to catalogue them all. But two stand out in my memory, as particularly brutal and sadistic.

Regulation sheets for the bathing of patients by nurses were pinned on a few walls. Among the instructions were that the cold water was always to be turned on first, that the temperature was to be 'ascertained by the thermometer', that every care was to be taken to avoid fright or distress by unnecessary submersion, and that 'not more than one patient is to be bathed in the same water'. It was a cold and dreary November morning when I was shown, by my superior, how to supervise and carry out the weekly bathing ritual. At that moment there were only seventeen men present as, at mid-morning, the rest were ploughing the fields or welding metals. 'Run the water and shove 'em in, one after the other'. I couldn't believe it: the same water for all seventeen. He could see my displeasure so, to make whatever point he was really trying to make over and above the fact that he was in charge, he also proceeded to shave all seventeen men with the same rusty and dangerous razor blade.

The other incident occurred in one of the secure units, a locked ward on the fourth floor, in which the only fellow-traveller I met at that hell hole was employed as an auxiliary. We were spending a few minutes talking about the state of affairs we found ourselves in and in particular he was telling me of an almost surreal incident which had occurred in his unit the previous day. A male patient had tried to cut his own throat with a reinforced-plastic urinal bottle. This failed to complete the intended task so he had, somehow, locked himself in the kitchen and turned on the gas; unfortunately he also lit a match. There was a small explosion and a large fire. By now terrified and ironically anxious for his own safety, he smashed the kitchen window and leapt from it, landing in a water tower. He drowned before anyone could save him. After the trauma of that conversation, we swapped notes on our respective superiors. He believed that his charge nurse easily had the worst reputation in the hospital, excelling in brutality. Just at that moment, as if on cue, he appeared in the unit, at which point he immediately set to work on a patient, an ex-professional middleweight boxer who had been diagnosed as suffering from the 'punch drunk state'. Whether or not this was actually a coincidental diagnosis of someone suffering from either a neurological or psychiatric condition, or a mixture of both, the man certainly was unsteady on his feet, was slow in movement and, apparently, was extremely irritable. He was, in addition, prone to bouts of tearfulness. The charge nurse decided to stimulate such a bout: he retrieved a bell from his office and walked toward his prey, the bell tantalisingly silent in his hand although the patient knew what was in store. The fear in his eyes was visible from where we were standing. The nurse pretended that he was going to ring it at least three times. The patient winced. Then the nurse struck the bell and the patient began a clumsy yet impassioned bout of shadow boxing, then – almost too painful to watch – slithered down the wall in tears. And the charge nurse laughed.

It was easy to make 'friends' with the patients. They had time on their hands, were often lonely and, providing there was no reputation for sadism, believed that we, the carers, would provide good company. I made quite a few friends among the patients during my time at Hatton. Most of them were broken and damaged individuals who were further maimed by what passed for 'treatment'. The little dignity they possessed on entering the hospital soon disappeared after being subjected to the treatment they received in Shakespeare Ward. Some of them, however, enjoyed celebrity status. A man I knew quite well had an almost profound ability to impersonate *any* bird that sang in the hospital grounds. He would tell me of the precise differences between one sparrow and another; he claimed he knew many of them, and enjoyed conversations with them. He told me that it was preferable to talking with his family who, whenever he reminded himself of them, would reduce him to tears. I bought him a copy of the *Observer Book of British Birds*. 'Tiny' was a man who appeared for the majority of the time to inhabit another universe altogether. He was, of course, almost seven feet tall and spoke an esoteric language that no one I knew could understand, not that many tried. The first time I encountered Tiny, he terrified me. I was introduced to him by Ginger, of whom more later, who said I was a 'friend'. Despite his hearty recommendation that I was 'ok' I still felt nervous as Tiny hovered over me. He then proceeded to measure me, which he did as one does a horse: hand upon hand. He smiled at me, said 'forty two', and left us. Ginger laughed.

Not all patients were easy to get along with, or as easy to like as Ginger or indeed Tiny. Michael, for example, was Hatton's own public enemy number one. The voices that frequently and without warning played havoc inside his head always gave him the same instructions. He was to kill cats. In a Victorian hospital, an amalgam of buildings with cavernous cellars, cats were aplenty. One census put the figure at two thousand. When Michael was on the prowl he reduced the figure by at least fifty before being caught. Skinning them alive, he would then hide, leaving the remains in full sight of anyone who cared to pass by. Only once did I have the misfortune to stumble across his handy work, but it was unforgettable.

As an instructor in the rehabilitation unit my job was to work with 'schizophrenics used to labouring work and fit enough to continue such work'. In a hospital that counted Coventry in its catchment area, this invariably meant that I actually worked with Irishmen. Patients had helped the economy of the Hospital with their labour since its early days in the previous century. Their work on the farms and in the laundry meant less expense for the ratepayers. In 1931, for example, the farms provided for the Hospital's kitchens 100,473lbs of beef, 45,690lbs of mutton, 529lbs of lamb, 10,219lbs of pork, almost 60,000 eggs and 40,000 gallons of milk – mostly through what amounted to little more than slave labour. Later, there would also be 'employment' available in wrought iron work, carpentry, leather work and building. Of course, patients were remunerated but this was hardly a living wage, and neither was it necessarily 'therapeutic'. Many patients would return from the farms completely exhausted and that fatigue, combined with their largactil, guaranteed a life-long stay.

Ginger was assigned to the 'team' that worked with me. If this were not so utterly sad, it would without doubt be entirely comic. This team of 'schizophrenic ex-building labourers' was to work with me in manufacturing 'crazy paving' for use in the nurses' houses. I thought someone was having a joke at my expense but, no, this was what the Head of Nursing (and, *de facto*, Head of Rehabilitation) believed would be useful work for the men. In addition, it would help landscape the somewhat untidy gardens of the nurses' quarters. The irony was not for one moment lost on Ginger.

We, the twelve of us, would assemble in a small hut on the edge of the Hospital. Inside it was *always* cold, whatever time of year and whatever temperature outside. I would make them all a cup of hot tea and give them a biscuit each. Collectively we would look for excuses not to venture outside, but eventually we would have to do so. They worked for about four hours then received their lunch, followed by largactil, and a drug-induced sleep. The work they were required to undertake was mindless which is why, I suspect, it was given them to perform. Sometimes there would be special requests. I remember, for example, that we unsuccessfully tried to construct a fish pond for the Medical Superintendent, with comic results. The only respite these poor patients had from their toil, and the often atrocious weather conditions, was in early summer when the orchards would be aflow with apples which my team was required to pick. It was on one of these balmy sunny days that I first came to the attention of the Medical Superintendent.

I led my band of merry men to the orchard, over the lawns on which many patients aimlessly wandered, past the cricket ground and to the small patch of healthy-looking apple trees. To begin, things went according to plan. With our assortment of garden tools we enthusiastically shook the apples from the branches. But one of my team whom, in a previous existence, had driven a bulldozer, decided on a more radical strategy. I tried to coax the spade out of his hands and suggested, in my best empathetic voice, that digging up the tree was not required. He disagreed and began to fight me: I was heroically defended by a couple of the others who were then, themselves, attacked by two others. Soon a crowd gathered around, later joined by my fox-hunting superior along with other male nurses, all alerted by the brouhaha. My team where all led away, some forcibly restrained, others crying. Even Ginger, who had been merely observing the mini drama, was taken back to the ward. All were subsequently sedated, and I was asked to meet the Medical Superintendent.

'They are dangerous people, not sometimes, but *invariably* so', were his words after he had chastised me for allowing myself to be put into what he clearly considered to be a dangerous situation. I used the meeting as an opportunity to raise some of the matters which were causing me moral and psychological distress, in particular my superior's vindictiveness. Again I was told what a difficult and exhausting job nursing was, and that 'yes, things do go wrong from time to time', and that he'd 'look into it'. I know a hypocrite when I see one, so I didn't pursue the matter, acted contrite and left him nodding sagely. I was to meet him again.

When I next met Ginger he was not as friendly and open as usual. After a few cups of tea, he eventually told me that he was saddened I had allowed the nurses to take him away from the orchard by force and sedate him. I told him, honestly, that it all happened so quickly and I was uncertain what to do. I tried my best to convince him that I *was* still his 'friend', an alien concept in this alien world.

I was stung by Ginger's relative indifference toward me. *I* needed him to be *my* friend. Action is always preferable to words alone, so I decided to act. I knew that he was an aficionado, as well as a lover of post-impressionist paintings, despite having no education in fine art. I presumed that, were he to know about it, he would be interested in an exhibition taking place in Coventry. Of course, very few patients read newspapers or knew of the rare cultural events taking place in the nearby city, and indeed for many of them Coventry might well have been on the other side of the Moon. Before speaking with Ginger I got permission to take him out of the hospital for the weekend, and I also got my mother to agree to him staying a night. When I raised the matter with Ginger he did not believe me. When he realised I was serious, he could barely conceal his joy. It is perhaps worth saying that many of the conversations I had with this 'paranoid schizophrenic' were just like the conversations I might have with you, the reader.

Like me, Ginger was surprised how small the paintings were when hung on the wall, in comparison to reproductions in a book, or one's imagination. He managed the streets of Coventry remarkably well, given that he'd been incarcerated for over a year. He was a little tentative and the noise bothered him slightly, but on the whole, he adapted himself with ease. At my mother's he didn't eat, much to her consternation. He watched the TV and chatted away harmlessly enough, without incident. He neither embarrassed my parents, nor they him. In fact, I was proud of them all that day.

On returning to Hatton on Sunday afternoon, Ginger was extremely agitated. He'd enjoyed a taste of freedom, companionship and civility, yet he was also used to the regime and the environment by which he had become institutionalised. He was finding the conflict difficult to deal with, as was I, especially when on the top deck of a double-decker bus he started simpering then wailing. At Hatton I was given the 'told you so' routine, that 'these people' were better off where they were, that it wasn't good to 'raise their expectations'. It *did* all end in tears, and Ginger was uncommunicative for weeks. When he did talk to me, he was clearly and visibly suspicious of my intentions.

My outrage at the way in which this institution had made Ginger the way he was and, perhaps, provided the opportunity for my sadistic superior and his fellow nurses to practise their sadism on the weak and vulnerable, led me to try and do something about it. But what exactly? There were very few individuals in the hospital who believed that patients were being mistreated. The majority of nurses felt that they were doing the best they could, given the conditions in which they worked and the state of mind of the patients with whom they were dealing. Moreover, they seemed to believe that violence – by the patients on other patients, patients on staff, staff on patients – was part and parcel of the job, an occupational hazard. The psychiatrists were a different species. They were for the most time elusive, and then when found tended rarely to make much sense. To my untrained eye, they did not appear to be blessed either with compassion or genius. No doubt they would complain about the number of patients they had to deal with and the conditions in which they worked yet a bad workman blames his tools, and their behaviour was often less than exemplary.

When I was not making crazy-paving or herding men into baths, I was sometimes asked to collect patients for their 'reviews'. This was when those patients who had been admitted for twenty eight days were reviewed by a psychiatrist to determine whether they should return home or remain incarcerated. I would be asked to find the patients in question and deliver them to the interview room. On many occasions the psychiatrist would run out of his allotted time, scribble something down on their file and leave them hospitalised for another twenty eight days. I have also seen relatives coerced into signing consent forms, not really understanding that they had given permission for their loved one to be electrically shocked, and indeed I have seen doctors forge signatures on such consent forms. I did not leave Hatton with the view that psychiatrists were, in the main, heroic creatures.

Eventually I took direct action. On an official visit to the hospital by Richard Crossman, the Coventry MP and Minister of Social Services, I decided that I would bring to his direct attention the iniquities I felt I was witnessing on an almost daily basis. As he swept down one of the corridors, surrounded by an entourage which included the Medical Superintendent and the Head of Nursing, I stopped him in his tracks. 'Do you know what's behind that small door?' Before he could reply, he was told that it was merely a linen cupboard. It was, in fact, a ward full of chronic patients, bed-ridden women who were about six inches away from each other, with no room to breathe or to have personal possessions. The Rt Hon. Crossman was not interested in pursuing my question. After all, his party was currently in government at the time, not in opposition, therefore exposing a scandal would have been somewhat counterproductive.

*

From January 1951 to October of the same year, Laing worked as an intern at the West of Scotland Neurosurgical Unit at Killearn, not far from Loch Lomond and merely a few miles north of Glasgow. The vacancy had appealed to him as it involved clinical work which would help him further understand the issues most concerning him, namely the relationship between the brain and the mind, and the interpersonal nature of the patient/doctor relationship. His work included neurological examinations, ward rounds with consultants and assisting in theatre. As before at Stobhill, two particular cases intrigued Laing. One involved a small ten-year-old boy who suffered *hydrocephalus*. Twice a day, Laing would insert a needle into his skull to drain off the excess fluid, a procedure which would increase the pain he was already enduring. Yet the boy tried to conceal his pain, crying quietly to himself. He only asked that God allowed him to finish reading *Pickwick Papers* before he died. Sadly, for Laing too, he only managed half of the volume. The other case involved a nineteen-year old circus performer, thrown from her horse and subsequently severely concussed when the horse rolled on her. The horse was destroyed. She regained consciousness a few days later, and as she did so, she '*was* a horse. She looked like a horse. She had horse's eyes. She neighed. She grazed on the grass outside the ward, naked, on all fours'.[1] This equine behaviour would continue for about a month, and would then disappear when she reverted to being human again for two days. Then, she would become a horse again, and the cycle continued. Such a conundrum of neurology and psychology intrigued and stimulated Laing.

Lobotomies were still practised on certain violent or deeply disturbed and depressed patients at Killearn, though two out of the three senior neurosurgeons refused to perform them. Laing himself saw them as barbaric, a savage act of destruction against a defenceless creature. The surgeon who did carry out the procedure did so in the classic ice-pick and hammer method.

In the 1950s lobotomies were still being routinely performed, and perhaps they will in time be recycled. Who knows what the future might bring? Who is to say. It is perhaps worth reminding ourselves of what was once believed to be a form of 'treatment'.

In 1890, Dr Gottlieb Burckhardt, a physician in a Swiss psychiatric hospital, drilled holes into the heads of six severely agitated patients and extracted sections of their frontal lobes, altering their behaviour with varying degrees of success. Two of the patients died. One of his successors was Professor Walter Freeman, a neurologist at George Washington University. He 'refined' the 'treatment' and regularly featured on the front page of the *New York Times* alongside optimistic headlines – 'Wizardry of Surgery Restores Sanity to Fifty Raving Maniacs' and, tragically incorrectly, 'No Worse Than Removing a Tooth'. In 1945, he devised the 'ice-pick lobotomy'. To cut a long and grisly story short: Freeman anaesthetised his patients with rapid busts of electric shock. He then drew the upper eyelid away from the eyeball, exposing the tear duct. The sharp point of the ice-pick was placed in the duct, and then, as Freeman put it, 'a light tap with a hammer is usually all that is needed to drive the point through the orbital plate'. The ice-pick was plunged into the brain. When it was about two inches inside, Freeman would pull the ice-pick about thirty degrees backward, as far as he could without cracking the skull, and then move it up and down in another twenty-degree arc, in order to cut the nerves at the base of the frontal lobes. The procedure took only a few minutes. The damage it wreaked lasted a lifetime. Freeman's post-operative advice to relatives was restricted to the order – 'buy them some sunglasses'.

1948 was Freeman's most celebrated year, in which he hammered his ice-pick into the head of Frances Farmer, film star and political activist. She was thirty four when Freeman operated. Later that day she lay supine on her bed, crying quietly and unable to speak. The personality that *was* Frances Farmer had been effectively terminated. She was reduced to a state of turgid, generalised mediocrity by the surgery. Society had won its battle with her, and she would never again be a threat. She ended her life as a clerk in a hotel, dying of cancer in 1970.[2]

Of course, ECT was also routinely used at Killearn and its inclusion as an established treatment in the everyday psychiatric practice alarmed and appalled Laing. Indeed, on one visit by Johnny Duffy, Laing asked his friend to type a letter on his behalf to the *British Journal of Medical Psychology* in which he compared ECT to a radio set not working properly – sometimes it did, sometimes it didn't. The letter wasn't published, yet years later the doyen of British psychiatry, Sir William Sargant, explained that ECT worked in the same way that a radio does – sometimes you just have to tap it and it works. Sargant believed that like the average wireless, the depressed mind may too be jolted back to life with a good shock, and he required no technical or conclusive proof to justify the procedure.

One of the senior neurosurgeons who objected to lobotomies on ethical grounds was Dr Joe Schorstein who became as close if not closer to Laing than his own father. Born in 1909 in Austria, the son of a Hasidic rabbi, he was eighteen years older than Laing. He was a perfect mentor for him, well-read and musical. They met in the ante-room of the operating theatre following surgery, in the early hours of the morning. Schorstein questioned Laing on the philosophers they both claimed to have understood – Hegel, Heidegger, Husserl and Nietzsche – and subsequently they became close friends. He sang the Hasidic songs of Central and Eastern Europe to Laing, shared whisky and pondered the unanswerable metaphysical questions which preoccupied them both. Schorstein, like Laing, was a troubled and tormented soul. He claimed to believe in the Crucifixion yet could not bring himself to believe in the Resurrection, a concept which Laing believed was the worst imaginable cosmic nightmare. It has been suggested that part of Schorstein's torment is related to a story that Laing would tell about an un-named colleague from Vienna. The man's mother was diagnosed, just before the First World War, as suffering from anxiety. Instead of seeing Freud, whose reputation she disfavoured, she consulted an eminent neurologist who suggested she was suffering from tertiary syphilis. An orthodox Jew, she was, of course, deeply upset at the diagnosis, but nevertheless accepted the word of this eminent physician. Her treatment was the administration of a dose of malaria, from which she subsequently died. The post-mortem showed *no* syphilis.[3]

Another of Schorstein's attractions was his well established connections with people whom Laing admired from afar, like the existentialist philosopher and psychiatrist Karl Jaspers. Formerly a professor at Heidelberg, he had been persecuted by the Nazis and stripped of his chair. Subsequently he moved to Basle. It was Schorstein's suggestion that Laing went to study under him in Switzerland. This proposal appealed to Laing on at least two grounds, primarily that he could work with a man who, like himself, believed that schizophrenics might well have insights and experiences far more intelligible than credited and, secondly, it enabled him to be closer to his French girlfriend Marcelle, whose family home was relatively near by in Annecy, France. Glasgow University were approached and they agreed to financially support the idea of Laing working with Jaspers and at the Neuropsychiatric Department of the University of Basle.

Unfortunately, Laing was called up for two years National Service, as a non-combatant. He would not be compelled to fight, should such a situation arise, but he would have to work as an army doctor instead. His appeal to work in Basle failed. Due to the Korean War, qualified physicians were in demand. He was interviewed by the Armed Services Board in Edinburgh who informed him that his two years as an army doctor would be counted as one of the years required towards his Diploma of Psychiatric Medicine. Laing was then enrolled into the Royal Army Medical Corps.

To begin his military career, Laing was sent to Millbank in London for a series of lectures, some of which appalled him, especially those concerned with the burgeoning trade in weapons of germ warfare. After this brief introduction he was posted to Aldershot for a more formal initiation and a period of officer-training. When asked to specify his religion,

Laing replied that he was an atheist. When told it was obligatory to be religious Laing replied that he was a member of the Church of England, as this was the closest thing to atheism he could think of.[4] Following his sojourn at Aldershot he received his first lengthy posting, to the British Army psychiatric unit at the Royal Victoria Hospital at Netley, in Hampshire.

At Netley, Laing came face to face with the full and total horrors of the psychiatric practice of the 1950s: ECT, insulin comas, tube feeds, amytal abreactions, straight jackets, padded cells, pre-tranquilliser drugs, barbiturates, chloralhydrate and paraldehyde. Indeed, Laing himself was routinely required to administer such 'treatments', including ECT and insulin comas. This latter procedure in particular concerned Laing. The patients were subjected to a dose of insulin sufficient to reduce blood sugar levels and induce a hypoglycaemic coma. The theory behind this was that the patients would then be free of the inhibitions which previously prevented them from remembering and talking about their 'experience'. Laing would pour glucose into the patients' stomachs to prevent the comas from becoming irreversible. However, the curtains were closed to prevent any possible epileptic seizure and the dark conditions made the task difficult: was the tube in the stomach or in the lungs? And needles were inserted into veins which had already collapsed.

This crude attempt to 'rebirth' patients, by taking them to the edge in order to bring them back mentally cleansed, appalled Laing. Apart from the inhumane nature of the treatment, he also felt it might well be counter-productive: that the 'unintelligent gibberish' that was being washed out might actually contain sense – 'desperate, encoded messages that ought to be heard and deciphered'.[5] However, the greatest iniquity, as Laing saw it, was Netley's policy and procedure *not* to communicate with the patients, on the grounds that such conversations would inflame their delusional systems and aggravate their psychosis. ECT and insulin comas were administered to deaden the mind and reduce cognitive and thought processes. Conversation would, therefore, merely excite these deadened minds. Laing knew in his heart that such practices were ethically wrong and inhumane, let alone the fact that they failed in their own terms. He knew that no psychiatrist, should they fall ill, would wish to be treated in a similar way. He also reasoned that such treatments, ECT and insulin comas for example, were an affront to a so-called normal person, so why on earth should disturbed patients be subject to them? Laing also discovered that the patients were beaten by the staff on a regular basis. What with the other procedures he had experienced and found unacceptable, he began to feel for the first time that perhaps these so-called treatments were merely methods of 'destroying people and driving people crazy if they were not so before, and crazier if they were'.[6]

A moment of epiphany arrived when, after hearing the loud and incoherent rantings of a patient, Laing went to routinely administer tranquillising medication. Instead he decided to sit down with the patient inside the padded cell. The man calmed down sufficiently for the medication to be redundant. Laing repeated his visits almost nightly and felt 'strangely at home there', lounging on the floor, feeling relaxed and comfortable. Against procedure, he would claim that what he was doing was research. After some time it became clear to Laing that not only did he feel at home, enjoying being with the patient more than he liked being with the staff, but that *listening* to patients was therapy, as was treating them as *individuals, human beings.*

In his memoir, *Wisdom, Madness and Folly*, Laing describes the extraordinary cognition of a patient whom he called 'John'. John could be 'anyone he cared to be merely by snapping his fingers ... but most of the time he was a gentleman catburglar and safe-blower in Manhattan or London or anywhere'. His loot or 'treasure, usually in gold and gems, was distributed to the poor. He was never any the richer. I became his companion in some of these escapades. I was a sort of Sancho Panza to his Don Quixote'.[7] John, once more, raised in Laing's mind the conundrum of the mad/insane dichotomy. He discussed the matter in one of the many letters he sent to his girlfriend Marcelle:

> In his life he has had virtually nothing of the things he had set his heart on; he is well aware that he is regarded as mad but he says that why should he not be: now he is anyone he wants to be: has anything he wants: does everything he likes: why should he return to a world where he is unable to satisfy every one of his fundamental desires? Why indeed I find it very difficult to give him an answer. Insanity, suicide or sanity. In the specific sense in which Sartre uses the word, we are 'free' to choose insanity or suicide. And more and more people are exercising their freedom in this direction.[8]

Listening to John was no easy task, but practice made it increasingly possible for Laing to get the gist of some of what he was talking about. Indeed, he would often feel that he knew all too well what the patient was saying, and the point of view he was expressing. Laing compared his affinity with John as one with music, getting in rhythm with another. He later took another patient, 'Peter', back home with him to Glasgow for three days to prevent him from suffering shocks or insulin. Soon after his return to Netley Peter left the army, an invalid but without having suffered psychiatric 'treatment'. He later created a successful career for himself in education: the three days, short in hours but long in humane care, proved decisive.

While at Netley, Laing developed an interest in 'malingering', those case in which soldiers allegedly faked illness in order to be excused duty. It became apparent to Laing that it was almost impossible to determine with any conviction or certainty whether or not symptoms like mutism and deafness were hysterical or schizophrenic, organic or functional, genuine or faked.

One of the few consolations of his time at Netley, other than the affirmation through his own experience that *listening* was indeed therapy, was that in the medical library he found and read the work of Harry Stack Sullivan. Like Laing, Sullivan was also interested in a *mésalliance* between neurological and psychological approaches in the study and treatment of mental distress. Intellectually, Laing's time at Netley was also characterised by his continuing interest in existentialist literature and philosophy, as witnessed by his many letters to Marcelle Vincent.

... I was reading Dostoevsky in large chunks – he had much the same to say about science as Kierkegaard. The same rebellion against these cold, impartial, irrefutable, objective facts of the natural scientist ... Unless a fact has significance for me, one way or another, I have no curiosity about it.

... for reading matter I am involved in Camus's *Le Mythe de Sisyphe* ... Camus at the outset of his book has to ask himself why he is still alive if his existence is so absurd. I must say he doesn't seem to me to have given any very *logical* reason for his continued existence. It seems to me that the final absurdity is that he remains in his place of torture, and anguish, and despair.

... Our actions are taken out of our hands. They are never, and cannot be entirely our own. Whether a young woman in Paris in a few days time does not set down a long letter to a doctor in a Military Hospital in the South of England – and what she says in it – may be decisive in the destiny of them both.[9]

His relationship with Marcelle was constantly interrupted by geography. It was difficult for them to spend sufficient time together for their relationship to develop to the next stage. Laing busied himself in work and extra-curricular reading and also enjoyed the company of friends, including Anne Hearne, a nursing sister from Netley, with whom he played tennis. Meantime, after spending one year at Netley, Laing was promoted to the rank of captain and posted to the Catterick Military Hospital, Yorkshire.

At Catterick one of his duties was to examine new recruits who had entered the army with a criminal record, and assess whether or not the recruit was likely to resume his previous criminal career whilst in the service of Her Majesty. Another letter to Marcelle throws some light on Laing's attitude towards the task.

My present work does not concern 'treating' these people – and in fact I am convinced that the only 'treatment' is prevention. There are numerous statistical surveys which make it pretty clear that poor, insecure economic conditions, unhappy homelife (e.g., parents drunk and quarrelsome), low education standard associated with under-average intelligence, and a number of other factors, are almost constantly present in those people who commit crimes at an early age.[10]

The letter is concluded with a question, 'Will we be able to meet at the end of the year?' The answer would be no, simply because his tennis companion informed Laing that she was six months pregnant. After seeking less than helpful advice from others, in the knowledge that nothing was certain with Marcelle, and given the prevailing social norms of the time, Laing did the 'honourable thing' and married Anne. The ceremony took place on October 11th, 1952 at the Richmond Registry Office, Yorkshire. Neither Amelia nor David Laing attended the wedding, shocked and disappointed at the turn of events, and nor did Laing inform Marcelle of the event until afterwards. When he did so, by letter, he said that he couldn't cry, so painful was the decision and its consequences. His first daughter, Fiona, was born soon afterwards on the December 7th.

While he was based at Catterick Laing published his first refereed article, in the *Journal* of the Royal Medical Corps in July 1953 on the subject of the 'Ganser Syndrome'. This unusual condition has four features – psychogenic physical symptoms, hallucinations, apparent clouding of consciousness and, most importantly, the giving of 'approximate answers'. These are answers which are plainly wrong but which strongly suggest that the correct reply is known. Thus a patient when asked how many legs has a dog, might reply five. The condition is believed to be a result of unconscious psychological mechanisms, and can often be mistaken for malingering. Laing's article was based on a case that was referred to him while he was stationed at Netley. Following a car crash and subsequent hospitalisation, a young soldier had deserted from the army. He spent time at home with his family, and time working on fairgrounds. Although his behaviour was abnormal, his family put it down to him just not being his old self. Eventually the soldier gave himself up to the authorities, and he came to the attention of Laing. To begin with, he was mute. He was given an intravenous injection of pentothal which resulted in the soldier bad mouthing both the army and also his wife, who had given birth to a child by another man, and whom the patient had subsequently divorced. Later he was unable to give correct answers to the simplest of questions and, for example, called an orange an apple, and stated that two times two was two. He became obsessed with his mother, whom he appeared to see and hear much of the time, particularly in the mornings. He regressed to the physical and mental state of a two year old. Clinically, Laing concluded that the patient's Ganser-like reactions rendered him unfit to plead in his proposed trial by court martial. Laing continued to observe the patient, and eventually hypnotised him and administered pentothal. Eventually, after some six weeks or so, he appeared to make something of a recovery. However, the detailed observations that Laing made of this young soldier merely reinforced his earlier idea that mental distress could be understood only if the physician could enter the patient's inner world, even if the physician or the patient himself could not immediately recognise the processes at work in that internal world.

Laing left the army in September 1953, still a young man of twenty five, but wiser in the knowledge he had acquired of mental suffering and the traditional psychiatric response to it. He had been particularly disappointed by his experience of army psychiatry: he had learned some skills in man management, administration, organisational institutional power and structure, but little new in terms of medical practice. A few months earlier, on May 18th, he had somewhat bitterly made a diary entry in which he recorded that he had achieved 'fuck all' in the army. However, he was married with a child, had done 'perhaps inestimable harm to one person', and had become more reconciled to both his parents. But he certainly had not furthered his career.

Gartnavel Royal Mental Hospital, Glasgow, was Laing's next stop *en route* to completing his psychiatric internship, of which two years was left. A nineteenth-century asylum, Gartnavel still maintained a division between fee-paying and non-fee-paying patients. Those with money were able to vegetate in a Victorian conservatory amidst palms and aspidistras, while the others were packed together like sardines. Laing, as one might imagine, worked among the latter. He also worked on the female refractory ward, full of over sixty women all stripped of any signs of personal identity and some of whom had been wasting away for over half a century. They were bathed once a week, their backs scrubbed painfully, and they hardly ever saw a physician except to satisfy the requirement that they were physically examined twice a year. Records were kept to a minimum and staff were rotated thereby negating any possibility of meaningful personal relationships between staff and patients. ECT was *de rigueur,* as were insulin comas, and some of these women had suffered lobotomies. Completely institutionalised, many of them manifested the behaviour they believed was expected of them, hearing voices and talking to themselves.

Three months was all that Laing needed before he proposed an experiment to the hospital authorities. He wanted to establish a room away from the refractory ward where the emphasis would be on developing personal relationships between staff and patients. Once his proposal had been agreed Laing chose twelve patients, all 'schizophrenic' and all of whom had not endured a lobotomy and only a minimum of ECT. Significantly they were also the least liked on the ward and therefore were those who had received least human contact and conversation. These women were to spend their days in this brightly decorated room, complete with magazines and art materials, and then return to the ward in the evening. Both the patients and the nurses were allowed to wear normal clothes, and the patients were allowed to wear make up, and even have their hair styled. Two nurses were given the job of exclusively and consistently caring for and interacting with them. After a disappointing response on the first day – hardly surprising given their previous experiences – the second day saw a most significant development. An hour before the door was due to be opened, the women were laughing, talking and fidgeting outside of it, eager to get inside. Laing later recalled the moment as one of the most moving of his entire life. These distressed, disturbed and incarcerated women were, for the first time, being treated like other human beings.

One minor but nonetheless significant event remained in Laing's mind. On one occasion the patients baked some buns and, in a spirit of generosity, took them to the doctors' sitting room. Only a tiny number of doctors were prepared to 'break bread' with these patients, the others perhaps believing that a schizophrenic-baked-bun might well be contagious and they themselves would develop schizophrenia. Laing wondered who were the crazier, the patients or doctors? Some eighteen months after the beginning of the experiment *all* twelve women had been discharged from the hospital, yet within a year all were back inside. After a life of institutionalisation it was invariably difficult for them to cope in the outside world. Moreover, as Laing surmised, perhaps family life was worse than life inside the hospital.

Together with his co-authors Cameron, McGhie and Freeman, Laing published their report on the project in the December 12th, 1955, issue of *The Lancet*, concluding that the beneficial therapeutic element had been the opportunities of meaningful relationships between staff and patients.

Johnny Duffy recalls a visit he made to Gartnavel, where on one evening when Laing was on-duty all night they shared some whisky and Laing played the piano. As the night progressed a woman was ranting from her overcrowded ward, and shouting that she wanted out of 'this fucking place'. Duffy recalls that the moment she saw Laing she *calmed*. While two nurses were restraining her in order to sedate her with medication, Laing simply said 'hello Jennie'. The three of them, Laing, Duffy and Jennie, went to an adjoining room where Jennie smoked a cigarette. Then, some time afterwards, Laing gently coaxed her back to bed, then remarked to his friend 'these bastards would get her down on the floor, give her a jab, but it wouldn't do her any good. Next day she wouldn't be any better'.[11]

While at Gartnavel, Laing's family was expanding. In September 1954 his wife gave birth to another daughter, Susan, and by early 1955 was pregnant again. His reading too was continuing and, in addition to his staple diet of Kierkegaard, Jaspers, Minkowski, Nietzsche, Sartre, *et al.*, he added Tillich, Huxley, Bergson, Simone Weil, Dylan Thomas, Tolstoy, and numerous others.

In 1955 he left Gartnavel to take up a position at the Southern General Hospital, where the Department of Psychological Medicine of Glasgow University was located. He was appointed as a Senior Registrar, working under the direction of Professor Ferguson Rodger. Surprisingly, given his youthfulness, Laing was given his own department, the youngest person to have held such an office. Despite Rodger's apparent high regard for Laing he opposed the latter's idea for another experiment similar to the one he had introduced at Gartnavel. He also disapproved of Laing seeing patients while in his armchair rather than from behind a desk. This was the nucleus of the condemnation which would follow Laing throughout his career.

Laing's third daughter, Karen, was born in November 1955. Two months later Laing's name was entered into the register of The Royal Medico-Psychological Association, recording him, at the age of twenty eight, as a formally qualified psychiatrist. When he discovered that his former colleagues from the Gartnavel experiment were expanding their collective paper into a book, without consulting him, it fuelled him to write. And after the publication in May 1956 of Colin Wilson's *The Outsider*, he vowed that he too would complete an existential study of his own.

3

We Are Our Own Question Mark

Viewed pathetically, a single second has infinite value; viewed comically, ten thousand years are but a trifle, like yesterday when it is gone. If one were to say simply and directly that ten thousand years are but a trifle, many a fool would give his assent, and would find it wisdom; but he forgets the other, that a second has infinite value.

Søren Kierkegaard

Kierkegaard tells the story of the man so absent-minded and abstracted from his own life that he hardly knows he exists until, one fine morning, he wakes up to find himself dead.[1] *Existentialism* is *the* major philosophical inspiration behind Laing's work. It is worth describing the major features of the approach, as its importance in his thought and actions will become all too apparent.

Unlike many other systems of philosophy, it is the existentialist view that there are 'always loose ends'.[2] Reality is not easily packaged. Our experience as well as our knowledge is always incomplete and fragmentary. Indeed, the father of modern existentialism, Søren Kierkegaard, significantly titled two of his major works *Philosophical Fragments* and *Concluding Unscientific Postscript*.

The basic tenet common to all existentialist thinkers is that 'the person is more than a thing and cannot be adequately formulated in the terminology of natural science'.[3] Existentialism is a philosophy of how man makes himself. As Sartre puts it: 'if man, as the existentialist sees him, is not definable, it is because to begin with he is nothing. He will not be anything until later, and then he will be what he makes of himself'.[4] Accordingly the themes one encounters in existentialist thought are those of freedom, decision and responsibility. These matters constitute the core of personal being. It is this exercise of freedom and the ability to shape the future that distinguishes man from all the other beings that we know on earth. Although, in the main, existentialists are concerned with the 'individual whose quest for authentic selfhood focuses on the meaning of personal being', they also are aware that man exists as a person only in a community of persons: interpersonally. Martin Buber's *I and Thou*, is perhaps the most obvious example of such awareness.

Another difference between this style of philosophising is that all existentialists appear aware of 'the tragic elements in human existence'. Existence ends in death. Perhaps, then, it is not surprising that existentialism, unlike all other major philosophical systems, focuses on the *emotional* dimensions of human existence. Indeed, from Kierkegaard to Heidegger and Sartre, the existentialists have provided brilliant analyses of states such as anxiety, despair, boredom and nausea.

Yet there is great diversity to be found among existentialist thought – the atheism of Nietzsche, Kierkegaard's Christianity, Sartre's fascination with Marxism. John Macquarrie has argued that 'the fact that so many different points of view are found among those commonly called existentialists simply shows that existentialism offers no shortcuts towards the solution of metaphysical or ontological problems'.[5] No quick answers to perennial questions: who am I? Does God exist? Is there life after death? Laing himself exquisitely puts it thus: 'we are creatures whose being is in question to ourselves – we are our own question mark'.[6]

In 1956, Laing clearly knew where his interest lay – in the field of mental misery, as he personally termed it. An opportunity was about to arrive which would, theoretically, enable him to immerse himself more into the *understanding* of such states of mind. It began after he had met and been influenced by the German Protestant theologian Paul Tillich whose acquaintance Laing had made in Glasgow. Tillich defined religion itself as the object of man's ultimate concern; nothing more, certainly nothing less. Philosophy, in Tillich's view, was to concern itself with ontological questions, and theology with existential ones. Here was a man who appeared to share the concerns that had been at the centre of Laing's intellectual life – Who are we? What are we? Where do we come from? And in Tillich's most well-known book, *The Courage to Be,* he had placed 'courage' at the centre of man's quest to stay sane in the face of the painful and relentless existential anxiety.

Supremely impressed and influenced by Tillich, Laing wrote a paper on the theologian and sent it to Jock Sutherland, editor of the *British Journal of Medical Psychology*. Sutherland, Medical Director of the Tavistock Clinic, was most interested in the paper. Fortuitously for Laing, Sutherland was in the process of establishing a scheme whereby psychiatrists from the provinces were brought to London to train. After sufficient elucidatory experience and psychiatric practice in the capital, they could then return from whence they came, and practice on the natives. Accordingly Laing was one of the first intake of Sutherland's scheme.

In 1956, the Tavistock Clinic was situated in Beaumont Street, having moved from its original location in Tavistock Square. Laing was appointed a senior registrar. Together with his family, which was soon to be expanded with the birth of two sons, Paul and Adrian, he moved to Harlow, an Essex new town some twenty miles north of London, and commuted daily into London. In addition to his daily work at the Clinic, it was part of the relocation package to the Tavistock that he was seconded to the Institute of Psychoanalysis. This was the first time that Laing had encountered psychoanalysis on a practical basis. He attended lectures and seminars, and ran a psychoanalytic clinic five times a week, under the supervisory auspices of the Institute. It was also a condition that he submit himself to the psychoanalytical process.

The Tavistock was an immediate and profound disappointment to Laing. For some reason he had anticipated that it would be an environment similar to those he had previously encountered. In particular, he imagined he would be working with severely disturbed and distressed individuals. Instead he realised that the Tavistock was exclusively an out-patient clinic, whose toilets were differentially marked 'staff' and 'patients'. Crucially he was not seeing people whose mental distress involved disturbances of the body as well as the mind. He felt that he was spending his time just sitting and talking with people whose problems appeared less severe than those to which he was accustomed. He believed that at the Tavistock he had 'really fucked up' and that from that moment on, he believed his career went 'down the drain'.[7]

Glaswegian Laing, immersed in continental philosophy and deeply empathetic with the craziest of people, found it problematic working alongside Tavistock luminary as John Bowlby, Cambridge-educated, cold, dispassionate, and Victorian in outlook. Bowlby had received world-wide recognition with his 1953 book *Child Care and the Growth of Love,* and in particular his view that 'maternal care in infancy' was as important 'in magnitude to that of the role of vitamins in physical health'.[8] This appalled Laing. He abhorred the notion that without the right kind of maternal care someone was destined for mental ill-health. He saw it as a terrible condemnation of those who had suffered from a poor childhood – as if they hadn't enough to cope with.

The Institute of Psychoanalysis similarly proved less than satisfactory, despite Laing being in the presence of such psychoanalytical luminaries as W. R. Bion, D. W. Winnicott and Melanie Klein. He realised that he was indeed among the most well-respected and influential analysts, but he found their teaching often didactic and authoritarian, and devoid of a sense of humour.

*

Whether this is the right moment to introduce this note of caution, I am unsure. However it should be noted that many of the people who have written and continue to write about Laing appear to simply assume without question that institutions such as the Tavistock Clinic, or the Institute of Psychoanalysis are, given their longevity, beyond criticism. Likewise, it also appears to hold true for the practice of conventional psychoanalysis, and indeed the very theory of psychoanalysis itself. I find it difficult to converse or debate with those who defend such theories and practices on the grounds that they are either beyond the scope of any test of validity, or more simply beyond the comprehension of the uninitiated – a sermon only for the converted. What is particularly unsettling about such postulations and suppositions are their very certainty. It appears almost impossible to disagree with a psychoanalytic interpretation without it being merely further proof of the patient's inability to see straight, or to admit to a particular psychological shortcoming. Psychoanalytical theory and practice is resplendent with hypotheses, ideas and concepts nearly all of which, to borrow Karl Popper's phrase, are unable to be *falsified.* This is not to say that I absolutely and unequivocally reject all Freudian notions but merely to emphasise that the certainty and, at times, the arrogance of the psychoanalytical world is based on flimsy foundations. Laing, mischievously perhaps, argued that the greatest contribution Freud made was making it possible for someone to earn a good income out of listening to people.

*

Laing himself was analysed by Charles Rycroft, a fairly orthodox man in his practice, who was less so in his theory. Five times a week for over four years Laing would submit himself to Rycroft for the 'Freudian hour' of fifty minutes. Once those minutes had been exhausted Rycroft would finish the session, even if Laing was earnestly talking or questioning. Laing would lie down on the couch and tell Rycroft of dreams he had remembered from the previous night. Rycroft would make little or no interpretation and when he did so would apologise in advance. The analysis was, in Laing's terms, 'undramatic'. Interestingly Rycroft did remark to Laing, after he had been talking about a situation at the Tavistock which had unsettled him, that 'you know one of the things about when you talk, you appear to mean it'.[9] In other words, it is almost impossible for an orthodox analyst to accept anything at face value: which, apart from anything else, might well result in a somewhat depressing and negative view of humanity.

Given Laing's insistence on trying to understand the patient's point of view, one can only marvel at the way in which he appeared to take this five-times-a-week medicine, despite it being administered by a somewhat congenial and non-dogmatic Rycroft. It has been argued that the analysis was unsuccessful by virtue of the fact that it failed to uncover Laing's deep-seated and profoundly destructive depression.[10] The question can reasonably be posed: why should a practice in which someone may or may not talk about and perhaps re-experience the important emotional, familial, personal and social moments of their lives, *necessarily* uncover and deal with something like depression? Additionally, perhaps Laing did not have the necessary psychological make-up to deal with the procedure, perhaps he was unable to suspend any doubts he might reasonably have had about psychoanalysis. Consider it for a moment: the patient might talk about almost anything, or nothing, and whatever he does, or does not, say, is then put through a theoretical mincer that includes such seemingly bizarre concepts as penis envy, the Oedipus complex, castration anxiety, or whatever. Of course, as always, there is an escape route mapped out in advance for the psychoanalytic sensibility and, not surprisingly, it was prepared for Laing. For as Marion Milner, one of Laing's supervisors at the Institute, put it, perhaps Laing was 'unanalysable', in other words, he was unreceptive to analysis. Heads they win, tails you lose.

On January 3rd, 1959, Douglas Hutchinson, best man at Laing's wedding and his close friend, fell off the snow-covered ridge of Ben More and was killed. Having encouraged him to go on the climbing trip Laing felt obliged to break the news to Hutchinson's widow, which he duly did. He wept uncontrollably at the funeral, and felt that he had lost the brother he did not have. John Clay, in his biography of Laing, states, without comment, that his behaviour at the funeral, the profuse weeping, caused more 'raised eyebrows among his professional colleagues'.[11] *Why?* Here was a man who felt he had been partly responsible for someone's death, someone for whom he cared greatly, and someone whose widow was left with a new-born baby. Surely it would have been unforgivable if he *didn't* weep? The incident characterised one of the many differences between Laing and his psychoanalytic colleagues: he was a man of passion who could and did express his feelings openly, they were detached professionals who analysed individuals and emotions objectively as if they were pieces of a jigsaw puzzle which needed rearrangement.

Laing wrote his first book, *The Divided Self,* whilst he was working at the Clinic and the Institute. It was written mostly in the early hours of the morning at his home in Harlow, and typed by his secretarial staff. This was one of the reasons why he frequently skipped lectures, seminars and other meetings at the Institute, absences which eventually called into question his right to qualify as a psychoanalyst. Many other reasons have been cited for his absences, usually variations on the same theme of his anti-authoritarianism, and his inability to accept discipline. A more simple explanation is that he saw through the absurdity of what passed for his psychoanalytic education, and believed that his own intellectual and clinical education was better served completing other tasks, and reading elsewhere. In the Spring of 1960, an attempt was made to postpone his qualification. In his defence Rycroft, admirably, argued that Laing was easily the most intelligent candidate he'd analysed, one who was independently minded and one who was aware of the importance of the unconscious in human behaviour. Marion Milner also supported Laing as did another luminary, D. W. Winnicott who, nevertheless, added the caveat that in his opinion, Laing would benefit after qualification by a continuing personal analysis.

Eventually the Institute's Training Committee relented, and Laing graduated as a qualified psychoanalyst on schedule in 1960.

A major factor contributing to why Laing encountered problems at both the Tavistock Clinic and the Institute of Psychoanalysis, in addition to his frequently expressing opinions on what he was being told and taught, was the considerable professional envy at his energy and originality. This centred on *The Divided Self*, drafts of which he had previously circulated among Tavistock colleagues. Some of the more established and less threatened of his colleagues, like Winnicott and Bowlby, were quietly enthusiastic. Winnicott was excited partly because he felt that Laing made so 'much use of the sort of things I think important' and, interestingly, that he had gained an insight about 'paranoid states' from the manuscript which led him to realise that one of his own patients was 'being watched by a projection of her true self'.[12] Bowlby also said that he liked it, though disapproved of the usage of the words 'existentialism' and 'phenomenology' as he did not fully understand their meaning.

The book had originally been started in Glasgow, when Laing was reflecting on his Gartnavel experiment. While in Glasgow he also circulated an even earlier draft of the book to the friends with whom he met at a weekly discussion group, especially Joe Schorstein and Karl Abenheimer, a practising Jungian therapist. The group shared the same interests and the same fascination with so-called continental philosophy – Sartre, Camus, Tillich, Martin Buber, Kierkegaard, Jaspers and Miguel de Unamuno, the little-known Spanish existentialist who believed that 'faith' meant the hope that death does not annihilate existence, yet the fact that it may well do so creates in man 'a tragic sense of life'. Such were the concerns of this small group.

After abandoning the title 'The Ghost of the Weed Garden', Laing settled on the later title, itself derived from William James's *Varieties of Religious Experience*, in which he posits a psychological explanation for mystical experience, suggesting that mystics and saints were themselves divided selves, responding to their own repressed guilt rather than to

God. The clinical evidence for the book emerged out of his work both in the army and at Gartnavel, and initially from meeting Edith Edwards, 'Julie', the 'ghost of the weed garden'.

Laing prefaced his book stating that its basic purpose was to make madness, and the process of going mad, comprehensible. 'Specifically, no attempt is made to present a comprehensive theory of schizophrenia. No attempt is made to explore constitutional and organic aspects ... A further purpose is to give an account in *existential* terms, of some forms of madness'.[13] Laing elaborates, and adds that schizophrenia cannot be understood without understanding despair. It is clear that his approach neither romanticises or idealises madness, nor does he view the schizophrenic as suffering a physical disease.

> The kernel of the schizophrenic's experience of himself must remain incomprehensible to us. As long as we are sane and he is insane, it will remain so. But comprehension as an effort to reach and grasp him, while remaining within our own world and judging him by our own categories whereby he inevitably falls short, is not what the schizophrenic either wants or requires. We have to recognise all the time his distinctiveness and differentness, his separateness and loneliness and despair.[14]

In a perceptive analysis of an interview with a patient described by Emil Kraepelin who, in 1897, first coined the term *dementia praecox,* Laing demonstrates that the psychiatrist is too preoccupied with categorising the behaviour of the patient to notice that the 'psychotic' utterances he hears are reasonable, if disguised, objections to being merely classified and not treated as a person.

The central concept for Laing is that of *ontological insecurity*. Meaning? An ontologically *secure* person will encounter the hazards of life from a 'centrally firm sense of his own and other people's reality and identity'. An ontologically *insecure* person suffers a fundamental insecurity of being, an insecurity that pervades all of his existence. He is thereby forced into a continuous struggle to maintain a sense of his own being. In this weak and vulnerable position he fears 'engulfment' by others, the 'implosion' of external reality, the 'petrification' of becoming no more than a *thing* in the world of the other. The individual's total self, the 'embodied self', faced with disadvantageous conditions, may be split into two parts, a disembodied 'inner self', felt by the person to be the real part of himself, and a 'false self', embodied but dead and futile, which puts up a front of conformity to the world.[15] Laing's final chapter, 'The Ghost of the Weed Garden', presents a case study which illustrates his central thesis.

By the time Laing encountered 'Julie', she had been incarcerated in Gartnavel for nine years, since she was seventeen. She had been labelled as being 'a typical inaccessible and withdrawn chronic schizophrenic', and upon admission had been diagnosed as hebephrenic and given a course of insulin treatments. To no avail. She hallucinated and acted in the most bizarre yet stereotyped ways. She was mostly mute but when she did speak it was in 'schizophrenese'. For example, Julie, in her psychosis, referred to herself as Mrs Taylor. Laing asks, what does this mean? It means, he asserts, 'I'm tailor-made', 'I'm a tailored maid; I was made, fed, clothed, and tailored'.[16] In other words, cut up and shaped by her mother. In his chapter, 'The Ghost of the Weed Garden', Laing presents a clinical case study of Julie, in which he breaks the code of her behaviour and language, interpreting it as an almost logical consequence of Julie's life and experience of life – and particularly family life.

Prima facie, Julie came from a close, loving family, normal in every way; Julie had an older married sister, and an almost doting mother. Her relationship with her father was a little less 'normal', but otherwise seemingly predictable. Throughout Laing's interviews with all family members, many different views and experiences of Julie emerged, but there were three points on which all agreed. There was a time when:

a) Julie was good = normal
b) Julie was bad = not normal
c) Julie was bad beyond all comprehension = mad

Julie spoke mostly through many separate entities, but primarily three:

a) the peremptory bully, who ordered her about and criticised her. 'This child is wasted time. This child is just a cheap tart'. Laing identified this quasi-autonomous partial system as the Bad Internal Mother, which he characterised as 'an internal female persecutor who contained in concentrated form all the bad that Julie ascribed to her mother'.[17]

b) the advocate on Julie's behalf, who buffered Julie against persecution, referred to her as 'her little sister' (although Julie's sister is in fact older, that is, bigger) and to whom Laing referred in phenomenological terms as 'her good sister'.

c) the good, compliant, propitiating little girl, whom Laing identified as a derivative of an earlier system similar to the false-self system he had previously encountered in schizoid cases.

Sadly, there were also remnants of what appeared to be an 'inner self', visible in moments when Julie appeared precariously sane, at which time she spoke in a scared almost inaudible voice. Given the above codes, Laing gives an example of one of Julie's more coherent utterances:

> I was born under a black sun. I wasn't born, I was crushed out. It's not one of those things you get over like that. I wasn't mothered I was smothered. She wasn't a mother. I'm choosy who I have for a mother. Stop it. Stop it. She's killing me. She's cutting out my tongue. I'm rotten, base. I'm wicked. I'm wasted time.[18]

Which Laing then interprets.

The first six sentences are spoken 'sanely'. The black sun is an ancient and sinister image which may have arisen totally independently in her mind, as it was unlikely she would have encountered it in any reading matter. She had left school at fourteen, had read little and was not considered 'particularly clever'. For Julie, this image is recurrent, and appears to symbolise her destructive mother. As we have seen, Julie's mother was doting, but upon closer examination Laing saw that she had never facilitated the child to learn independent behaviour, to become autonomous, and therefore to have a concrete image of herself in 'the world'. Therefore Julie begins to convert existential truth into physical facts, and in her delusions makes the basic psychotic accusation, that her mother has murdered a child, a child which was wearing Julie's clothes when it was killed. She elaborates that her mother didn't want her *ab initio*, that her mother smothered her and most significantly perhaps, did not want her to become a person. In fact, through interviews with the mother discussing Julie's infanthood, Laing concludes that none of the adults in Julie's world knew the difference between existential life and death. On the contrary, when Julie was at her most existentially dead, she received the highest praise – that she was never a *demanding* baby; she was weaned without trouble; she had perfect bowel and bladder control from the moment she was taken out of nappies; she was always obedient; she was never 'trouble'. Far from being a perfect child – a good and a normal child – Julie paradigmatically characterised a non-child, a child with no will or desires for gratification. Julie in fact referred to herself as 'a tolled belle' or 'told belle', too terror-stricken to become a person, merely *a thing*.

Therefore Julie sees her mother as crushing her out, meaning both the birth process and the extinction of spirit. Her mother could only truly love a false, compliant self, and Julie consequently feels she has been murdered. To be able to live, Julie feels her mother needs to admit her mistakes, and to admit that *Julie might be right*. In clinical terms, she needs to be allowed to project some of her bad-self into the mother, and then be allowed to *take* goodness out of her mother, and not be passively *presented* with it all the time. Julie needs her mother to be a *mother* so that she can in fact be a real child.

It was typical of Julie's rants and critiques of her mother that they would be followed by catastrophic reactions. Halfway through her rant, she appears to be under attack presumably from the bad mother, whom Julie has always acknowledged as 'the Boss'. Then, follows the defensive denigration of herself as base, worthless and rotten. As Laing pointed out to Julie on a later occasion, Julie was afraid of being killed by herself, for saying such things. 'Yes', agreed a quiet voice, perhaps Julie's 'self', 'yes, that's my conscience killing me. I've been frightened of my mother all my life and always will be. *Do you think I can live?*'

Given that much of Julie's perception or delusion of what was right or wrong in her world centres on the mother, perhaps we should discuss the concept of the 'schizophrenogenic mother'. To the contrary of what some of Laing's critics have written about him, he did not advocate a witch-hunt against mothers. His hypothesis is quite clear:

There may be some ways of being a mother that impede rather than facilitate or 'reinforce' any genetically determined inborn tendency there maybe in the child towards achieving the primary developmental stages of ontological security. Not only the mother but also the total family situation may impede rather than facilitate the child's capacity to participate in a real shared world, as self-with-other.[19]

He asked – what happens if the mother's or family's scheme of things does not provide an environment in which the child can thrive and breathe? He answered – the child has to develop its own piercing vision and to be able to live by the code of that vision – or else go 'mad'.

With Julie, Laing believed it quite possible that she was born, due to some genetic factor, with her organism so formed that instinctual need and need-gratification did not come easily to her. Added to this, she was surrounded by people who took this very deficit as a *token of goodness,* and, as Laing said, stamped with approval this absence of self-action. He stated that this almost total failure of the child to achieve self-instinctual gratification, married to the mother's total failure to realise that this was *abnormal,* was a recurrent theme in the early relationships of mother-schizophrenic child.

Julie didn't have a true perception of 'self', or position in the world. Laing described her as a girl 'possessed' by the phantom of her own being, having no freedom, autonomy or power in the real world. Terrified of many things, but perhaps most of all the concept of 'life', Julie saw Laing as identical to life and was consequently at times terrified of him. She felt she was the 'Destroyer of Life', and terrified that life would destroy her.

Julie saw her existence purely in terms of absence of life, in images of arid barren ground. Laing termed it a death in life, and indeed Julie succinctly describes herself, in the third person common to schizo-phrenese, 'she's the ghost of the weed garden'. Sadly, Julie sees herself as a *ghost* i.e., a manifestation of something which once existed, but is in addition the ghost of a *weed* garden. She is the mere ectoplasmic remnant of something which, even in life, had no value. Julie's world is empty and dead, in which there is no future or hope of possible gratification/satis-faction. *Even Julie's dolls died.*

At the age of seventeen, Julie had a doll which she had retained from infancy and had never outgrown. In total secrecy, she treated it as if it were a human child – perhaps the human child she was not or could not become. It was called Julie Doll. Naturally her mother was concerned that her seventeen-year old daughter was still playing with dolls, and insisted with increased frequency that she 'give it up'. Perhaps she was jealous of the attention Julie gave it. Whatever. One day the doll disappeared and Laing never solved the mystery of where it had gone, and by whose hand. Both Julie and her mother denied ever removing it. Shortly afterwards, Julie heard a voice which said that a *child wearing her clothes* had been beaten to pulp by her mother. Julie wished to report the matter to the police. Laing entertains the possibility that Julie's internal mother, the bully and archetypal destroyer, disposed of the doll, or maybe her real mother did. As might be imagined, the loss was cataclysmic to Julie, who, there can be no doubt, identified closely with it. And again there is the recurrent imagery of a murder of a child by a mother, in Julie's case metaphorical, the existential translated into the physical.

The sad phenomena of both the Julie Doll and the Ghost of the Weed Garden is that they embody succinctly, Julie's desperation at feeling existentially and therefore physically dead in and to this world.

Laing did perceive that Julie believed (however psychotically) that she had an intrinsic value, buried deeply within herself. But whether Julie could ever find an environment, in all its meanings, which would allow her to become alive, was another matter. Perhaps the saddest set of words in the chapter is Julie's description of herself – 'she's just one of those girls who live in the world. Everyone pretends to want her and doesn't want her'.[20]

The plight of all the Julies in our world which insists on a quick-fix remedy is a sad one. 'This child's mind is cracked. This child's mind is closed. You're trying to open this child's mind. I'll never forgive you for trying to open this child's mind'.[21]

The above quotation comes from Julie's 'good sister'. But it could just as well come from a spokesperson for orthodox conventional physical biological psychiatry. Although Laing does not spell it out, his solution for the person who has *actively* created a false self in order to survive in an intolerable situation is for them to find a way – with appropriate guidance and support – to be *themselves*, to regain their sanity through authentic interaction with others.

The book was turned down by six publishers, including his first choice

Victor Gollancz, who sympathetically decided against publication. Eventually Laing found a home for it with Tavistock Publications, who published it in 1960, two years later. The book was critically well-received, perceived as a thoroughly professional and original approach to understanding psychosis and in particular schizophrenia, yet in hardback the book sold a mere sixteen hundred copies. It was only later when, in 1965, a Penguin edition was published that it sold in thousands, to a public who could recognise themselves and those around them in Laing's pages. By the time of his death in 1989, the book had sold over three-quarters of a million copies world-wide, translated into numerous languages.

In 1961, while he was still employed by the Tavistock, Laing also, quite legitimately, established a private practice in Wimpole Street, at the hub of the private medical fraternity. In his tranquil consulting room, chairs were scattered at random creating a more relaxed and less orthodox atmosphere. There *was* a couch but this was more for the purpose of a patient taking a rest than for a reconstruction of conventional analysis. A print of Bruegel's *Fall of Icarus* hung on one wall. This parable of the fate of those who foolishly aspire to rise above their rank in life amused Laing who, nevertheless, was determined to rise above the established view of his work and standing. There were other prints and drawings elsewhere. His desk was not centrally placed. Patient after patient visited his consulting room, endeavouring to gain enlightenment in order for their mental misery to dissipate. Unlike a conventional analyst, Laing would not insist that a patient saw him for a protracted period of time; sometimes one session would suffice while on other occasions he might suggest that a person saw him regularly, but for a short period of time. As time went on he began to abandon the stricture of the 'Freudian hour', seeing patients for longer periods and sometimes, albeit infrequently, for shorter.

LSD had first been used therapeutically in the UK during the 1950s at various institutions, notably Powick Hospital, Malvern, which had a purpose-built LSD unit. At Wimpole Street Laing began to experiment, tentatively and responsibly, with LSD, both on himself and with consenting patients. Although he had taken other somewhat milder drugs, especially marijuana, it was the first time he had taken a psychedelic substance. Laing tried the drug with friend and erstwhile colleague Dr

Richard Gelfer. He found that it apparently enabled him to somehow re-experience the sensations he might well have enjoyed as a young boy – a *primary* sort of experience, in which new perspectives would unfold and reveal themselves to him. His interest in LSD and other psychedelic substances was first aroused after reading Aldous Huxley's *The Doors of Perception* and *Heaven and Hell,* both published in the mid-fifties and both of which describe Huxley's own experiences with LSD, mescaline and peyote. In his writings, Huxley saw the psychedelic experience as one in which the mind's awareness would be expanded to new horizons through the use of hallucinogenic drugs, and other naturally occurring substances.

Huxley believed that the places visited by the minds of the 'insane and the exceptionally gifted' were so far removed from the normal man's landscape that it was difficult for either to communicate with the other. And he believed that the mescaline experience was, for example, helpful in shaking someone out of the 'ruts of ordinary perception, to be shown for a few timeless hours the outer and the inner world'. Importantly for Laing, Huxley compared the visionary psychedelic experience with that of the schizophrenic experience and argued that schizophrenics too have their times of heavenly happiness. But Huxley concluded that, unlike the mescaline taker, schizophrenics do not know when, if ever, they will be 'permitted to return to the reassuring banality of everyday experiences' which causes 'even heaven to seem appalling'. According to Huxley many such individuals spent most of their time 'neither on earth, nor in heaven, nor even in hell, but in a grey, shadowy world of phantoms and realities'. However on occasions such schizophrenics *did* descend into hell. Huxley cites the case of a young schizophrenic girl, Renée, whose vision was *not* a source of bliss but a nightmarish sense of unreality – 'the intensity of existence which animates every object, when seen at close range and out of its utilitarian context, is felt as a menace'. Significantly Huxley then reports her 'horror of infinity'. Compared to the healthy visionary whose perception of infinity is safely experienced as a revelation of the Divine, Renée's perception of the infinite was experienced as a vast cosmic mechanism which existed only to 'grind out guilt and punishment, solitude and unreality'. 'Sanity is a matter of degree', Huxley concludes, 'and there are plenty of visionaries who see the world as Renée saw it, but contrive, none the less, to live outside the asylum'.[22]

It is hardly surprising, therefore, that Laing was so interested in the possibilities that LSD might offer in his understanding of the schizophrenic experience, particularly when he felt that conventional methods were so vastly limited. LSD was able to take someone to terrifying experiential states of mind. Places with no exit. Hell. Someone might feel that they were really only a fragment, that they were in bits and pieces, wandering around the world aimlessly with nowhere to go. Conversely, such experiences and states of mind tend to be illusory, and they pass. They are transient. The sense of hopelessness that seems permanent disappears. The person emerges from the experience. Then again, what may be experienced is a sense of awe, of wonder, an almost spiritual state.

In the early years Laing utilised, under licence, Czechoslovakian-manufactured LSD which had been used therapeutically for a number of years. He diluted the LSD in a glass of water and then the session would unfold, for a time of not less than six hours. Some of the features of the session that Laing insisted upon were that there was to be an atmosphere of trust, quiet and security, and that, especially, the end of the session was to be free of disruption. It was important, Laing asserted, that someone was able to return to their previous consciousness, rather than some other state of mind. It is, of course, difficult to establish with any reliability the precise effects, both in the short and longer time scale, that such therapeutic drug-taking had on any individual patient. Some claimed that such six hours achieved more than a lifetime of conventional treatment, whilst others had less sanguine experiences. Laing claimed that by 1965 he had conducted over one hundred therapeutic LSD sessions and had himself taken the drug over thirty times. Mina Semyon has written movingly and informatively of her own LSD experience with Laing. She begins by recounting that when he suggested she take some LSD she admitted that she was unsure of what it actually entailed. Laing responded with 'it's probably better if you don't know much about it; would you like to try it?' Because he was the first 'human being who made me feel that such a thing as *trust* exists', she nervously yet enthusiastically agreed. At the agreed time, with Laing's proviso that her husband was to collect her afterwards, the six-hour session began. He poured the substance into a glass of water which she drank, then he added some more water to her glass, which he drank. Russian by birth,

her experience or 'trip' in psychedelic parlance, found her back in her
homeland.

> I found myself sitting on the floor curled up in a little ball, in a damp cold
> room in the Tartar Republic. I am four years old, my father is dead, my
> mother is lying in bed with covers over her head crying, and the Tartar
> landlady, whose son was just killed in the war, was lying behind the Russian
> oven wailing. I am sitting with shoulders hunched, sandwiched between
> their grief, my dress feels cold and damp, almost standing up, I am feeling
> a nobody, not considered, beaten down by life and abandoned.[23]

Despite the difficulties in describing her actual experience the words
are, nonetheless, extremely powerful and evocative. On returning to
normal consciousness Semyon felt that Laing too had experienced what
she had just experienced, as if it had been projected onto a screen. She
asked him if the events she had witnessed could have been as bad as she
felt them to be, and of course he replied 'probably worse'. She believed
that by being allowed to re-experience, as it were, the full horror of her
traumatic childhood, to see again the excruciating difficulties her mother
endured in addition to being unable to love her vulnerable four year-old
daughter, and by recognising her own resentment, she reached a turning
point. She knew that it was time to let go, if that were possible – to fully
accept the pain of her life, and move beyond it.

She recalls that although she experienced no psychedelic colours,
Laing himself changed before her eyes, from a samurai to a Turkish
pasha, and back to himself. The experience, carried out in an environment of safety and care, did not immediately solve all her problems, but
it did bring them clearly into focus.

My own experiences taking LSD on a therapeutic basis were less
enjoyable and far less enlightening, somewhat low key yet desperately
disturbing. On each of the four occasions, my head quickly lost its shape
and possessed no firm parameters. It was as if it could have floated away
from my neck at any given moment. Soon afterwards, each time, I
appeared to turn into an orange. Particularly distressing was the sensation of a hidden hand attempting to peel my skin.

*

Some years later Laing visited Timothy Leary, the chief spokesman and advocate of LSD, at his sprawling Millbrook estate in upstate New York, following an introduction by Allen Ginsberg. On a superficial level the two men enjoyed each others' company and appeared to speak a similar language. Leary recalled that Laing talked about shamanic medicine and compares him to Magister Ludi, the character from Herman Hesse's novel *The Glass Bead Game*, who would weave 'science-religion-art-experience' into the 'slickest bead game of our time'.[24]

In the early 1960s, it became common knowledge that Laing was therapeutically experimenting with LSD, news which was inevitably received by his peers with neither understanding nor approbation. Bowlby, for one, believed that such work would ruin Laing's potentially successful conventional and scientific career. But by that time, *The Divided Self* was reasonably well-known in professional circles, its sequel, *Self and Others* was being published, and Laing was in a position to accept criticism with equanimity.

Self and Others was an attempt to show that every relationship implies definition of self by other and other by self. In particular Laing was concerned with the role of fantasy in interpersonal perception and the consequences for the formation of identity, untenable positions and other malformations of interpersonal experiences. The book established Laing as a pioneer in the development of social phenomenology.

In the early 1960s the Laing family had moved out of the Essex suburbs into London. Laing was still putting himself under pressure with his research, writing and therapeutic practice and his marriage began to feel the strain of his apparent workaholism. The Tavistock also continued to frustrate and anger him. One of the many incidents which convinced him he should look for work elsewhere was the Clinic's reception of two separate but soon to be related papers. The first was written by two well-known biological psychiatrists, Kallmann and Slater, who posited that sterilisation might be appropriate for 'incorrigible schizophrenics'. The second was Laing's paper 'A Critique of the so-called genetic theory of schizophrenia in the work of Kallmann and Slater', in which Laing argued that Kallmann and Slater had a hidden agenda – eugenics – which was absolutely indefensible and inhumane. Indeed, yet another case of who was crazier, the patients or the psychiatrists? Bowlby's reaction to Laing's paper was shamefully predictable, namely that he should have been more 'scientific' in his condemnation of Kallmann and Slater's arguments, less rhetorical and, significantly, that if he wanted to change fundamentals he should do so from within the system/language/protocol, not from without.

With five children's mouths to feed, and in the certain knowledge that his private practice could not supply all the necessary income, yet feeling utterly disenchanted with the Tavistock, Laing faced an impasse. It seemed he had nowhere to turn. He had been a senior registrar for almost five years and would soon, in all likelihood, be promoted to consultant psychiatrist. Salvation came through the friendship he had previously forged with Eric Graham Howe, a fellow aficionado of Buddhism and director of the Open Way Psychotherapy Clinic. Laing was impressed with Howe, who had studied under Krishnamurti and whose message of spiritual self-responsibility he had accepted, and who had written the introduction of the Buddhist text the *Satisampajanna Sutra*. And Howe also felt that in Laing he had met a kindred spirit. Within a short time Howe offered Laing the position of clinical director of the Open Way Clinic. He accepted and left the Tavistock Clinic. Changing the name of the Open Way to the Langham Clinic, he organised and administered a programme of psychoanalytical and Jungian psychotherapy at affordable prices. Despite this definite career change, he was not quite finished with all things Tavistockian. Earlier, he had set in motion an important piece of research which was to lead to *Sanity, Madness and the Family,* one of Laing's most controversial books.

The idea for the project came about originally in 1958, because of Laing's feeling that, unlike the Tavistock technique which separated adults and children into different departments, families should be seen together and, preferably, in their own environments. *At home.* Accordingly he developed research plans to observe two cohorts of families, one set of 'schizophrenic families' and the other, 'normal'. Quite simply, yet controversially, the point of the research was to measure the degree to which the family environment might contribute to schizophrenia. The Tavistock Institute of Human Relations approved the proposal and agreed to fund it. Co-researchers on the project included Aaron Esterson, Russell Lee and David Cooper of the Belmont Hospital, who was to become a close friend and colleague of Laing's. Cooper, a South African born psychiatrist, later established an experimental unit named Villa 21, at the Shenley Hospital in St Albans, the purpose of which was to attempt to establish more humane relationships within the hospital at the expense of rigid demarcations between doctor and patient.

Once a week, all those involved would meet in a seminar with Laing to discuss the various approaches and methodologies they might employ in their research. One such approach which actually *emerged* from the seminar was written up in Laing's 1966 co-authored book, *Interpersonal Perception*. The authors, Laing, Herbert Phillipson and Russell Lee, argue that 'over a hundred years ago Feuerbach effected a pivotal step in philosophy', when he discovered that it had been previously been exclusively oriented around 'I', and that 'no one had realised that the "you" is as primary as the I'.[25] In other words, 'I am not the only perceiver and agent in my world'. The others are 'you, him, her, them, etc'. The presence of these others, the authors assert, 'has a profound reactive effect on me'. The book is an exploration and an explication of such patterns and cycles of positive and negative feedback in interpersonal relationships. As Laing *et al.* formulate it, through 'my behaviour I can act upon three areas of the other: on his experience of me; on his experience of himself; and upon his behaviour. In addition, I cannot act on the other himself directly, but I can act on my own *experience* of him'. For example, a central idea of the book is that in any room consisting two people, there are actually at least six; the two of them, together with four 'ghostly' presences: what I think of you, you of me, what I think you think of me, and you of me.

The authors constructed a questionnaire titled 'The Interpersonal Perception Method'. It attempts to elicit people's perceptions of 1) what they think of themselves, 2) what they think of the other person in the relationship, and 3) what they think the other person thinks about both parties to the relationship. The dimensions along which the questions are asked include issues of dependence and autonomy, concern and support, contradiction and confusion, and denial of autonomy within a relationship. The potentially beneficial nature of the procedure is that, in addition to the economy of time involved in administering the questionnaire, it shows exactly where each party does or does not understand that there is agreement or disagreement. Within the context of marital counselling, for example, no one is blamed: pathology is located in the spirals of reciprocal perceptions and misperceptions, not attributed to one or the other parties involved. The book's sensibility and approach was later incorporated, to an extent, in Laing's *Knots*.

In 1962, and in connection with the family research project Laing, financed by the Tavistock, made the first of many visits to the USA. On the trip he met family researchers and therapists like Lyman Wynne, Ross Speck, Murray Bowen and others, but especially important for Laing was a meeting with anthropologist Gregory Bateson who in 1956, with colleagues Haley, Jackson and Weakland, had produced a landmark paper titled 'Toward a theory of schizophrenia'. The paper described and operationalised the process of the 'double bind', in which an individual is placed in a situation that he or she perceives to be one in which he or she simply cannot win. Bateson *et al.* hypothesised that such a person caught up in the double bind may develop schizophrenic symptoms. An example Bateson *et al.* offer is that of a young schizophrenic man, in recovery, visited by his mother. When he sees her he instinctively and warmly embraces her, upon which her body stiffens. He feels that she does not want to be embraced – at least by him – and, sensitive to her wishes, he releases her only to be met with her remark, 'Don't you love me any more?' In response the young man blushes, to then be met with his mother gently chiding him with the words 'You must not be so easily embarrassed and afraid of your feelings'. The result is dramatic: he can only stay with her for a few minutes and, after she leaves the hospital, he assaults a nurse and is restrained. The situation could have been avoided if the man had been able to say to his mother something like 'I know it's difficult for you when I put my arms around you', however the schizophrenic patient does not have that option open to him. As Bateson argues, 'his intense dependency and training prevents him from commenting upon his mother's communicative behaviour, though she comments on his and forces him to accept and to attempt to deal with the complicated sequence'.[26] In essence, the impossible dilemma faced by such a person trapped in such a double bind can be expressed as follows – *If I am to keep my relationship with my mother I must not show her I love her, but if I don't show her that I love her, then I will lose her.*

The double bind made defensive and anxious schizophrenic individuals even more so. Behind every question was a hidden and potentially dangerous meaning, aimed at undermining their well-being. Hence the schizophrenic's overt concern with such hidden meanings and his ability to find them. He thus becomes suspicious and defiant, and eventually 'gives up trying to discriminate, and then reacts inappropriately, for instance laughing at the wrong moment, or becoming excessively serious, or detaching himself, or withdrawing into extreme paranoid or catatonic states'.[27] A never-ending spiral, the individual's behaviour becomes diagnosed as schizophrenic and their psychiatric career commences.

Bateson's approach, interviewing family members as well as the individual patient, was endorsed by Laing. He also wished to interview *en famille,* with as many family members present, in their own homes and with as little interference as possible from clinicians or researchers. He was equally stimulated by Bateson's generic theory that schizophrenic symptoms may well result not from biological factors, but rather disordered and disturbed patterns of communication. To begin, Laing, Esterson, *et al.* specified their selection criteria for the subjects whom they would observe: they were to be women who had been diagnosed by at least two psychiatrists as schizophrenic; be between the ages of fifteen and forty; have received less than fifty shots of ECT in the previous year; and have at least one living parent. Once the patient and her parents and other family members had agreed to participate, Laing and Esterson conducted interviews with the patient alone, then together with the other family members, and then finally alone with her parents. All the interviews were recorded and subsequently transcribed. Over one hundred families were interviewed over a period of three years and then, and only then, were the findings and observations analysed. The central point of the research was, as with *The Divided Self,* to demonstrate that the often bizarre symptoms of schizophrenia were far more intelligible to an outsider than conventionally believed. In the introduction to *Sanity, Madness and the Family,* Laing and Esterson claim their case studies demonstrate that 'the experience and behaviour of schizophrenics is much more socially intelligible than has come to be supposed by most psychiatrists'.[28]

In their observations Laing, Esterson and the other researchers tried their best to avoid objective interpretation, especially of what various family members *might* have been either thinking, feeling or planning beneath what they *actually said* when observed. The researchers believed that conscious and overt forms of disordered communication were, in themselves, sufficient to lead to confusion, mystification, paradoxes, tangential communications and double binds which, in turn, created anxiety, and led to schizophrenic symptoms.

One such case study was that of the 'Eden family'. Laing examined the family history of seventeen-year old Ruby, who was admitted to hospital in an inaccessible catatonic stupor. Gradually persuaded first to eat, and then to talk, Ruby rambled incoherently, often contradicting herself, at times hysterical about and at times completely indifferent to her recent unwanted pregnancy and subsequent miscarriage. She was convinced that 'people' disliked her, and talked disparagingly about her. She heard voices, calling her 'slut', 'dirty', 'prostitute'. Moreover, she believed that even her own family disliked her and wanted to be rid of her. Ruby didn't even know who she was, unable to decide between the Virgin Mary and the wife of Cliff Richard.

During his twenty two hours of interviews with Ruby and her family, Laing uncovered a miasma of deceit, at the very foundation of which were falsehoods about the consanguineous relationships between family members. Ruby herself was the illegitimate offspring of a liaison between Ruby's mother – whom she called 'mummy' – and a married man who visited occasionally, whom Ruby called 'uncle'. Cast out by her own father, Ruby's mother was given sanctuary by her own sister – whom Ruby called 'mother' – and her brother-in-law whom Ruby was encouraged to call 'daddy'!

All of the family colluded in the false representations made to Ruby. At times the family disagreed violently about Ruby's putative knowledge of the true state of affairs, in effect – does Ruby know who she really is, or does she believe she is whom we say she is? Or even the further possibility that Ruby might know we are lying but she is pretending to believe us. As Laing says, 'the most intricate splits and denials in her perception of herself and others were simultaneously expected of this girl and practised by the others'.[29]

During the interviews, it can clearly be seen how Ruby's family, in full knowledge of the truth, would distort the facts and verify statements which they knew to be false. And then, when they thought the time was right, they would actually tell the truth without further reference to what had gone before. Of course, the family's version of events was dictated not by moral concepts of wrong or right, but by the omnipresent phantom of scandal and gossip.

It appears that Ruby was fully cognisant of the truth, perhaps the only person capable of recognising it in this cesspool of liars. Ruby found the truth unbearable; she literally could not bear the weight of it. She could only face it, acknowledge and refer to it whilst in a state of 'sickness'. Then when she had perhaps received some cathartic release, she 'recovered', and felt remorseful about having inflicted pain and incurred displeasure by referring to the truth; by not playing her allotted part in the game. Consequently, she adopted the rules and once again became fully compliant – and just when she was at her most sick her family perceived her as most healthy. In fact, the family made Ruby feel mad or bad for actually perceiving the truth – the truth about herself and others, and the attitude of others to her. For example, in her distracted paranoid state, she voiced her fears that all of her family disliked her, made her a scapegoat, mocking and despising her. Upon recovery, Ruby regretted the things she had said. She acknowledged that not only did she have a 'lovely' family, but that they had been 'really good' to her. And of course the family perpetuated this myth about itself, increasing Ruby's guilt at suspecting the true state of affairs, expressing dismay and horror that she should think they didn't love her.

To Laing, the family vehemently expressed their true feelings – which of course they denied to Ruby – that she was a slut, little better than a prostitute. But of course when Ruby again became sick enough to tell them, in her own way, that she knew their true feelings, they made her feel mad and bad.

If Ruby was ever at any time in doubt about her true parentage, the illusion would have been shattered as her mother and aunt revealed her illegitimacy whilst attempting to abort her child, flushing soapy water into her vagina.

Laing implies that the root of the problem lay with the uncle's inability to deal with the sexual attraction he feels toward Ruby. He sublimates his desire and it is expressed as irritation, dislike: 'she won't leave me in peace – she's always stroking me, just like that, pawing me. She knows it gets on my nerves, but she does it deliberately'. Ruby of course thinks he likes the stroking, running her hands over his trousers, and she is probably right. Significantly, the uncle does not act to stop the behaviour: 'I won't pamper her like her mother and aunt. If I pampered her she'd stop pawing me but I don't'.[30] Yet he claims to be sickened by the 'pawing'. His wife coolly notes that he doesn't appear sickened at the time. And therefore a second string is added to this fiddle of duplicity; the uncle is sexually attracted to the seventeen-year-old Ruby, to the extent that he carries a photograph of her.

> I used to take her photo to work – she used to be very pretty, she looks terrible now. I used to be proud of her looks. I'd take her photo to work and show it, and my mates would say: 'That's a fine bit of stuff there', and I'd say, 'Just watch it, she'd scratch the eyes of any man that tried that sort of thing'. It was a terrible business. There's no excuse for it [the pregnancy].[31]

And of course, his wife doesn't like her husband taking an interest in a sexually nubile young woman living in intimate proximity of him. She resents Ruby and scapegoats her. Ruby's mother is in an uncomfortable position; her tenure at the house, in which she has a furnished private room, is reliant on her colluding with her sister and brother-in-law, by turning on her daughter. She is, in effect, caught between protecting her own child, and protecting her tenure. Denied the protection of the one true friend she should have, Ruby is left open to attack from all quarters. She is seen as competition by her cousin – to whom she refers as 'brother' – who is jealous of the attention everyone gives Ruby. Therefore he too colludes in the lies told about Ruby, exaggerating her misdemeanours to further taint Ruby's image in his parent's eyes. Laing says his criticisms get more expansive, even out of hand.

> *Cousin*: She's indecisive. She's not allowed to make a decision.
> *Aunt*: Yes, she won't make any decision. Do you remember when she left that job? I told her but she wouldn't do it.
> *Cousin*: She wouldn't sit any examinations. She gets ill before examinations. She won't take a decision.

It is clear that the truth is that Ruby *does* take decisions, and *acts* as opposed to *says*. The family cannot accept that her decisions and her actions do not accord with their opinions of what she should do. Therefore the fact that Ruby does not make the decisions they have taken for her, or takes her own independent decisions, becomes translated into 'Ruby won't take decisions'.

This kind of Orwellian 'double think' – saying one thing while deliberately meaning another – is reflected in virtually every instance of recorded conversation. For example, Ruby's pregnancy. *Cousin*: 'Pregnancy? I've got nothing against her for that. It could happen to anybody, nice people, respectable people ...'[32] And almost in the same breath, the same cousin reveals his actual fear of being disgraced by association. *Cousin*: 'I wasn't surprised. My cousin Edith was at that party and a couple of days after she said to me, "You should have seen Ruby". I hushed her up because there was someone else there at the time. I didn't tell anyone because I didn't know if it was true. Edith's a trouble maker'.[33] Interestingly, it is Ruby's uncle who rushes her to the doctor for a pregnancy test, 'to make sure'.

The family were then asked by Laing to clarify the issue of the neighbours, as a great symptom of Ruby's 'sickness' was her delusion of reference, that the 'whole district' was talking about her while pretending not to be. This does of course suggest a paranoid state – until the family do indeed clarify the issue:

> *Mummy*: They are so kind to her. They're all interested in her welfare. No one has said a word to her about it or going into hospital, not a word, there's no gossip. I don't know why Ruby should think the neighbours are talking about her.
> *Aunt*: Ruby once asked if I thought the neighbours talked about her, if they knew she was in hospital, and I said, 'of course not'. Ruby is the one who can't keep things to herself. She'll tell everyone her business. Whenever she comes home on leave from hospital, they greet her, 'Hello Ruby, home again?' Nobody's ever been unkind to her.[34]

It is her cousin, who sees her as his most direct rival for his mother's attention and his father's affection who actually states that 'they don't talk in front of her. It's like a coloured person coming to stay here. Nobody will say a word against her to her face, but they'll have plenty to say when she's not there. They talk about her all right'.[35]

As Laing presents the scenario, one can perhaps begin to perceive how a sensitive vulnerable person could be overburdened by her family's guilt, conceits and delusions. Unable to trust her own perceptions and also those closest to her, Ruby cannot tell what is reality and she cannot locate herself within the reality of the family.

The claustrophobic nature of many of the families suggests a 'form of subtle emotional blackmail, a killing by kindness' – families in which daughters feel restricted, with no life of their own and unable to healthily separate from their parents.[36] Crucially it was the *denial* of any conflict within the family that created the most harm, pushing daughters into further and further extremes, as no one would affirm, or confirm, what they were experiencing and feeling. Daughters would find themselves in 'no win' situations but feel unable to respond. Mystification processes would keep things as they were and ought to be. In this book, Laing continued to consistently maintain that schizophrenia was a strategy which a person invented in order to live in an unliveable situation.

Importantly, Laing discovered that within the so-called 'normal families', mystification, confusion and disordered communication also occurred but not to the same degree, nor with the same intensity, and obviously not to the extent of creating a situation which an individual member found untenable. However the proposed second volume examining such families failed to appear, much to the dismay of many who believed that a comparative volume would have clarified the impression they had that Laing believed *all* families created pathology. Laing's justifications for not publishing the second volume were manifold, but centrally related to the material itself. Quite simply he believed that it was too boring to be of interest, in short – unpublishable.

> When it came to looking at the families of so-called normal people, there wasn't anything to redeem it ... Every member of the families *totally fitted* – getting up and going to work and going to school and coming back and watching television and doing nothing and going to bed ... They thought about nothing, they said nothing very much, they were just fucking dead and there was no edge or no sharpness or no challenge ... It was like Samuel Beckett, reams and reams and reams of nothing.[37]

The controversy that followed the publication and media coverage of the book, amounted to the accusation that Laing had claimed families 'caused' schizophrenia. Of course another controversial element was the fact that within Laing and Esterson's arguments was the clear implication that the desired autonomy of the patient was to be accepted – including sexual autonomy. Laing and Esterson therefore took the step, when the second edition was published, of writing an explanatory preface. They asserted that they did not 'accept "schizophrenia" as being a biochemical, neurophysiological, psychological fact, and we regard it as palpable error, in the present state of the evidence, to take it to be a fact'. Rather, their central question was, 'are the experience and behaviour that psychiatrists take as symptoms and signs of schizophrenia more socially intelligible than has come to be supposed?' Laing and Esterson then reported that one common reaction had been to argue that 'eleven cases, all women, prove nothing'. Their response was forthright. They posed the question, what was the 'social intelligibility of the fact that no one study has been published, so far as we know, of a comparable kind before and since this one?', for, if 'we were wrong it would be easy to show that we are, by studying a few families and revealing that "schizophrenics" really are talking a lot of nonsense after all'.[38]

By the early 1960s, Laing's family life, and particularly his relationship with Anne, was less than fulfilling, and at times excruciatingly painful. In short, his marriage was foundering. Both he and Anne expected different things from their partnership, and they each continued to be disappointed both in themselves and in each other. Unresolved, their differences grew as the gap between them widened. They argued so loudly and ferociously that their neighbours complained. And around them, cultural differences were taking place which sanctioned less inter-personal restraint, and more freedom in relationships. This emotional *laissez-faire* may have improved stronger, more loving partnerships – but it was a death knell to the Laing's marriage.

In 1962, Laing met journalist Sally Vincent and somewhat later embarked on a strongly companionable and sexual relationship with her. She recalled that she found Laing endearingly and emotionally very expressive, and that he would unselfconsciously burst into tears at the cinema or theatre. He convinced her that his marriage to Anne had effectively come to an end and, for a matter of a few months, he moved in with his new partner. She discovered, amongst other things, that his support made her feel positive about herself, but that at times he could be brutally frank, and refused to provide either socially-expected an-swers or conversation. At a dinner party held at author Alan Sillitoe's she recalls Laing stood up, declared that he thought he wouldn't 'bother with' it, and left.[39]

Laing's family had moved three times and were living, at the time of Laing's sojourn with Sally Vincent, in North Finchley on the edge of Hampstead. After his relationship with Sally Vincent petered out, he stayed for a short time with friends and then returned to Anne and the family home.

Laing was still in contact with Marcelle Vincent, his French love, with whom he had remained friends since the end of their romance. In 1963, he visited her in Paris and she arranged for him to meet Jean-Paul Sartre. The occasion was intended to be an opportunity to see if Sartre approved of the book on his philosophy which Laing and his colleague David Cooper were writing.

The meeting with Sartre was a relative success with Sartre doing most of the talking, Laing the listening and both the drinking. The two-hour conversation ranged in topic from Rachmaninov, to old age, to alienation and, of course, to Laing's proposed project.

The book that resulted is no easy read. Indeed, in their introduction the authors note that 'Marx is credited with the remark that he had no time to write short books', and that their own book could be said to be a 'long short book – long to write, no doubt long to read'. It was actually written in a relatively short, but intensive, period of time, following lengthy dialogues between the two men and published, a year later, as *Reason and Violence: A Decade of Sartre's Philosophy.* The division of labour was extremely specific: Laing wrote a synopsis of Sartre's *Critique de la raison dialectique,* Cooper the essays on *Saint Genet, comédien et martyr* and *Questions de méthode,* and together they wrote the introduction. In the readable preamble, Laing and Cooper argue that for Sartre, psychoanalysis is 'above all an illumination of the present acts and experience of a person in terms of the way he has lived his family relationships'. They proceed to criticise more conventional or orthodox Freudian theory for its neglect of existential concepts, and assert that it was important, central even, that a reconstructed psychoanalysis discovered the 'intelligible choice of self, the fundamental project of becoming a certain sort of personal being'.

Sartre himself wrote the foreword to the text and reinforced their ideas and practice – 'Like you, I believe that one cannot understand psychological disturbances from the outside, on the basis of a positivistic determinism, or reconstruct them with a combination of concepts that remain outside the illness as lived and experienced'. He added that he believed all patients were to be respected as human beings first and patients second, that he agreed that 'mental illness' was a response to an intolerable situation and that finally he hoped their work would help hasten the day when psychiatry was a 'truly human psychiatry'.[40]

*

'From the moment of birth, when the stone-age baby first confronts its twentieth-century mother, the baby is subjected to these forces of outrageous violence, called love'. So Laing began his 1964 lecture at London's ICA. He followed with another poetic assertion, that 'the initial act of brutality against the average child is the mother's first kiss'.[41] His theme, that increasingly violence masqueraded as love was, of course, absolutely consistent with many of his thoughts on family and interpersonal life. 'Wouldn't it be natural if someone ran off with your wife to want to do something violent to him?' was a question Laing faced from his mainly youthful middle-class audience. As was frequently the case, Laing's response was measured and precise – 'Do you really love your wife? Is it so unbearable to you to think of her finding happiness with someone else? ... [pause] ... To love another is to see oneself as an other to the other'.[42]

Such performances guaranteed Laing media status and, from 1964 onwards, he appeared frequently on both radio and television, and at numerous conferences and events. He was the darling of the burgeoning political so-called New Left movements, but consistently resisted being seduced by any of them, refusing to be anything other than tangentially involved. Laing's politics at that time were the politics of the personal, the politics of the family, the politics of the space between people, the politics of how it has come to pass that modern man possesses staggeringly huge amounts of knowledge about the external world but understands increasingly less about himself and our inner psychological and existential worlds. 1964 was also an important year for other reasons. On a trip to the USA to research communicational theories of schizophrenia, he came across two youthful physicians, Drs Joseph Berke and Leon Redler, who were to follow him back to the UK and work with him on later projects.

The following year was eventful and significant. In March, he received a telephone call from a young German graphic designer, Jutta Werner, some thirteen years his junior and a friend of Ralph Metzner, a colleague of Timothy Leary's. When Metzner had heard she was going to London he gave her a list of 'interesting' people he thought she should contact. One of those names was Laing's. Apparently, she had no idea of whom he was, or his profession, and had heard nothing of his reputation as charismatic, fashionable and 'difficult'. She called his number from a public telephone in a café. When he answered, she says she felt a sensation something akin to an electric shock, and dropped the receiver out of surprise. Eventually, with the café proprietor's encouragement, she picked it up and managed to speak to Laing, who was still holding on at the other end. On his suggestion, they met at a restaurant. She was young and attractive; Laing was no longer in love with his wife – if ever he had been – and moreover found their family life stifling. Jutta was in search of the novel. It was an obvious meeting of bodies, opportunities – and minds. Soon after, they had sexual intercourse on the Wimpole Street couch. She moved into an apartment in Earls Court where Laing could visit and stay, and a little later, he would tell her that he had a wife and five children.

Laing's marriage to Anne finally ended the following year. It is difficult to know with any certainty if both partners were relieved at the termination of what had become a loveless, painful and acrimonious marriage. Laing certainly felt that he 'couldn't stand her' and that the arrangement was solely 'for the sake of the children'.[43] For a passionate and decisive man, Laing took the unusual step of seeking opinion as to what his next step ought to be. He convened a meeting of three friends, one of whom brought along a friend, another psychoanalyst whose opinion it was that it would be totally dishonourable and insane to leave five children. Laing later recalled that he noticed the man was staring at him with what he termed the 'diagnostic look', as if Laing were a madman. Laing flouted their opinions and decided to leave. The following year, Anne and her five children decided to relocate back to Glasgow, after a brief attempt at a new life in France.

It has been suggested that *either* Laing was 'punctual' with maintenance support payments to the family, or that he 'sent *little* money to support them'.[44] Perhaps what actually happened was that he punctually sent them little money. It *appeared* that Laing's contact with the family was, for a number of years, quite minimal and his son Adrian has commented that when he received a visit from his father some two years after he left the family home he had 'almost forgotten what he looked like'.

Indeed, among the many criticisms levelled against Laing are those along the lines that although he could look after other people, he did not look after his own family, that he could spend time with the mad and the miserable but not his own children, that he sacrificed his family in order to pursue fame, etc., etc. I believe that it *is* important that individuals try their best to behave towards others as they would wish others to behave toward themselves. And that a person should be measured in terms of his or her *total* life and not simply one aspect of it. However I believe, partly because he was a psychiatrist, and especially because he was one who wrote about the family, and partly because he ruffled many establishment feathers, he has been unfairly treated. At the least it can surely be agreed that from the outset his relationship with Anne was based on a sense of duty rather than reciprocal love, that the joint decision to bring further children into the world was a brave attempt at continuing a marriage that was doomed, and that their radically different lifestyles, skills and sensibilities invariably led to quite different expectations. Knowing Ronnie Laing I cannot for one moment believe that he left his wife, in the full knowledge that by doing so he would be also leaving his children, without pain in his heart. As is the way, especially now that Laing is dead, we hear only from those who have been 'wronged' and we are not made fully aware of all of the circumstances involved. In hindsight it has actually been clearly demonstrated by numerous researchers that the communicational patterns in families where parents are out of synch with each other are less conducive to children's mental health than a family where there is only one parent but no animosity. Indeed, given Laing's strictures on the consequences that may occur through patterns of disturbed and confusing communication within families, perhaps he had the courage of his convictions before he, or someone else, did even more damage. It would be absurd to imagine that Laing was merely calculated, callous and heartless and that he did not suffer himself from the separation from his children.

*

Perhaps most importantly, we should always remember the Gospel according to John 8:7. The Pharisees and scribes sought Jesus's opinion on an allegedly adulterous woman, whom, according to Mosaic Law, was about to be executed by stoning. After first choosing silence, Jesus was provoked into a response – 'he that is without sin among you, let him first cast a stone at her'. *Or,* expressed somewhat differently, 'when a pickpocket sees the Buddha, he only sees his pockets'.

*

In 1965, *The Divided Self* was published successfully as a paperback, and became an almost immediate best-seller, especially among the young, the disaffected and those who felt that no one was speaking out on their behalf. Individuals who believed that their own voices had been stifled or deemed insane or irrelevant. In the new edition Laing was more assertive, more confrontational. The language Laing employed in the preface to the second edition was more challenging, and was evidence that he had broadened his concerns:

> I am still writing in this book too much about Them, and too little of Us ... (and) ... In the context of our present pervasive madness that we call normality, sanity, freedom, all our frames of references are ambiguous and equivocal. A man who says he has lost his soul is mad. A man who says that men are machines may be a great scientist. A man who says he *is* a machine is 'depersonalised' in psychiatric jargon. A little girl of seventeen in a mental hospital told me she was terrified because the Atom Bomb was inside her. That is a delusion. The statesmen of the world who boast and threaten that they have Doomsday weapons are far more dangerous, and far more estranged from 'reality' than many of the people on whom the label 'psychotic' is affixed.[45]

The end of 1965 witnessed the termination of Laing's contract at the Langham Clinic, following Eric Graham Howe's disapproval of his therapeutic usage of LSD and other rumours circulating about Laing's interest in other drugs of one kind or another. By this time, however, he was already engaged in a therapeutic project that was to have both immediate and long-term consequences and which was to bring him varying degrees of fame and notoriety.

4

Brotherly Love

There was once a tree in the forest who felt very sad and lonely for her trunk was hollow and her head was lost in the midst. Sometimes, the mist seemed so thick that her head felt divided from her trunk. To the other trees she appeared quite strong but rather aloof, for no wind ever bent her branches to them. She felt if she bent she would break, yet she grew so tired of standing straight. So it was with relief that, in a mighty storm, she was thrown to the ground. The tree was split, her branches scattered, her roots torn up and her bark was charred and blackened. She felt stunned, and though her head was clear of the mist she felt her sap dry and she felt her deadness revealed when the hollow of her trunk was open to the sky. The other trees looked down and gasped and didn't know whether to turn their branches politely away or whether to try and cover her emptiness and blackness with their green and brown. The tree moaned for her own life and feared to be suffocated by theirs. She felt she wanted to lay bare and open to the wind and the rain and the sun and that, in time, she would grow up again, full and brown from the ground. So it was that, with the wetness of the rain, she put down new roots and by the warmth of the sun stretched forth new wood. In the wind her branches bent to other trees and as their leaves rustled and whispered, in the dark and in the light, the tree felt loved and laughed with life.

Mary Barnes

Soteria House was a twelve-bedroomed house situated on a busy street in San Jose. It was the central focus of the Soteria Project, a twelve-year experiment which began in 1971, the brain child of American psychiatrist Loren Mosher. As head of the Centre for Studies of Schizophrenia at the National Institute of Mental Health he set in motion a project which, in essence, involved sending half of those patients newly diagnosed as schizophrenic by the local psychiatric services to the local general hospital psychiatric wards, and the other half to Soteria House which was *not* staffed by doctors and nurses. Reviewing the findings of the Soteria House project, as well as the results of similar establishments

like Emanon in San Mateo, Crossing Place in Washington DC and
McAuliffe House in Maryland, Mosher concludes that during his twelve-
year study of alternatives to mental hospitalisation, the Soteria Project
resulted in four major achievements. It dehospitalised madness, through
taking care of patients/residents in a homelike setting in the community;
it demedicalised madness, through its focus on interpersonal help; it
deprofessionalised madness, because it required of its workers no mental
health training or experience; and it dedrugged madness, by declining to
treat most residents with antipsychotic medication.[1]

The research into Soteria House showed that, after two years, its
patients were in no way worse than those who had been admitted to
hospital and who had received powerful medication. In fact, on many
measures, they were actually better. Soteria House, despite its success,
was forced to close in 1983 due to lack of funds. The Washington-based
Crossing Place houses a wide variety of 'long-term mad people', all poor,
psychotic and deemed in need of hospitalisation, two thirds black, a third
HIV positive and a third homeless. By 1998 it had admitted over two
thousand individuals, only five per cent of whom were not successfully
returned to the community. Despite the evidence of their success, the
work of the Soteria Project goes unnoticed in the USA, especially within
the psychiatric profession where there is so much financial investment in
the medical-pharmaceutical-institutional model. Few psychiatrists wish
to work outside of the conventional hospital setting, nor do they wish to
lose their monopoly on 'treating' the mentally distressed. Most importantly, psychiatry is literally owned by the pharmaceutical industry.

The Greek word 'Soteria' has been translated along the lines of
'deliverance', and also on occasions as 'salvation' or 'protection'.
Mosher's project has indeed led to the protection of thousands of
individuals and has resulted in the establishment of similar projects, in
both Switzerland and in Germany where, in the year 2000, it is anticipated that many more Soteria-like projects will be established.[2]

All of these projects were inspired by Kingsley Hall, a project initiated
by Laing and others, formally established in 1965. 'Asylum' means a
place where you are not seized or violated, a place of sanctuary. A place
of protection. It had always been Laing's aim, since he first encountered
seriously distressed individuals, to provide protection for such people.
His experiment with the women from the refractory ward at Gartnavel

was, however slight, an attempt at doing exactly that. More poignant were those occasions on which he gave sanctuary at his parent's house to those psychiatric patients whom he believed were in danger, should he not have done so. Now was the time to physically and wholeheartedly provide such sanctuary in an environment over which he would exercise control and authority.

From as early as 1962, Laing had been pursuing this idea, through conversations with his erstwhile colleagues Drs Cooper and Esterson and others, most notably psychiatric social worker Sidney Briskin. In addition Laing had convivial discussions with Elly Jansen of the Richmond Fellowship. His aim was to establish a centre where schizophrenic breakdowns and recoveries could be more closely monitored, and one from which recovered individuals could subsequently move on to one of the Fellowship's half-way houses. Laing had previously visited Jansen's Denbridge House, the therapeutic community she had established in Bromley. Laing was impressed and when, sometime later, he was asked for the reasons behind its success he replied 'simply love. Elly loves the people there'. Specifically he argued that he believed she did not have any 'preconceived notions of what they should be like, they weren't made to fit in with spurious codes of conduct, they felt accepted and knew that their views were valued'.[3] Despite their mutual admiration, nothing concrete was created. Another influential role model was the revisionist psychoanalyst Harry Stack-Sullivan and, in particular, his work at the Shepard-Pratt Hospital in Baltimore. Sullivan believed that a person could recover from 'madness' within a matter of months given an appropriate environment. He cited the need for such a unit to be small, with staff chosen on the basis of their ability to 'interact non-destructively with schizophrenics', and the elimination of those hospital procedures which humiliated and degraded the new patient and further reduced their sense of identity and self.[4]

Laing and his colleague Esterson recognised the need for those people defined as schizophrenic to heal themselves, in their own time and in their own way, in a safe and protective environment. Unfortunately, their proposal to provide such a sanctuary – a London Centre for the Study and Treatment of Schizophrenia – fell on deaf ears. In conversations with colleagues and in the pages of academic journals Laing began to refer increasingly to this alleged process of self-healing as 'metanoia', the term from the New Testament for conversion or repentance. He had come across it in Jung's *Symbols of Transformation* in which Jung had used the word to describe the parallel process between what was called a psychotic episode and a mythological journey or transformation of the soul – with its central drama of the night sea journey, the hero's struggle with the monster of the deep, his transformation and rebirth.

In the *mélange* of ideas which flowed between Laing and his colleagues, they drew on Esterson's experiences from his kibbutz in Israel, and Cooper's experiences of Villa 21, at Shenley Hospital. The theory was given its first practical application by another of Laing's colleagues, Sidney Briskin, who in October 1964 opened his own front door to four former residents of Villa 21. Soon after, another home – coincidentally one of Laing's previous houses – was opened up to ten former psychiatric patients. It was run by an ex-carpenter whom Leon Redler had met when working with Maxwell Jones, the famous Scottish psychiatrist who had pioneered the open-doors policy at Dingleton Hospital. Of course in Dingleton's case the only reason the doors were allowed to remain open, in the 1950s, was because of the use and consequences of ECT – people were unable to escape even if they wished to do so.

When the idea became an irresistible force, Laing and his colleagues decided that an administrative framework was necessary. Consequently in April 1965, the Philadelphia Association was established. Taking its name from the Greek, meaning 'brotherly love', the aim was for the Association to research the causes of mental suffering or illness, in particular those relating to what was termed schizophrenia, and to find ways in which to relieve it. Its founders, Laing, Cooper, Esterson, Briskin, Clancy Sigal, Raymond Blake and Joan Cunnold, all held the view that mental suffering, including schizophrenia, was not to be seen as inevitably caused by biological, neurological or genetic factors, but rather as a response to interpersonal and social, as well as existential factors, and that 'natural healing' might well take place given time and the right circumstances.

The premises had already been obtained. Sidney Briskin had found Kingsley Hall in London's East End, originally a church and built in 1923 by two pacifist sisters, Muriel and Doris Lester. They had created a community centre, of sorts, and renamed the building after their recently deceased brother, Kingsley. In 1931 Mahatma Gandhi had stayed in one of its four sheltered rooftop rooms, when he was attending a London conference on the vexed issue of Indian independence. In the 1960s the Hall had been under-utilised. By the time it came to Briskin's attention, it was in a general state of disrepair. Laing agreed to pursue the matter further and, with Briskin, visited Muriel Lester to present his case for the use of the premises: that they were intending to help those people who were currently being violated by the psychiatric profession, and about whom no one cared. Convinced of Laing's integrity, decency and intentions, Lester agreed and the Philadelphia Associated were allowed to use the Hall for five years at a token rent, on the condition that Laing would continue to provide access to those community groups which still occasionally used the premises.

When Kingsley Hall first opened its doors in June 1965, Laing was on holiday with his family in another of Anne's fruitless attempts to salvage her marriage. The Philadelphia Association took initial charge, and sometime later the American psychiatrists whom Laing had met in New York, including Joseph Berke and Leon Redler, also moved in. Laing himself finally moved into Kingsley Hall on a full-time basis six months later with Jutta Werner. They lived together in a small and cramped room which, together with the communal rooms, served as their home.

Mary Barnes, whose life was later immortalised in print, on stage, and also through her own writing and painting, was the first Kingsley Hall resident whose healing process was to be guided by Laing *et al*. She had previously received conventional treatment in a psychiatric hospital, and this, as might be expected, had failed. What she received at Kingsley Hall was the freedom – and all this entailed – to physically and mentally regress, to 'go down into herself'. At times she demanded to be treated as if she were a baby, seeking baby food and caresses. Later she played with her faeces, painting both herself and the walls with them. She would, at times, be carried to the bath as and when her weight fluctuated. When her weight became perilously low there was a collective fear that she might die. The only other alternative would be to readmit her to a medical ward for tube feeding, an action that would constitute an admission of defeat. Nevertheless Laing himself put it to her that it was her decision – eat or die. The person whom Laing particularly encouraged to take care of Barnes was Joseph Berke who, with what appeared to be pure love and dedication, helped her with her depression, anger and madness, and in so doing helped her express her feelings through painting and writing. Much later her paintings of Christ-like figures and other spiritual and pagan symbols were exhibited as she slowly and partially recovered from her regressed state. Other less-fêted residents included both men and women who, at Kingsley Hall, were able to be themselves, whatever that meant for both them and the other residents, including those who were unofficially designated as the carers. One woman would spend her time trailing ghosts, one man spent his time laughing with terrified joy at his escape from ECT, others appeared to live in unfathomable places and behaved in bizarre and crazy ways. Kingsley Hall was noisy, unpredictable, at times dangerous, ecstatic, and often unclean. But, for most of the time, it *was* an asylum, a place of sanctuary. It was a place where 'treatment' was not offered in any conventional sense. Rather, what was exercised was a kind of 'benign neglect', a concept based on a fundamental respect for those personal freedoms, and which the residents of Kingsley Hall had all too often experienced as under-threat from a medical establishment which served only to invalidate their sense of self. Leon Redler, who appeared in the film *Asylum* with resident David Bell, recalls his time at Kingsley Hall as one of excruciatingly hard work, sometimes it was like 'hell'. Redler admired Bell's poetic language, and indeed 'loved' Bell. He 'helped' him by simply enabling Bell to understand some of the features of his life which had upset and 'disturbed' him. For instance, every time a new resident entered the household Bell would be extremely upset. Redler simply but effectively pointed out to him that, as the first of six children in his own family, he probably had resented the birth of each sibling, seeing it as a rival for his parent's love and attention, and that it was these feelings of displacement and jealousy and insecurity that Bell re-experienced at the arrival of every new resident.[5]

One of the organising principles of this apparent chaos was what Laing was later to term 'autorythmia': that of allowing individuals to become aware of and live according to their natural rhythms, as opposed to trying to conform to conventional or inappropriate rhythms. Each person, it was held, had his or her biorhythm and a *right* to this rhythm, and no person has a right to interfere with the rhythm and tempo of anyone else if it was not doing anyone harm. As Laing put it, 'where in the world are lunatics allowed to bathe naked in the moonlight?'[6] Someone felt easier sleeping in the day, another through the night. It was, however, all well and good in principle and theory, but it did also lead to further chaos, as basic housekeeping duties were frequently left unattended. Despite attempts to ensure that there was a distribution of domestic duties among the residents, this was often impossible to achieve, by virtue of the states of mind of those present. Perhaps the only rule or norm that was established and that was attempted to be adhered to, was that there was to be no transgressive behaviour. A resident was entitled to live in whatever world they chose, be it the sixth dimension or planet Zog, but they were *not* entitled to deliberately harm one another.

There was little if any structure to any particular day, and even the regular yoga sessions didn't always take place. Evening meals were taken together, especially in the early period of Kingsley Hall, with Laing seated at the head of the table. Proper food, not hospital food, was served and the residents were treated like fellow human beings, albeit disturbed and sometimes disruptive ones. Despite some reports that music was played constantly and that there was nightly dancing, from free-form to flamenco, this was not the case, although Laing did dance, as did others. He would, if the mood took him, dance with anyone including smelly and unwashed men as well as his *coiffured* and perfumed girlfriend. There were to be no boundaries and no distinctions and no privileges. Similarly, the idea that Laing acted as a Svengali-type figure was also incorrect, as both residents and carers were not prevented from seeking their own salvation from whatever route they so chose.

The potentially cathartic, curative qualities of the state of regression was a central theoretical concept adopted into everyday therapeutic practice of Kingsley Hall. It was accepted that self-healing could, potentially, occur if one were to 'go down and back into oneself', and then return, re-born, purged and free of the scars of the past. Metanoia.

One of Kingsley Hall's most valiant features was its policy allowing the residents considerable decision-making powers over intake. Thus, when a resident was discharged or left, the remaining residents usually decided on the replacement and only rarely did Laing and the Philadelphia Association exercise their veto. Invariably, they would collectively agree to accept the most disturbed applicant, rather than the least. As time went on, Kingsley Hall opened its doors to transitory individuals who were in fear of conventional psychiatric admission and who would, if possible, be given accommodation for the night and sent away with advice and encouragement. Visitors too were welcomed, and Laing would sometimes systematically invite visiting psychiatrists, artists, academics, writers and others. Such visits invariably meant moments of high drama and absurdity, as well as periods of conversation and debate. No one was segregated, everyone was able to participate. Discussions ranged widely, from Bob Dylan's lyrics, and Tillich's theology to the *Diamond Sutra* and Hesse's *Steppenwolf*. Not all visitors were impressed, though in the main most open-minded individuals could see a unique experiment unfolding before their eyes. No one could avoid the acknowledgement that a *community* was in the process of being established: where the madman could be himself without fear of enduring punishment masquerading as treatment. No one was ever told that they were there for 'their own good': *everyone* was entitled to be there and to partake of a journey the destination of which was, as of yet, uncertain.

In addition to Kingsley Hall's more well-known visitors, including celebrities both minor and major, people like Timothy Leary, Alex Trocchi, Fritz Perls, Sean Connery and playwright David Mercer, there were also those who were associated with the Philadelphia Association in an advisory capacity, a legal requirement of its charitable status. They included Maxwell Jones, Jock Sutherland and social work professor Dame Eileen Younghusband. It is impossible to know what all or each of them made of Kingsley Hall, as one can imagine that much depended on the circumstances of any particular evening. What *was* certain, however, was that the local working-class citizens disliked it immensely. Their reactions ranged from the benevolent concern of those people who believed that the residents needed 'proper medical care' rather than being allowed to walk around the streets in freezing weather without shoes or socks, to those who expressed anger and alarm at the sight of Mary Barnes performing a sun dance on top of the roof, naked and smeared with excrement.

From the very beginning there were, understandably, many differences of opinion as to the most appropriate and effective way of organising and managing the chaos, the residents and the building. Sidney Briskin, wholeheartedly committed to the project, was anxious that there were too few policies of administration and accountability, and that Kingsley Hall had an insufficient economic base. David Cooper's involvement appeared to wane quite soon after the project commenced. His immersion in various forms of Marxism and other so-called revolutionary ideas continued to grow. Esterson and Laing had a serious and acrimonious difference of opinion, based less on policy issues than on personal dislike and envy. Laing himself came to realise that the democracy he had unfurled meant he would not always get his own way. Although usually he did. When he didn't, his reason was supplanted by his emotions, especially his anger which would unleash torrents of verbal abuse and disappointment. At times like this, it must have been difficult to distinguish him from the other residents.

At the end of 1966, Laing, together with Jutta, moved out of Kingsley Hall, to an apartment in Belsize Park Gardens, his home for the next decade. Drs Berke and Redler, together with Morton Schatzman, began to exercise more authority, and eventually Kingsley Hall became their responsibility. Both Laing and his colleagues had felt the difficulties he experienced over his year long residency at Kingsley Hall. For a start, it was neither the most appropriate nor the most desirable place for a relationship to flourish, amidst such bizarre surroundings and spectacularly bizarre behaviour, nor was there much privacy. In addition, Laing continued to see patients at Wimpole Street, his time being in greater demand than ever as his name and reputation grew. There was also his commitment to writing, to which he stubbornly adhered. Perhaps most significantly, the experiment at Kingsley Hall was based on the principle that everyone, residents and 'carers' alike, were 'in it' together. It had become clear that not only the avowedly mad residents sought sanctuary from this milieu – others did too, and with varying degrees of success. Perhaps Laing could no longer get what he felt he needed from the community. Perhaps he decided that a more conventional environment would afford him the sanctuary and protection *he* needed, and perhaps he felt himself to be too vulnerable there, too exposed.

This unique and courageous experiment came to an end when the lease expired in 1970, although Leon Redler had managed to acquire some Archway households which ensured continuity for residents. In Laing's day-to-day absence, Kingsley Hall had continued to adhere to its principles and continued to receive publicity and local condemnation. When it was time to finally close the doors, the premises were in a sorry state of affairs, in need of extensive repair. It is indeed fair to say that the local community was glad to see the madmen taken away. In a world in which people still expect the mad to be hidden from view behind the safe walls and fences of hospitals, and in which they prefer to see the mad lethargically wandering around like human zombies, it is to the credit of Kingsley Hall that it survived for so long in the face of such hostility. Medical opinion, also, was decisive and undivided in its condemnation of the project, and one well-known psychiatrist believed that Laing had, at last, committed professional suicide.

In matters of the mind and the soul, statistics mean little. Nonetheless they do show that Kingsley Hall admitted over one hundred and twenty people in its five-year existence, with the average length of stay being something like three months, though other residents stayed over four years. As far as any one can conclusively demonstrate, the experiment appeared to do no harm, and possibly considerable good. Certainly many of the residents returned to the world outside of Kingsley Hall and were able to make their way in it. Laing himself argued, some twenty-five years later, that the work was 'still in progress' and that it certainly had not been a failure. Surely such experiments are proof enough that the alternatives – people being left to walk and wander the streets, aimless, confused and estranged, in danger of being rendered homeless and vulnerable; or of being hospitalised with no guarantee of a return to self-knowledge or even a calmer state of mind, despite medication – are no improvement on Laing and his colleagues' bold venture?

> For the time it went on, people lived there who would have been living nowhere else – except in a mental hospital – who were not on drugs, not getting electric shocks or anything else, who came and went as they pleased. There were no suicides, there were no murders, no one died there, no one killed anyone there, no one got pregnant there ... You might have thought that everyone would have died of starvation or pneumonia or by killing themselves or raping each other or beating each other up or wasting away on drugs or overdoses. But people didn't do that.[7]

Despite such incontrovertible evidence, almost daily Laing encountered rumours about both himself and also Kingsley Hall: that he himself had actually received ECT while there, that he had in fact committed suicide, that he was sleeping with the women residents, that he was always on LSD, that the residents were raping each other. Perhaps the most surreal moment came when someone wrote a letter to the magazine *New Society* under the name of R. D. Laing, at which point Laing telephoned to protest that it wasn't he who had written. They replied, 'how do you know?'

From the 1970s onwards and despite the closure of Kingsley Hall, the Philadelphia Association continued to thrive, and indeed by that time other, smaller, households had been established which continued the work in the same spirit. In the USA, in addition to the Soteria Project, establishments based on the spirit and the methods of Kingsley Hall were opened, like John Perry's ill-fated Diabasis in San Francisco, but also Burch House, in New Hampshire, opened in 1978 by David Goldblatt, one of those who had worked for the Philadelphia Association in London. Goldblatt argues that the theoretical ideas on which Burch House was predicated included the central notion that the 'true healing of psychic ills occurs naturally, through supportive relationships', taking place in an environment which validates and accepts the 'psyche's dark side', and is a process which 'occurs in its own time'.[8] Moreover, he argues that he believes in taking a stance which is 'heartening rather than disheartening, encouraging rather than discouraging'; that he listens to what an individual is saying without assumption or presumption, so that 'those who are suffering can utilise the natural healers within themselves'. Finally, that he pays respect to 'people's experience, thereby laying a fertile ground for developing a relationship'. Burch House, despite a distinct lack of encouragement from the orthodox psychiatric establishment, continues its work into the next Millennium.

The Philadelphia Association's London houses were run by people like Leon Redler, John Heaton and Hugh Crawford, a fellow Scottish psychoanalyst reputedly more pragmatic than Laing. He was perhaps the only man whom Laing saw as approaching his equal. One of the numerous individuals both he and Laing encountered through their work in such households and communities, was 'Jerome', whose own particular experience is a salient illustration of such an approach to healing.

'Jerome' was a twenty-year-old man referred to Laing by a local psychiatric hospital. He had been removed from his home, parents and siblings because of his refusal to leave his bedroom. At hospital he refused to speak, not knowing why but simply knowing he must. Diag-nosed as suffering catatonic schizophrenia with depressive features, Jerome was 'treated' with ECT and subsequently returned home a more personable and social person. This improved state lasted merely six months before he once again became withdrawn, received more ECT, returned home for a temporary improvement before once again with-drawing. This cycle lasted over two years. The prognosis was pessimistic – the next hospitalisation might be a permanent one. After reading *The Divided Self,* he implored his parents to let him see Laing who was the only man he believed he could trust not to 'treat' his condition. Jerome entered one of the Philadelphia Association's houses and they agreed to his terms: that he was to be allowed to stay in his bedroom until he himself decided to come out.

Jerome never left his room nor did he eat, nor did he visit the lavatory. Amidst the stench he was asked if he would eat and, reluctantly, he agreed to do so providing the food was placed outside his door. Six months passed and it became evident that Jerome's body weight must have become dangerously low – only no one had been able to see him to verify this suspicion. In desperation Hugh Crawford and Laing decided that something had to change. They moved him into a room with one of the carers, psychoanalyst Mike Thompson who, with others, took turns to feed and bathe Jerome, change his bed sheets and give him therapeutic massages to relieve the loss of muscle tone and to increase physical contact with him. After all, it was precisely this dimension of physical contact and sense of community that was believed to be so important in the healing process. Thompson himself became depressed at enduring the stench and the silence, and found cohabitation with a living ghost almost unbearable. As a remedy he invited another schizophrenic to share their room: a young man who believed himself to be Mick Jagger. Over five hundred days passed and nothing changed. Depressing though the situation was and as alarmed as Laing and Jerome's family were, his pattern of behaviour became commonplace and an accepted part of the household.

Hardly anyone noticed when Jerome came downstairs to use the bathroom, saying 'hello' before returning to his room again. One hour later he came back down to say he was hungry, and sat and ate. The following day he was as sociable as, for the previous five hundred and forty seven days, he had been withdrawn and almost mute. He was asked gently why he had chosen to isolate himself for all this time. Jerome replied that it was because he had to count to a million, and then back to zero, uninterrupted, in order to obtain his 'freedom'. That was all that he had wanted to do and no one had allowed him to, until now. 'But why had it taken so long?', he was asked. Jerome acknowledged that he had been left alone for some of the time but that there were, nonetheless, interruptions and interference. Every time he reached one thousand or more his concentration would be distracted by a song, a massage, an attempt at conversation. Then he would have to begin the task all over again. 'So why didn't you tell us?', was the reasonable question Jerome was asked. 'That wouldn't have counted. You had to give me my way, without my having to explain why'. The mad compulsion which had compelled him to conquer his numerological Everest had been satisfied, and he could now get on with his life.

Twenty years on, Jerome lives a contended and ordinary existence, with no concern for numbers or in any need of any psychiatric or medical help whatsoever. Once deemed a hopeless case, his life has proven quite the opposite.[9]

*

Gregory Bateson, Ross Speck, David Cooper, Ronald Laing, Stokely Carmichael, John Gerassi, Herbert Marcuse, Jules Henry, Paul Sweezy, Allen Ginsberg, Julian Beck, Paul Goodman, Simon Vinkenoog, Gajo Petrovic, Igor Hajek, Lucien Goldman, Francis Huxley and Thich Nhat Hahn were among the impressive list of speakers who performed at the Congress of the Dialectics of Liberation, held in London, at the Round-house in Chalk Farm, from July 15th to the 30th, 1967. Other speakers were invited, like sociologist Erving Goffman who, at the last moment, withdrew. This all-male collection of academics, economists, psychiatrists, political activists, literary critics, anthropologists, sociologists, theatrical directors and Buddhist monks, came together at the request of Laing, Cooper, Redler and Berke. The four men planned and administered the Congress from Laing's Belsize Park Gardens base and from there, sent out invitations world-wide to both speakers and their potential audience.

Given the impressive collective reputations of those assembled, spear-headed by Laing – who was, by this time, one of the most sought after performers on the academic and media circuit – it was hardly surprising that the Congress received widespread media coverage, drawing a large crowd on each of the fourteen days. Subsequently a number of films were produced covering the event, notably one by an American filmmaker, in addition to a series of long-playing records of the major performances.

The Congress itself was no academic conference. Instead it was a series of public lectures, discussions and seminars, some poetry and music, films and documentaries. There were also spontaneous, informal gatherings and discussions, many of which took place outside of the Roundhouse, in surrounding cafés and restaurants. The avowed aim of the Congress was to reconcile theory and practice, to focus on the role of violence in the world, and to find ways of changing repressive and oppressive circumstances at both the macro and micro level: to create what was termed dialectics of liberation.

Laing's own contribution was a lecture titled 'The Obvious', a lengthy and discursive and, at times, fragmentary critique of what he termed a 'totally irrational social world system'. The two major features of the lecture, in addition to his dramatic and well-presented performance, were that he remained faithful to the ideas he had previously expressed concerning the importance of the context of experience and behaviour, and secondly that he developed more stringently his critique of so-called 'normality'.

His concern was the *context* of behaviour. The apparent irrationality of behaviour, argues Laing, becomes somewhat more intelligible when seen in context. The psychotic's irrationality can be rendered intelligible within the context of the family whose own irrationality can be rendered intelligible within wider encompassing contexts and networks, and so on and so forth, up to the context of the total world system. In a sense Laing was anticipating the later 'hyperglobalisers' who currently argue that we live in a world in which social processes operate predominantly at a global scale. However, these contexts and networks are either infinite, or they stop. And if they do stop, what was the consequence, the meaning of the *final* instance of irrationality? Laing attempted to address this question, hypothesising: 'more than one person has said – and usually been regarded as mad for having said it – that perhaps God is not dead: perhaps God is Himself mad'.[10]

Laing illustrates the central idea of the importance of social context through the perspective of conventional psychiatry. 'Someone is gibbering away on his knees, talking to someone who is not there. Yes, he is praying'. Without the social context and therefore the social intelligibility of this behaviour, it can only be described as mad, and for which treatment would be required. The result of this so-called 'treatment' subsequently has the opposite effect to that intended.

> Many patients in their innocence continue to flock for help to psychiatrists who honestly feel they are giving people what they ask for: relief from suffering. This is but one example of the diametric irrationality of much of our social scene. The *exact* opposite is achieved to what is intended. Doctors in all ages have made fortunes by killing their patients by means of their cures. The difference in psychiatry is that it is the death of the soul.[11]

Laing argued that it would perhaps be more fruitful to examine the experience and behaviour which is accepted by society as 'normal' as opposed to that which is condemned as 'abnormal'. He illustrates his argument with an image he was to repeat over and over again in other circumstances. A mother holds her three-year old child out of a sixth-storey window. She makes it clear to the child that although she *could* drop him, she will not. 'See how much I love you', she tells him. She means the child to understand that if she didn't love him, then she would have no compunction in dropping him. According to Laing this was no psychopathology, the mother meant what she said. It was to show her child that she loved him. An extreme example of normality, argues Laing. 'The *normal* way parents get their children to love them is to terrorise them, to say to them in effect: "Because I am not dropping you, because I am not killing you, this shows that I love you, and therefore you should come for the assuagement of your terror to the person who is generating the terror that you are seeking to have assuaged" '. Because it is terrified, the child is seen as ungrateful.

Laing then returns to the importance of context, because to understand the behaviour of such a normal mother we would have to go back to her parents. The normal mother is clearly upset that her child is ungrateful, when she believes he should be *grateful* she didn't drop him. We have to understand *her* experience of parental love. Perhaps she herself was *not* held out of a window as she perhaps felt she should have been. And why not? For the answer to that we would have to know how *her* own parents were loved by her grandparents. Generation after generation of relatives and kin are part of the social context that might offer clues to the seemingly irrational behaviour observed.

Many of the relationships between the speakers were less than congenial, as might be anticipated, given that these were people with quite different perspectives and agendas. Laing found Marcuse cold and uncommunicative, for example. But the major source of conflict was between Laing and the Black Power representative Stokely Carmichael, who presented a passionate yet simplistic monologue about the colonialism of the West, and also what he termed 'the system of international white supremacy integrated with international capitalism'. Carmichael and Laing disagreed about almost everything but particularly with what Laing saw as Carmichael's superficial rejection of the individual as a focus of analysis and, by implication, his reification of the term 'system'. Laing believed that Carmichael was as guilty of racism as any white man could be, with his continual rejection of all things white including any white political support that might come his way, and also his rejection of non-revolutionary black politicians. And Laing certainly objected to Carmichael's accusation that his fellow participants were guilty of 'intellectual masturbation' – all words and no action. On a personal level they also failed to gel: Laing was cynical about the clear hypocrisy of Carmichael's vitriolic condemnation of the white race, whilst he simultaneously raced away from London to have sex with some specially selected white Swedish women. Any notion that there would be positive long-term relationships forged between particular individuals over the two-week period was quickly dispelled. Laing spent time with those he already knew and whom he felt shared his sensibilities, like Gregory Bateson and Jules Henry and, effectively, ignored the others.

There was, however, one unanticipated consequence of the proceedings. The following year, the major presentations from the Congress were published, edited and introduced by David Cooper and titled *The Dialectics of Liberation*. In this slim and commercially successful volume, Cooper achieved a number of his aims, especially in defending Carmichael's position, claiming that it was not in fact counter-racist. More significantly for Laing, he managed to label him as an *anti-psychiatrist* like himself, a label Laing abhorred because of the radical differences between his own position and Cooper's. By 1967 their differences had already become visibly apparent. Cooper's politics were becoming increasingly unconventional, his perspective eventually leading him to the somewhat extreme view that schizophrenics could be viewed as proto-revolutionaries useful as foot soldiers in the struggle for liberation. Laing, conversely, was more concerned with his traditional preoccupation – the social intelligibility of schizophrenia, the social contexts of schizophrenia and other forms of mental distress, and of course the concept of the schizophrenic journey *or* metanoia: schizophrenia perceived as a spiritual or existential death followed by rebirth. Two years later, Cooper was to publicly announce his final parting of the ways with Laing, stating that unlike Laing who was preoccupied with spiritual matters he was to travel to Latin America to take up the struggle against imperialism.

Although the Congress was commercially successful, it proved to be critically and politically irrelevant. Hot on its heels came the so-called Anti-University of London, established by Joseph Berke, at which Laing revealed his interests by offering a course on 'inner space in Greek, Christian and Egyptian mythologies'. The Anti-University was short-lived and did little to increase any particular individual's intellectual or social credibility.

1967 ended with Laing becoming a father again, Jutta having given birth to a son, Adam, and with increased demands on his time, especially for media and conference appearances, his opinion canvassed on LSD, religion, schizophrenia, politics, childbirth, violence and love. His celebrity was based, in addition to the Kingsley Hall project, on the book which had just been published and was to catapult him to international recognition and continued notoriety.

5

Them and Us

The structure of psychotherapy is such that no matter how kindly a person is, when a person becomes a therapist, he or she is engaged in acts that are bound to diminish the dignity, autonomy, and freedom of the person who comes for help.

Jeffrey Masson Against Therapy

The Politics of Experience and The Bird of Paradise is described by one of Laing's biographers as being not one of his better books. It is often characterised as the pre-eminent symbol of his decline and fall from *intellectual* grace, a book which marked the end of his serious work and his disengagement from the issues that had occupied him for almost a decade. Personally, I couldn't disagree more. In my view it is crucially important that one does not read the book as if it were simply a continuation of his earlier ideas on experience, relationships and psychiatry. Not only is it wider in its scope, it is, additionally, stylistically quite different. For me it was *the* book that excited me, moved me emotionally and intellectually, which I read as if he were writing specifically of my life and of the society I reluctantly inhabited.

It was, in fact, two books published under the same cover. The latter, which was a much shorter contribution, appeared to many readers to be a stream of consciousness(es) written while on LSD or another mind expanding substance. Laing's description of the text was somewhat less esoteric. He argued that he saw it more as a prose poem of the genre of *Aurélia* by Gérard de Nerval or like Serafino d'Aquilano, or similar to a Herman Hesse piece. One page, he argued, which he only included after considerable thought, could not have been written had he not experienced mescaline. However, the rest of the text emerged from material he remembered from his dreams and states of minds that occurred between sleep and waking. Both books benefited from the short but dramatic vignettes Laing inserted, most of which were recollections of his experience of psychiatry from the 1950s onwards.

Laing had already laid the ground in early 1967, when he delivered a series of lectures at the William Alanson White Institute of Psychiatry, Psychoanalysis and Psychology, New York. He invited his professional audience to consider the following possibility: that the patterns of mystification, confusion and invalidation commonly found in the families of those labelled schizophrenic were themselves part of a wider pattern of oppression, integral elements of the cultural and psycho-social fabric of capitalist societies. This critique of particular aspects of capitalist social structure was forcefully expanded in the first part of the *The Politics of Experience and The Bird of Paradise*.

These ideas were not new to Laing. Indeed, with the exception of the first chapter, the book itself was a compilation of articles he had written and presentations he had given throughout 1964. For many readers what was startling about the book, not simply in terms of its place in Laing's *oeuvre* but more generally, was the fulsome and unrestrained attack on almost every conceivable social institution including the family, psychiatric hospitals, the church, schools and the educational system, political and scientific organisations and, of course, the processes of conformity and so-called 'normality'. His language was angry, violent, political and apocalyptic. It was a call to arms, not in the manner in which someone like David Cooper would respond, but rather an appeal for *us all* to understand what was going on and to do something about it, if that were possible, before it was too late. He wrote as if he anticipated thermonuclear annihilation and the end of the world at any moment.

'Was it mad to be normal, or normal to be mad?', was merely one of the many mantras which emerged from Laing's book which was, one might say, an attempt to make sense of a world which no longer makes sense. Amusingly, Laing himself was wont to claim that Richard Nixon was one of many senior American politicians who had read the book, in an attempt to understand the dissent of the sixties. Some reviewers believed that the book's commercial success, especially among the young on both sides of the Atlantic, lay in the fact that it was indeed a powerfully written critique but one without any answers. Professionals who shared the same terrain as Laing, especially psychiatrists and psychoanalysts, believed that this time Laing had strayed too far and that any possibility of him resurrecting a conventional career was now out of the question. Indeed, as Laing himself has remarked, some colleagues believed that the book was perhaps a demonstration that he had ruined his 'brilliant mind', and that he might have been 'moving into a schizophrenic form of paranoid psychosis'.[1] A Harvard academic was even awarded a grant for a linguistic analysis of the book to see whether it showed any signs of 'mental disorder' and subsequently published an inconclusive paper on that very subject.

It has been suggested that among Laing's reasons for writing the book the way he did was that it provided a cathartic release for him, that it was an act of revenge and that it was an attempt to gain further popularity, a wider audience.[2] This appears less than generous – the book was written about the social world as he saw it, expressed in a language that was certainly incisive and powerful, and not in the passionless and impenetrable language of the scientific journal written in a justificatory spirit and replete with dependent clauses. Laing's *style* does not invalidate his arguments or observations.

The Politics of Experience is brimming with ideas. A cursory summary can not do it justice. However. It is, first and foremost, a lament: 'Humanity is estranged from its authentic possibilities'.[3] 'We are born into a world where alienation awaits us', writes Laing. In other words, we are born into an *un*-welcoming and hostile world, in which we feel estranged and lonely, because the 'normality' to which we are expected to conform is anti-human and *un*-natural.

His first theme is our alienation from experience. *Pace* Freud, Laing describes how we are merely a fragment of our true possibilities. 'As adults', he writes, 'we have forgotten most of our childhood, not only its contents but its flavour'; we hardly know of the 'inner world'; we barely remember our dreams and make little sense of them when we do so; 'as for our bodies, we retain just sufficient proprioceptive sensations to co-ordinate our movement and to ensure the minimal requirements for biosocial survival – to register fatigue, signals for food, sex, defecation, sleep'; our capacity to think, except in the service of what we are 'dangerously deluded in supposing is our self-interest, and in conformity with common sense', is pitifully limited; our capacity even to see, hear, touch, taste and smell is so 'shrouded in mystification that an intensive discipline of un-learning is necessary for *anyone* before one can begin to experience the world afresh, with innocence, truth and love'.[4] What is even more remote, Laing argues, is the likelihood of an immediate *experience* of the spiritual realm of demons, spirits, 'Powers, Dominions, Principalities, Seraphim and Cherubim, the Light', and as such domains become more alien to us, we need 'greater and greater open-mindedness even to conceive of their existence'.[5]

This condition of alienation, of being unconscious or asleep, of 'being out of one's mind', is the condition of the 'normal man'. Creatures that have killed perhaps 100,000,000 of their 'fellow normal men in the last fifty years', argues Laing. Importantly, he adds that because this so-called 'normality' is a result of the destruction of our capacities to experience, the more 'senseless it is to continue with generalised descriptions of supposedly schizoid, schizophrenic, hysterical "mechanisms" '.[6]

Laing believes that the institution responsible for ensuring conformity to this state of mind of so-called normality is the family *as found* within the capitalist economy of the affluent early-1960s. Its function is to socialise infants, the young and the impressionable, programming 'each new recruit to the human race to behave and experience in substantially the same way as those who have already got here':

> The Family's function is to repress Eros: to induce a false consciousness of security: to deny death by avoiding life: to cut off transcendence: to believe in God, not to experience the Void: to create, in short one-dimensional man: to promote respect, conformity, obedience: to con children out of play: to induce a fear of failure: to promote a respect for work: to promote a respect for 'respectability'.[7]

A few pages later Laing broadens his attack, to include another agent of socialisation, namely the educational system, especially through a succinct and logical passage worth quoting in its entirety:

> A child born today in the UK stands a ten times greater chance of being admitted to a mental hospital than to a university, and about one fifth of mental hospital admissions are diagnosed schizophrenic. This can be taken as an indication that we are driving our children mad more effectively than we are genuinely educating them. Perhaps it is our very way of educating them that is driving them mad.[8]

In the two chapters titled 'The Schizophrenic Experience' and 'Transcendental Experience', Laing simply yet profoundly outlines some of the ideas he had already previously developed on the nature and process of madness. He remarks that the American psychiatrist Harry Stack-Sullivan would suggest to those who came to work with him that, 'in the present state of society, the patient is right, and you are wrong'. Laing asserts that it is as much an outrageous simplification as is the idea that the psychiatrist is right and the patient wrong. But, he adds, 'I think, however, that schizophrenics have more to teach psychiatrists about the inner world than psychiatrists their patients'.[9] Laing asserts that the work that he and his colleagues embarked on in the early 1960s was prompted, in the first place, by those psychotherapists who formed the impression that, 'if their patients were *disturbed*, their families were often very *disturbing*'.[10] Laing describes the conclusions that he, Aaron Esterson and David Cooper reached after studying over one hundred circumstances around the social event when one person comes to be regarded as schizophrenic:

> … it seems to us that *without exception* the experience and behaviour that gets labelled schizophrenic is *a special strategy that a person invents in order to live in an unlivable situation.* In his life-situation the person has come to feel he is in an untenable position. He cannot make a move, or make no move, without being beset by contradictory and paradoxical pressures and demands, pushes and pulls, both internally, from himself, and externally, from those around him. He is, as it were, in a position of checkmate.[11]

Laing goes further and asserts that there is no such 'condition' as 'schizophrenia', the label being no more than a social fact and the 'social fact a *political fact*'. This political event imposes definitions and consequences on the labelled person. Other individuals – psychiatrists, doctors, nurses, social workers – are medically empowered and legally sanctioned to deal with the labelled person who is then inaugurated into the career of patient. The hospitalised person labelled as patient, and specifically as 'schizophrenic', is 'degraded from full existential and legal status as human agent and responsible person, no longer in possession of his own definition of himself, unable to retain his own possessions, precluded from the exercise of his discretion as to whom he meets, what he does'.[12] The labelled person's time is no longer his own, nor is the space he occupies of his own choosing. *He is invalidated as a human being.* And, Laing adds, 'once a "schizophrenic" there is a tendency to be regarded as always a "schizophrenic" '.[13]

Perhaps the most controversial statement that Laing made, certainly as far as orthodox psychiatry was concerned is: 'Madness need not be all breakdown', it may also be 'break-through'. It is '*potentially* liberation and renewal as well as enslavement and existential death' (*emphasis added*).[14] This is perhaps *the* quote used by those who appear to deliberately wish to misinterpret Laing and attribute to him remarks and opinions he neither said nor held. Laing is quite simply stating the obvious: *some* individuals suffer the experience of madness and re-emerge somewhat the wiser, although many do not and suffer interminable existential death instead. Laing also argues that certain transcendental experiences appear to be the well-spring of all religions, and adds that 'some psychotic people have transcendental experiences'. However, he qualifies the statement carefully in adding that he was not implying 'psychotic experience necessarily contains this element more manifestly than sane experience'.[15]

The subject of the chapter entitled 'A Ten-Day Voyage' is Jesse Watkins, a sculptor and friend of Laing's. In 1940 he suffered a 'psychotic episode' that lasted ten days. In a taped interview with Laing he recounted, as best as he could, the experience he underwent. The following extract offers a flavour of his language:

> ... I felt as if I were a kind of rhinoceros or something like that and emitting sounds like a rhinoceros and being at the same time afraid and at the same time being aggressive and on guard. And then – um – going back to further periods of regression and even sort of when I was just struggling like something that had no brain at all and as if I were just struggling for my own existence against other things which were opposing me. And – um – then at times I felt as if I were like a baby – I could even – I – I could even hear myself cry like a child ...[16]

Laing's analysis of Watkins's journey leads him to reassert his view that we can no longer assume that such a 'voyage is an illness that has to be treated': 'Can we not see that *this voyage is not what we need to be cured of, but that it is itself a natural way of healing our own appalling state of alienation called normality?*[17] In the spirit of Kingsley Hall, he calls for places to be established whose express purpose would be to help people through the 'stormy passages of such a voyage'. And he characterises the direction of such a journey, or voyage, as one which involves going 'back and in', because it was 'way back that we started to go down and out'; there is a long way to go back to contact the reality 'we have all lost contact with'. Laing concludes the chapter with a remark aimed at conventional psychiatry – 'and because they are humane, and concerned, and even love us, and are very frightened, they will try to cure us. They may succeed. But there is still hope that they will fail'.[18]

The Bird of Paradise, Laing's fifteen-page 'prose poem', is a provocative collection of memories, observations and experiences. It is an extraordinary piece of writing, added on like a coda, but not yet a coda. Laing had published nothing like it before, and would not again. Earlier working titles included 'Entrances and Exits' and 'The Swordfish and the Moon'.[19] As in all of Laing's writings, *The Bird of Paradise* is highly stylised and carefully crafted. At times, it is lucid, touching, a depiction of physical and mental misery, whether on the streets of Glasgow or within the wards of a hospital. Recurrent themes emerge. He relays the story of Jimmy McKenzie, the pest who shadowed the psychiatric ward shouting and swearing back at his voices. Of course only one side of the conversation could ever be heard. It was decided, Laing reports, to alleviate his and 'our' suffering by giving Jimmy a leucotomy. An improvement in his condition was noted and he no longer walked around shouting at his voices. Instead: 'What's that? Say that again! Speak up ye buggers, I cannae hear ye!'

At other times, Laing recounts bizarre perceptual phenomena, some of which appear to be accounts of dreams: 'Two men sit facing each other and both of them are me. Quietly, meticulously, systematically, they are blowing out each other's brains, with pistols. They look perfectly intact. Inside devastation'.[20] Some of the prose reads like an uninhibited stream of consciousness, in which Laing appears to be pushing a linguistic experiment to its extreme boundaries.

> Fishes, washed up and out in their death throes twitching, rubbing themselves together for their own slime. Don't be a shy fish. This is no time for dignity or heroics. Our

> best hope is cowardice and treachery. I would rather even
> be white than dead.

I agree that the prose is bizarre, unconventional, but certainly no less comprehensible than, for example, the opening line of one of the reputedly greatest works of this century which goes, 'Once upon a time and a very good time it was there was a moocow coming down along the road ...', James Joyce's *A Portrait of the Artist as a Young Man*.

These sentences have been dismissed as the ramblings of a mind under the influence of mood altering substances. Which they may be, although Laing denied to me that this was the case. But on the face of things, these sentences are no more obscure or incoherent than the conversations he recorded with Julie, 'the ghost of the weed garden' in *The Divided Self*. Laing interpreted Julie's seemingly nonsensical verbal jigsaw to show how it accurately reflected how she perceived herself and her position in life. In the absence of any concrete alternative, perhaps one should admit the possibility that Laing tried to construct for us the day-to-day interior monologue of those persons labelled schizophrenic, so that we could share their thoughts. The reader who finds them tedious and incomprehensible has the option of removing him or herself from the situation, i.e., to cease reading. This is of course not a possibility for a person suffering mental disturbance, and whose existence in the world has been invalidated by those people who cannot understand what is being communicated to them.

It seems that Laing's greatest crime in *The Bird of Paradise* was daring to be different, when there was probably no other viable alternative for him. As he states on the final page, 'I have seen the Bird of Paradise, she has spread herself before me, and I shall never be the same again'.[21]

One of the consequences of the widespread success of the book was that, once again, it was used to reinforce the view that Laing was anti-family, and that at the feet of parents in particular he laid the blame for the ills of the modern world. But Laing has nowhere openly condemned the family *per se*. Rather, he has described those communicational processes which, in *certain* families consisting of *certain* individuals at *particular* times and moments, *might well* lead to the invalidation of at least one person's experience of themselves and the world, and which *might*, in turn, lead to madness. There is no doubt that Laing enjoyed conventional family life including, in the main, monogamous practices, and that he saw no superior alternative to it. One of the difficulties of Kingsley Hall was this precise lack of privacy, and an enforced communitarianism that he did not feel totally at ease with. Yet he condemned the manner in which the family was increasingly distorted in order to fulfil the requirements of a modern (capitalist) economy for obedience and conformity in a mechanistic age, with the result of turning people into automatons.

*

Darkness Visible, William Styron's memoir of his depression and his momentary thoughts of suicide, demonstrates movingly and profoundly the richness of human experience and the strength of spirit at such times of crisis. He recalls how on one bitterly cold night, the furnace broken, he sat wrapped up, almost to the point of mummification, against the chill. It was late, and he believed he would not live to see the following dawn. He was watching a movie on video, in which a young actress who had been in one of his plays was cast in a small part. The story was set in late-nineteenth-century Boston and in one scene the characters entered a music conservatory from which, beyond the walls, came a contralto voice, a 'sudden soaring passage from the Brahms *Alto Rhapsody*'. Styron continues to observe that for months previously he had been numbly unresponsive to such sounds, indeed to any music or other pleasure. But this piece of music

> ... pierced my heart like a dagger, and in a flood of swift recollection I thought of all the joys the house had known: the children who had rushed through its rooms, the festivals, the love and work, the honestly earned slumber, the voices and the nimble commotion, the perennial tribe of cats and dogs and birds ...[22]

These memories, and the people they recalled, saved him from abandoning himself and submitting to suicide. He realised he could not 'commit this desecration' on himself.

Anyone who has themselves fallen into the clutches of a blue mood or a deeper depression can recognise the desperation Styron describes, as well as the beauty his heart feels, and of which he talks – the presence of children, the perennial tribe of animals who shared his living space, and the sound of the Brahms *Rhapsody*. From personal experience Styron writes movingly yet ambivalently about the various therapeutic interventions he endured in an attempt to control his depression, especially the sometime competing approaches of pharmacology and group therapy. Other individuals experiencing and suffering depression might well take a route of salvation and 'treatment' diametrically opposed to the one Styron endured. This is one of the many major difficulties in discussing therapies of any kind.

It is has been suggested by Christopher Lasch and others, that the therapeutic outlook has begun to become a more dominant socially organising principle than the previous one of religion. Whether or not his argument is valid is a moot point, but what *is* certain is that the psychotherapeutic arm of the therapeutic industries is among the least investigated or understood enterprises that continue to develop. Very little is truly known about the actual processes involved. In the same way that no one returns after death to tell us of Heaven or Hell, very few people share with us their considered thoughts and experiences of the therapy they have endured or benefited from. Although the origins of supportive, skilful and beneficial *listening* date back to the beginning of time, psychotherapy, as we have to come to recognise it, formally starts with Freud. In this connection it is salutary to note that although we tend to consider the psychotherapeutic enterprise to be humanitarian in essence, this does not mean that the practitioners themselves recognise this. In an unguarded moment Freud himself wrote in a letter that he had found 'little good about human beings on the whole', and that in his experience most of them were 'trash'.

For Freud, *psychoanalysis* itself was an educational as well as a clinical experience, which someone purposively paid to receive. He leased his time. Many of the problems and dilemmas that Freud dealt with were those general problems of living and not necessarily life-and-death matters of madness. The fundamental rule of orthodox psychoanalysis is that the therapist is to be viewed as an anonymous figure *who cannot be faulted,* a sometimes frustrating experience for an individual who believes the interpretation he or she has been asked to accept is inappropriate. Equally problematic is the notion of 'transference' – the supposition that both analyst and patient are subtly emotionally involved – and one that is almost impossible to examine. It is, however, far easier to learn from those *failures* in psychotherapy, especially when the process goes spectacularly amiss, as in such cases, for example, where a therapist is accused of improper conduct. Implicit in every psychotherapeutic encounter there is a conundrum: will a patient who has undergone therapy and who has, in his or her own terms, emerged from the relationship successfully treated or indeed healed, wish to share this with anyone else and admit that he or she have been in therapy? Or will they prefer to remain silent or even take personal credit for any beneficial change that has taken place? And anyone who has endured an *unsuccessful* therapeutic encounter may well not wish to recount the painful or meaningless moments spent in such a relationship. More common, perhaps, is the situation in which a person, by the very virtue of the time invested and money expended, is more likely to perceive the experience in positive if not glowing terms *even if* it was actually unsatisfactory, mundane or even damaging. Karl Kraus famously remarked that 'psychoanalysis is that kind of illness of which it thinks itself the cure'. However, the people drawn to Laing tended not to seek to be in therapy *as if it were a substitute for life.* Rather they sought his assistance as they attempted to unravel and erase established patterns of pain and torment and to live a more fulfilled existence.

To write about 'Laingian therapy' is as difficult as writing about a coherent and formal Laingian 'theory'. Despite his own voracious reading and his ability to internalise and integrate various ideas and perspectives, the result was not one of a *systematic* set of concepts and ideas that were part of a specified theory. Laing had devoured many strands of existentialism and phenomenology, yet it would be inaccurate to simply term his thought existentialist or phenomenological. Similarly his reading of Freud and the post-Freudians from Klein and Stack-Sullivan onwards would not lead us to affix the label Freudian to his work. He was, of course, extremely well versed in Freudian theory and practice. He shared certain of Freud's sensibilities. But of course, for Laing, philosophers such as Schopenhauer and Nietzsche predated and were more interesting than Freud. Laing added to his 'therapeutic tool kit' such central ideas as unconscious motivation, defence mechanisms of the ego, and so on. And although he developed concepts such as metanoia further than many others had managed to achieve, such concepts were

R. D. Laing, Torquay, 1947.

R. D. Laing, conference in Leuven, 1965.

Marcelle Vincent, Loch Lomond, 1949.

John Bowlby.

Charles Rycroft.

D. W. Winnicott.

Mary Barnes, Summer 1971.

Leon Redler, Kingsley Hall, 1967.

R. D. Laing and Victoria Crowe, London 1974.

Victoria Crowe painting R. D. Laing for the Scottish National Gallery, London 1974.

Potrait by Hag (aka Ian Hargreaves) for the record sleeve, *Life before Death*, 1978.

Jutta Laing, R. D. Laing, Jill Purce and Fritjof Capra, Zaragoza, Spain, 1980.

R. D. Laing and others, Zaragoza, 1980.

R. D. Laing, Zaragoza, 1980.

R. D. Laing, Zaragoza, 1980.

R. D. Laing and Allen Ginsberg, Hampstead, 1985. Photo by Tom Pickard.

Thomas Szasz, Elly Jansen, R. D. Laing and Bernard Posner, London, 1984.

R. D. Laing in his study, Hampstead 1985. Photo and text by his friend, Allen Ginsberg.

Johnny Duffy and R. D. Laing, Glasgow, 1987.

R. D. Laing, Naropa Institute, Boulder Colorado, July 7th, 1987. Photo by Allen Ginsberg.

R. D. Laing and Marguerita — 'two days after Charles's conception' — Boulder, Colorado, 1987.

Charles, Marguerita and R. D. Laing, 1988.

Charles and R. D. Laing, 1988.

R. D. Laing with son, Benjamin, early 1989.

R. D. Laing, the day before he died, St Tropez, 22nd August 1989.

not central pieces of an already predetermined jigsaw. The label that one *is* tempted to affix to Laing is that of social-phenomenology, earned through his painstaking attempts to demonstrate patterns of interpersonal communications, and about which he so vividly wrote, especially in his earlier books. Perhaps the most that can be said with any certainty is that, in true existentialist fashion, he saw philosophising and theorising as *necessarily* incomplete and somewhat unsatisfactory activities. There is certainly no sign that he himself was especially satisfied with what theoretical work he had achieved, and unquestionably he believed that all of his work was *a work in progress*.

But it would also be a mistake to characterise Laing as someone who criticised yet attempted no reconstruction or alternative to that which he had criticised. He consistently attempted to provide alternatives to those theories and practices which he felt to be incomplete or incorrect. Kingsley Hall was a concrete example of metanoia, his alternative to the conventional psychiatric practices he believed failed individuals. And his concept of ontological insecurity was the idea which he believed explained aspects of the schizophrenic experience more accurately than traditional biological interpretations.

Another reason why it is problematic to discuss Laingian therapy is that at no time did he *codify* his approach or his actual behaviour in therapeutic situations. Indeed, on those rare occasions in which he toyed with the idea of specifying a term for his own therapeutic outlook or approach, he half-heartedly talked in terms of it being an 'integral' approach or one of 'synthesis'. But these were rare occasions and not whole-hearted. Essentially Laing was not totally convinced, perhaps in his arrogance or perhaps in a moment of accurate self-reflection, that anyone else could actually do what he did. When asked what people got when they saw him in therapy, he replied 'they got R. D. Laing', not existential therapy, not post-modern Freudianism, simply R. D. Laing. This is, of course, one of the many reasons that a priori make it extremely difficult to examine *any* psychotherapeutic practice because, quite simply, much of what goes on is *beyond words*. And in Laing's case this was doubly true for, unlike someone who may be orthodox or, say, Lacanian, he did not rely solely on *speech* as his interpersonal therapeutic data for examination or discussion. He did not consider his intervention as merely an approach based on a semantic theory developed solely to make sense out of words. Laing might well, within well-defined and previously agreed boundaries, physically embrace a patient, laugh and share a drink, and even conduct a session while taking a walk.

One of Laing's favourite sayings was from Confucius – 'The way out is via the door. Why is it that no one will use this method?' A derivation of this, used by Laing particularly when discussing how to free oneself from addictions, was, 'if you want to get out of prison and the door is open, why stay there and find out how you got there?' When he was asked to codify, to label the essence of the therapeutic encounter, he replied that, among other things, sometimes his patients wanted his view on them, which, when he had given it, they could then take away 'and make the best or the worst of it':

> I mean, I'm not saying that this is going to do you any good, but if you are coming to see me and if what you want to get from me is how I see your life and the situation you're in and you think that will help you well I don't mind giving you that. But I am not promising you that this is going to be therapeutic ... (and) ... One thing just one thing, don't kill yourself on my doorstep. If you can't take what I'm going to tell you, just fuck off in good order, and if you're going to think of that, give me a promise that you won't slit your throat until you've stopped seeing me for at least six weeks because I don't want any responsibility for what you do with your life.[23]

Laing adds, however, that to someone else he might be somewhat more tender. Each person would receive a different, particular and tailored response. Of course, Laing had been trained in classical psycho-analysis at the Institute of Psychoanalysis, and indeed, for over ten years spent something like twelve hours each week engaged in such work, out of a total of ninety hours per week in which he was seeing patients in one way or another. Someone would sit in a chair and someone else, or even a couple, would sit opposite him and talk. As Laing puts it, 'twosomes, couples, families, in their own homes, in my place in Eton Road, going out for walks eventually – perhaps – sitting on the top of Primrose Hill, looking over London while they talked about themselves'.[24]

Nevertheless Laing claimed that he was never truly imbued with any Tavistock or Institute concepts – 'I was never a convert. I never had to be de-converted'. He believed in the importance of the idea of 'transfer-ence', and considered it interesting – if someone was coming to see him, he would ask himself, 'who is this, who are they talking to, who do they think they are speaking to, their mummy when they're two-and-a-half years old, or are they treating me like a little baby?'[25] However, Laing would not *interpret* this, rather simply point it out – 'do you realise that by virtue of what you've just said, that you are treating me like your father. Now I want to point out to you that I'm not your fucking father!'[26]

Laing's approach was unconventional. It was also resplendent with a variety of diverse methods and techniques. Sometimes he believed that a patient merely needed to hear clearly and unequivocally what they had just told him, so he would slowly and deliberately repeat their utterance. In the course of listening to someone, he would be considering the future of that patient – should they see him regularly, or should they be referred elsewhere. Sometimes a problem that he'd envisaged would take years to resolve would be resolved in just one hour.

Open-mindedness was a key element of Laing's therapeutic thinking. Certainly, he did not envisage what he did was 'psychotherapy', since he simply attempted to contribute positively to his patient's lives, in whatever form that may take. Someone might be a physical disaster, and he would point out to them that 'smoking twenty cigarettes before breakfast is unhelpful, that they couldn't get anything straight unless they addressed themselves to that sort of thing'. One woman he saw was being beaten by her father, with whom she still lived. Laing: 'I mean, *you* haven't got a problem. When you walk out of here, we'll send a car round for you in twenty minutes, stay with that person at their house, and don't go back home. Right? When the dust has settled you'll be able to see what you've been living in'.[27] Essentially Laing came to work in the here-and-now, the present, without any preconceived overarching theoretical or methodological guidelines.

About half of the people who tried to see Laing were those who had read his books, and particularly when it was first published, *The Divided Self* and then, later, *The Politics of Experience and The Bird of Paradise*. There were those who had been hospitalised, or fearful of being so, many already physically destroyed by numerous electric shocks, others, especially the devotees of *The Bird of Paradise*, wished for Laing to open up the world of LSD for them, and, to a degree, he would oblige. Other patients came via other patients, doctors, social workers, family mem-

bers, friends, psychiatrists. He would sometimes refer patients to Philadelphia Association households, or to other colleagues, or see them
himself. What they would receive from Laing was '*Laing*. They've had
my company and attention, my *engagément* on their behalf', and my
'hopefully refined, trained, cultivated intuition, spontaneity and sensibility'.[28] But *Laing* did not claim omnipotence:

> I'm not claiming to be Jesus Christ or Buddha. So I'm capable of being
> unpleasant to you or to anyone else or to myself and striking notes and
> being out of key myself, and going through ups and downs in my life.[29]

On a number of occasions Laing mentioned that perhaps he ought to
conceptualise what he did therapeutically under the headings of Music,
Meditation and Martial Arts. Such experiences had always been central
to his life, therefore it would have been quite consistent for him to want
to include them in his healing.

The conventional definition of *music* is that it is the art of combining
vocal or instrumental sounds (or both) to produce beauty of form,
harmony, and expression of emotion. Indeed, we often use musical
terminology to describe our states of mind – that we feel off-key, or out
of time or step. Missing the beat, the rhythm, the tempo. Music is
sublime. One is moved and uplifted by its presence. It has been used to
encourage men to kill each other, or maybe to accept more easily a
certain death. When it is without words it requires and enables a purer
form of listening. It may soothe, calm. It may enable people to get out
of themselves and perhaps into others. In Beijing's mental hospitals,
ballroom dancing is taught to the patients as part of the therapy. And
music may bring us closer to the Divine. One simply has to consider the
music of Hildegarde of Bingen, or the mystical dance of the Mevlevi
dervish.

Meditation may enable the individual to de-programme him or herself
from the inappropriate way in which he or she have come to view the
world. We mis-take things. Meditative practise may, like music, effect a
calmness, may reduce anxiety and in so doing help both the person who
practises it in addition to those around him or her. It begins to address
the question – who am I? It helps rid the person of any number of
delusions surrounding his or her sense of self, the sense of identity. The

individual *may* come to realise that the world and others are, in a real sense, a figment of his or her construction. Meditation deconstructs 'reality'. Essentially: when practised profoundly, seriously, sincerely, and honestly, meditation leads to an awakening or a 'wising up'. The world appears fresher, one feels more contact with it, one experiences a sense of relief, happiness, compassion. One can acknowledge the one-ness of all. That other people matter.

Tai Chi, aikido, and other *martial arts*, involve one's whole being – including one's physical being – much more centrally than other therapeutic activities. Balance. Centre of gravity. Flexibility. *Grounded.* Through the increased energy flows that are created, fear is transcended. Or at least there exists the potential for it to do so.[30]

Imagine a therapeutic environment – a *community* of carers, of all sorts – in which one struggle could take place amidst music, through meditative practices and with one's feet planted firmly on the ground. This was one of Laing's unfinished projects.

The beginning of *all* truly valuable 'therapeutic' work is *listening*, something Laing believed he was good at:

> ... if you ask me what have I done or given to people, a lot of people who have come to see me have said that the main thing they have got from me is that I listen to them. They have actually found someone who actually heard what they are saying and listened ... For many people in life, there's no one listening to them, no one hears them, no one sees them, they are made up by everyone, they feel quite rightly that they are ghosts. They might as well be dead, as far as their nearest and dearest are concerned ... (and) ... so if they come to see someone who actually sees and hears them and actually recognises their reality, their existence, that in itself is liberating.[31]

*

Michael Acutt called R. D. Laing from a call box in San Francsico where Laing was currently staying. Following a severe emotional shock, Acutt felt that he was literally falling part, a feeling of which he was naturally deeply afraid. He asked Laing for help. Indeed, he felt that he was 'falling', and had difficulty standing. He pleaded with Laing to help – 'have I ever asked you for help in the seventeen years that I have known you?' Eventually it was agreed that he would go to Laing's rented house, situated in one of the more salubrious parts of the city. Throughout the course of the day, Laing managed to calm Acutt, and then they managed to spend a more pleasant evening. Eventually, Acutt was packed off to sleep on a guest bed in the living room. On awakening he found Laing sitting on the edge of his bed. Acutt himself was still 'falling'. They quietly drank coffee together. Then softly Laing informed him that, during the night, Acutt must have knocked over a vase on the way to the bathroom, and that now this expensive vase was shattered in hundreds of pieces. 'I don't want you to pay for this Michael, but the vase is part of the rental package so we have to fix it'. Laing suggested they went to a store, bought some Crazy Glue, and some green food dye to cover the cracks, and then they 'would put Humpty Dumpty together again'. Walking back to the house they stopped for a drink, started work on the vase, rolled a joint, and then spent a few hours laughing, arguing, repairing the vase as well as heart and mind. The vase was fixed. Acutt got to his feet and once more entered the streets of San Francisco. No longer falling.[32]

Death before Life, Life before Death

Which is it, is man one of God's blunders or is God one of man's?
Friedrich Nietzsche

Despite the international publicity surrounding *The Politics of Experience and The Bird of Paradise* Laing spent most of the late sixties doing what he had always done, giving lectures on subjects as diverse as Buddhism, family therapy, and regression. He spent the summer of 1968 on the Greek island of Patmos, on which John had written *The Book of Revelations.* Laing never actually visited the cave in which John was allegedly chained up and where he had written the book. He was working on his own book, provisionally titled *Patmos Meditations*, based on symbolic logic and the mathematical work he was pursuing, especially in set theory, which he was applying to family relationships. While at Patmos he also wrote notes intended for an autobiography and which almost two decades later were used in his 1985 memoir *Wisdom, Madness and Folly.*

Laing had planned the mathematical work as the basis of the Massey Lectures, a series of five radio lectures to be broadcast by the Canadian Broadcasting Corporation in the winter of 1968, and in which some of these ideas were to be incorporated. These lectures, in slightly altered format and with some additional essays, were eventually published as *The Politics of the Family* in 1971. One central theme that Laing was to elucidate was the importance of the inter-generational nature of families, and the manner in which past generations exercise influence on the present. He argues that families (of some kind or other, albeit *very* different from ours) have existed, say, for at least 100,000 years – 'We can study directly only a minute slice of the family chain: three generations, if we are lucky. Even studies of three generations are rare. What patterns can we hope to find, when we are restricted to three out of at

least four thousand generations?'[1] Laing discusses the common methodological problems a study of the family involves, especially within those
families which, at first glance, appear to be running smoothly. Laing cites
the most frequent circumstance he encountered was one in which what
he could see was happening bore almost no, if any, resemblance to what
family members thought was happening, or that they were experiencing,
irrespective of physical evidence or common sense.

> Maybe no one knows what is happening. However, one thing is often clear
> to an outsider: there is concerted family *resistance* to discovering what is
> going on, and there are complicated stratagems to keep everyone in the
> dark, and in the dark that they are in the dark. The truth has to be
> expended to sustain a family image. The family as a shared fantasy image
> is usually a container of some kind *in* which all members of the family feel
> themselves to be, and *for* which image all members of the family may feel
> each should sacrifice themselves. Since this fantasy exists only in so far as
> it is 'in' everyone who shares 'in' it, anyone who gives it up, shatters the
> 'family' in everyone else.[2]

Interestingly, in the chapter entitled 'Intervention in Social Situations',
Laing highlights an uncomfortable truism, namely that however sophisticated an intervention is, or the therapeutic sensitivity employed, *change*
is extremely difficult to facilitate: 'the strategy of intervening in situations through the medium of words by telling people what we think
they are doing, in the hope that thereby they will stop doing it, because
we think that they should not be doing what we think they are doing, is
frequently vastly irrelevant to all concerned'.[3]

For much of the rest of the year Laing continued to see increasing
numbers of patients at Wimpole Street, and he agreed to some of the
many requests he received from both print and broadcasting media.

From the summer of 1966 until early 1969 Laing had little, if any,
contact with his first family, who were still living in Glasgow. In January
1969 he *did* visit the city but it was primarily to see his father David, who
was suffering from Alzheimer's and was, by this time, in the psychogeria-
tric ward of the Leverndale Hospital. His father was unable to recognise
his son, but in the twisted logic of senile dementia believed Laing to be
the man who 'lived with my wife'. Laing was later to base a short poem,
'Return of the Prodigal (I)', on the painful encounter.

son	hullo dad
father	hello (*pause*) Who are you?
son	I'm your son dad
father	O you're my *son*
son	yes dad
father	and what's your name?
son	Peter
father	you're my son Peter
son	yes dad I'm your son Peter
father	you used to live with my wife
	I never thought I'd see you again ...[4]

In 1970, the same year that the Kingsley Hall project closed, Jutta gave birth to Laing's seventh child, a little girl whom they named Natasha. At the same time he produced what was destined to be yet another volume of work so novel and unexpected that it defied immediate categorisation. For a number of years he had been writing small phrases and poems, miniature dramas, all of which he later described as those 'tangles, fankles, *impasses*, disjunctions, whirligogs, binds' and indeed the *knots* that people entangle themselves in and find themselves among. Paradoxes, dilemmas, conundrums, expectations and counter-expectations and hidden meanings, all expressed in Pinteresque circular and self-reflexive language. He argues that the 'patterns delineated' had not yet been 'classified by a Linnaeus of human bondage'.

Laing himself was uncertain as to what precisely he was writing and what he would do with the material. Over a period of some five or six years he had collected the poems and vignettes he occasionally felt inspired to write, and without much thought, placed them in a folder for future reference. He *was* certain that they were something of a kind which he had never previously written, or indeed encountered by anyone else's hand. Maybe he would send a small number to the *Times Literary Supplement* or some other literary magazine or journal. That he himself was serious about the volume is evident from his introductory remarks:

> I could have distilled [these patterns] further towards an abstract logico-mathematical calculus. I hope they are not so schematised that one may not refer back to the very specific experiences from which they derive; yet that they are sufficiently independent of 'content', for one to divine the final formal elegance in these webs of *maya*.[5]

Just before he left for Patmos, Laing realised there was a possibility of publishing the unusual material in a small volume. He had already painstakingly reworked much of the writing, and whilst on Patmos he applied the finishing touches. At the same time he found time to make notes for his autobiography and to prepare for the Massey Lectures. The book's success was due, in no small part, to its design. It was a precursor of the 1990s when books increasingly are purchased as *objets d'art* in their own right, regardless of literary or intellectual merit. The title *Knots* came to him when he was browsing in a bookshop, trying unsuccessfully to find material similar to the type he was creating, i.e., psycho-poetry. He came across a translated sutra called *knots*. In some respects, *Knots* is consistent with much of his other explorations of interpersonal communication and the processes of mystification and confusion. Indeed, it might even be a useful teaching aid for therapists, a starting point from which they could discover the conundrums their patients' find themselves in. Certainly many people totally unacquainted with either the previous work of Laing or of the psychology of communication, could recognise their own dilemmas within the short book and, more importantly, could use the generic language as a way towards self-understanding.

> A son should respect his father
> He should not have to be taught to respect his father
> It is something that is natural
> That's how I've brought up my son anyway.
>
> Of course a father must be worthy of respect
> he can forfeit a son's respect
> But I hope at least that my son will respect me, if
> only for leaving him free to respect me or not.[6]

This *knot* describing how a son should respect his father emerged out of a discussion Laing had with Gregory Bateson, concerning how Japanese children were taught to respect their fathers as a form of practice rather than as a mark of true deference, simply so that they could learn how to respect others as they proceeded through life.

How clever has one to be to be stupid?
The others told her she was stupid. So she made
herself stupid in order not to see how stupid
they were to think she was stupid,
because it was bad to think they were stupid.
She preferred to be stupid and good,
rather than bad and clever.

It is bad to be stupid: she needs to be clever
to be so good and stupid.
It is bad to be clever, because this shows
how stupid they were
to tell her how stupid she was.[7]

In his biography of Laing, Daniel Burston argues that the book presents no solutions to those blind alleys that Laing so succinctly describes, that there was no clinical application, and that it was if he was 'admitting defeat' and 'retreating to a position of detached bemusement'. He goes further to say that, 'unlike his efforts in 1967 and 1968, which bristled with criticism of the social order, this work had no social or political relevance – further evidence of his deepening disengagement'.[8] This is somewhat missing the point. Laing was simply being *creative*. He did not consider that it was incumbent upon himself to either write and produce particular types of books or books written in a particular format or style. Why was it not possible, or desirable, or indeed *acceptable* for Laing to use anything other than the conventional language of psychiatry? Was he, unlike others less capable, to have glass ceilings placed on his attainments or on the literary devices open to him? Why could he not expand his literary and imaginary horizons – why could he not experiment with literary genres? The syntax he uses in *Knots* makes the complex cryptogram of human relationships *accessible, attractive* and *comprehensible* to those not versed in the Latinate language of psychiatry. Why is Laing to be pilloried as opposed to praised? Despite the reactionary views of critics like Burston, *Knots* was applauded by many reviewers, though not all, for his novel venture into psycho-poetry. *The Politics of Experience and The Bird of Paradise*, though more critical and politically radical, was published in 1967 although it was actually written at least three years earlier. By the time its publication date had arrived, Laing was already immersed in meditative, contemplative and spiritual activities. Yoga, meditation, music, prayer and poetry were *always* more central to his life than any *practical* social protest or active political involvement. In any case, by 1970 Laing had already accomplished a life-time; he had contributed significantly to the amelioration of the tortured psyches of many individuals; raised the awareness, through his books, of alternative conceptions of mental distress and illness; given succour to those who believed their experiences of themselves and others were invalid; and, most crucially, through the Kingsley Hall project, laid the foundations of an on-going experiment which continues today, both in Europe and the USA.

The suggestion that *Knots* is without social or political relevance is short-sighted. For a book of its type – without precedent, and therefore difficult to market – it sold extremely well, all over the world but especially in the USA, Germany and the UK. In the USA, despite some lukewarm reviews, the book's publishers, Pantheon, discovered that it was selling extraordinarily well in the run-up to Christmas, not to intellectuals or academics, but to secretaries and other women who were purchasing it as a Christmas present for their partners. Part of the attraction may well have been the book's distinctive black and white design and typography, though it is hard to imagine that they were not entranced by the vignettes that most readers could identify with. As Laing himself later admitted, he had always hoped that he would 'manage to write something that was accessible to any intelligent person'.[9] What could be more socially or 'politically' relevant in the struggle against gender, inter-generational and other injustices, than a book that people could actually read and understand, get ideas from and make them begin to ask questions?

Knots transferred to both the stage, celluloid and radio. Edward Petherbridge directed the stage version and Laing hoped that he would take the performance toward formal miming, or *commedia dell'arte*. In the film version it was Laing who, a little mischievously, gave the production the visual idea of a little boy with an arrow, who aims and then shoots it at his mother, piercing her through the breast at which point she says, 'mummy isn't angry, she's just very, very disappointed'. The BBC's 1973 radio version combined words and music, orchestrated by Humphrey Searle and produced by Martin Esslin who remembered Laing's 'boyish zest in entering into this type of show business and obviously greatly enjoyed the atmosphere in a studio with actors and musicians'.[10]

By the end of 1970, Laing was quietly exhausted. The celebrity he had achieved had taken its toll. He disliked lecturing and was often sick beforehand. Travelling was a mixed blessing, especially when the schedule was tight. More and more demands were made by the media, and also those individuals who wished either to receive analysis with Laing, or share some LSD. His own existing patients required attention and care, his colleagues sought advice and support, and others, only a few, increased his burden with their desire for fame by association. And then there was his writing, and his second family which included an infant. In the USA he was expected to make pronouncements about Richard Nixon and Vietnam, and he also felt that there were widespread hopes that he would become a demagogue or be a white Martin Luther King. Students continued to buy his books, which were to be found between Casteneda and Marx, and he was given the label 'Acid Marxist'. Laing was beginning to feel consternation concerning the existence of the figure of 'R. D. Laing', an entity which appeared to enjoy a life extraneous to and independent of Laing himself.

On March 30th, 1971, Laing, Jutta and their two children, Adam and Natasha, together with the *au pair* Brenda, left on the mid-afternoon flight to Ceylon (Sri Lanka). They travelled light, and Laing took neither books nor drugs of any kind.

For those who knew Laing, this was no great surprise. Even if the *precise* timing of his departure was unexpected, the desire to visit the geographic heartlands of Buddhism was not at all unforeseen. Within most of us there is a place or places for which we hunger: where we believe that some kind of sumptuous joy or unique pleasure, some form of new knowledge or education might take place, where some new start may commence, or where some form of awakening or enlightenment may occur. And so it was for Laing. He had yearned to visit India since he came across the life of Mahatma Gandhi and the writings of the Buddha as a teenager. In his writings he had made no secret of both Western and Eastern spiritual and mystical influences. The supplementary material he produced which accompanied his 1967 lectures in New York, was given titles, like 'a Sutra on going back and going out of one's mind', and another, 'a Sutra on remembering'. In his published books he had made passing references to ideas such as 'the veil of Maya'. He had made a brief comparison between 'the schizoid attitude toward the body and the Gnostic project of achieving disincarnate spirituality'. In 1966, he had opened *Interpersonal Perception* with an allusion to the Hindu myth of the jewelled net of Indra, which 'describes the observable cosmos as a plethora of multifaceted jewels reflecting one another's reflections, and reflections of reflections, generating an infinity of images and perspectives'.[11] In 1969, he had claimed that, through diligent meditation, he had 'finally relinquished the misguided identification of a man with his body'.[12]

On her forty-third birthday, writer Françoise Sagan remarked that the one thing she regretted was that she would never have the time to 'read all the books I want to read'. In 1971, Laing had also reached that year of his life, and knew that he had to take his chances, that after years of dedicated meditation and yoga if he was to take his practise any further perhaps it would be beneficial to learn from teachers other than himself. Besides which, in Ceylon and India there would be opportunities to immerse himself in Eastern literature more indigenous and esoteric than *The Tibetan Book of the Dead* and the other more commonplace Buddhist texts he had devoured already. He had learned from his erstwhile colleague Eric Graham Howe about a monk who lived at a mountain training-centre in Ceylon. This monk was a teacher and scholar of Satipittana meditation. It was to him, Nyanaponika Thera, that Laing decided to make his pilgrimage. He closed down his private practice and handed over the reins of the Philadelphia Association, and then travelled to Glasgow to visit his first family. After a tearful parting, he left for Ceylon.

Originally he had wanted to go alone. He craved *solitude,* especially at that time when he felt the world closing in. However Jutta was fearful that if he went alone there was the distinct possibility he might never return. As Laing himself concurred, 'she thought that if I really went off on my own in the mood I was in she might never see me again', that he might 'disappear into the depths of God knows where, and certainly a side of me felt like doing that'.[13]

In Ceylon, Jutta stayed at the Tourist Lodge at Bandarapola while Laing fearlessly took to the hills, to the Buddhist mountain retreat at Kanduboda. He was taught the technique of the Four Foundations of

Mindfulness, the practise based on the central idea of impermanence – that human suffering is a result of ignorance and that the emotions of desire, hatred and bewilderment may only be dealt with through giving up all attachments. To internalise this, the practise involved Laing sitting still in a small room, making as little movement as possible, and eating rarely and frugally. One bowl of rice and gruel a day. Seated in Lotus, the practise might last over twenty hours each day. This was but one of the various meditative practises he learned and mastered. Laing diligently studied Pali texts of the original teachings of the Buddha and, in a short time, came to be seen as a successful pupil.

The reunion with Jutta came some two months later. Another two months were spent in Ceylon before they all moved on to India. Already the trip had taken its toll. Jutta, in particular, found his absences, either in mind or body, difficult to adjust to. Besides which, at that time, her interest in Buddhism was quite minimal although not totally absent.

After some conventional tourism in Delhi, they moved to Almora, near the Himalayas, in the Kumaon foothills, mountains silhouetted against the sky, streams rippling through the silence of forests, and placid lakes reflecting the panorama of nature. They rented a small house two miles away from the nearest village. Laing would spend his time in meditation, fasting and Buddhist scholarship, while the children played happily, and Jutta busied herself domestically, learning a little Indian music along the way.

Among the many scholars, teachers and 'holy men' whom Laing encountered was a local sadhu Gangotri Baba, a fifty-one-year-old ex-doctor who for seven years had wandered through India with begging bowl and robe, and who now lived perilously perched half-way up a mountain slope on an overarching crag, his dwelling made of tree branches formed into a human bird's nest. One hour away from Nainital, the nearest town, he lived a mysterious life of contemplation and asceticism.

Laing described him as an Indian Baba who was a member of a branch of 'Indian holy men who lived up in the snow and ice of the Himalayas without any clothes and who never shaved. *Naked wild men*'.[14] All that they carried with them were six-feet long tridents. Fire was a central feature of their lives, upon which they would walk, eat and sit. They would also smear their bodies with the ashes. They were disciples of Kali, the Hindu goddess who appealed to Laing's sensibility. In Indian mythology this black/dark blue woman-like creature is represented as having a long, lolling tongue, dishevelled hair and is garlanded with corpses and severed heads. She dances on the lifeless body of her husband Shiva, thus dramatising the teaching that the male deity needs his female energy in order to function creatively. She is both a mother figure and a divine energy who brings in her wake bloodshed, pestilence, terror and death. In one visual image Kali is headless, and is holding her own head, while the mouth greedily drinks the blood that spurts uncontrollably from her neck.

At the time of Laing's pilgrimage to the Baba it was already the depths of winter. The human bird's nest in which the Baba lived was already almost cut off. Laing vividly describes his time with the birdman.

> ... I was right up there for three weeks without any other human beings, only the occasional leopard, monkeys – it was up in the ice mountain jungle – and we sat in front of the fire. My life depended on the fire being on all the time fuelled by tree logs that had to be got and carted up there. I had the job of getting the wood to keep the fire going. It was a major physical effort and we just had enough rice and grain to maintain supplies. He had just a loincloth on, and I had a Scottish pullover and a loincloth and that was it. So we sat in front of this fire, we hardly had any conversation or talked about anything for several weeks ... but he was congenial company.[15]

Before he left the nest and returned to his family, Laing was initiated into a particularly esoteric sensibility of the Kali tradition, in which the Baba produced a massive cake-like substance which symbolically represented Laing himself, and which was subsequently burned and eaten. He was smothered in ashes, ate the cake representing himself, and then spent the remainder of the night in a meditation to the moon. Some time afterwards, perhaps a week or so, Laing returned to Almora. On reflection, he believed that the encounter with Gangotri had taught him many things, and provided him with particular kinds of nourishment which he felt, at that time, he required. At a simple level it was a 'boy scout course of survival' which he was 'in the mood for'. The Baba had also shared with Laing some of the knowledge and experience he had acquired from his previous seven years spent living in the jungles of Nepal, where he had neither seen nor communicated with a single human being. Laing recalled the Baba had suggested to him that they were both half crazy, 'I was half and he was the other half'. When put together, 'we were either completely sane or completely crazy'. But, recalled Laing, 'he thought I was crazy to go back again to human beings because they were all completely crazy'.[16]

After leaving Gangotri Baba, Laing returned to Almora where Jutta and his family were still awaiting him. He spent some months studying Sanskrit language and literature, and consulted other scholars and lamas. He also encountered a Sufi, Mufti Jal-al-Ud-din, from whom he sought some illumination, some wisdom on the questions which had always been at the fore of his spiritual search, including the meaning and purpose of life itself, and the correct way to live. He was advised to renounce the world and to 'take up the robe and bowl'. This was an unsatisfactory answer for Laing who, already, knew that the key to spiritual edification was to be 'in the world but not of it', rather than to renounce it and remove oneself from it. That was, perhaps, too easy. With some sadness, he wrote down his thoughts and fears – 'it would be a blessing were I to find the right man for me ... [but] ... maybe there is not such a man, maybe I cannot recognise him'.[17]

After just over a year Laing's sojourn to Ceylon and India came to an end. During that time he had made pilgrimages to places and to people, and had immersed himself in meditative practices and Buddhist scholarship. In April 20th, 1972, the family returned to London. Before long Laing was once again thrust into the media and professional spotlight, partly by virtue of the fact that his income was dwindling while his expenses in London remained quite high. One of the consequences of this realisation was that Laing agreed, reluctantly, to undertake a lecture tour across the USA planned for the winter of the same year. *If* peace, contentment and tranquillity were the states of mind Laing was searching for, they appeared to be as far away as ever. Laing should have known better. As he would often say, if you want to make God laugh tell him your plans.

Dazed and confused he wrote a diary entry in early 1972 which stated that there was nothing he wanted to do, yet he didn't want to do nothing. His fame had increased while Laing himself was *in absentia* in the East.

Life magazine produced a five-page spread on the 'philosopher of madness', including some striking black-and-white photographs of both Laing and Jutta. *The Politics of Experience* had sold almost half a million copies, and *Life* claimed that Laing, like Timothy Leary and Marshall McLuhan, was a 'professional scholar transformed into an oracle and prophet'. Before long, Laing would become further disturbed and distressed by the seemingly independent life of the persona, R. D. Laing. Like him, and yet not of him, it was like his *doppelgänger*. Of course, Laing had courted the possibility of celebrity and fame, as any writer does simply by the act of putting pen to paper. And it cannot be denied that he enjoyed some of it, bathed in it. He was, after all, simply human.

In 1971, Ken Loach had released *Family Life*, a film portraying a young woman's treatment at the hands first of her family, as she experiences a schizophrenic episode, and secondly at the hands of the psychiatric profession, as she is coerced into ECT treatment and subsequently treated against her will in hospital. Featuring the actress Sandy Ratcliff, this fictional documentary was scripted by David Mercer on the basis of his theatrical play *In Two Minds,* written some four years earlier. No one was in any doubt that this was *cinema à la Laing*, except, of course, Laing himself who was paid for his advice, but refused to have his name on the credit roll. He perhaps did not appreciate fully the conventions and nature of cinematic 'truth'. The film's over-simplified scenario was not to his liking – 'as a piece of propaganda by David Mercer and Tony Garnett, it was not the sort of film that I would have stayed at very long'.[18] Despite this, the film was seen as a profoundly dramatic yet realistic example of what many people believed to be Laing's belief that the family 'caused' schizophrenia. A more realistic portrayal of the excruciating pain of the psychotic experience and the kind of response to it that Laing favoured, was the film *Asylum,* a documentary feature that focused on the relationship between Leon Redler and another resident of one of the Philadelphia Association households. Shown in 1972 in both New York and London, there were only fleeting moments with Laing on screen.

Ironically, one of the performances he delivered in the year of his return, at the Friend's Meeting House, London, was on the subject of families, with the sub-text that he was appalled to have returned to find people using the name Laing in support of their own and quite different ideas. David Cooper's *The Death of the Family* was one such example, with Laing erroneously sharing the label 'anti-psychiatrist' with its author. He reaffirmed the position that he had attempted consistently to hold over the years with varying degrees of success, that although he castigated *dysfunctional* families, in themselves families could be nurturing and supportive and, importantly, in the absence of anything superior, are the best that we can expect.

A lonely hearts ad in the New York *Village Voice* read 'Two chicks who dig Coltrane, The Grateful Dead and R. D. Laing seek compatible mates', while bumper stickers proclaimed that they were totally 'mad about R. D. Laing'. This was the America that Laing encountered when he arrived in November 1972 for his five-week long lecture tour.

The tour was organised from America. The road manager was experienced in the world of rock music. Danny Halpern was appointed Laing's all-round minder, and was there to take care of all his needs, both administrative and personal. Performances would last for an hour followed by time for discussion. On each occasion Laing would courageously and theatrically remain silent, until he was ready to perform. He would be alone on-stage, framed by a single spotlight. His audiences, invariably young, and fresh from the pages of *The Politics of Experience* and *Knots*, appreciated the first psychiatrist they had probably ever encountered who talked in a manner that they understood and could identify with. 'Consciousness won't be found at the end of a microscope', was simply one of the hundreds of phrases that Laing threw at his audience.

The tour comprised a series of lectures given in fourteen cities, one of which was of course New York, where Laing stayed at Dorothy Parker's old haunt, The Algonquin Hotel. He failed to be impressive during his television appearance with Norman Mailer, but was more focused later when he took part in a televised debate about the nature of schizophrenia. Anthropologist Margaret Mead, ex-wife of Laing's colleague Gregory Bateson, piously refused to appear on the same radio show with him because he had deserted his first family of five children. At Santa Monica he performed before over four thousand devotees, a week after Bob Dylan had pulled in the same number. Tickets were hard to come by. 'Sold out' signs were a regular feature. In between performing and drinking, he would fit in some practice at his piano and the occasional bout of sleep. His immense energy impressed all those around him, though some wondered how long it would last.

In New Orleans Laing bayed like a wolf at the moon, understandably telling the Apollo astronauts to 'get the fuck off' and leave it alone. The drinking that had enabled Laing to be more than usually expressive continued on a flight to Salt Lake City, during which he had a hot dispute with one of the air hostesses on the need to wear shoes on the flight. As the confrontation developed, he was almost put off the plane when it made a stop to refuel. Later he would brawl with his minder Halpern, but was still able to continue with media engagements soon afterwards.

Despite the media hype and Laing's alcohol-induced 'playfulness', regardless of the fact that many of his audience would touch him as he walked past them treating him like a prophet or a guru, and although some of the performances and subsequent exchanges with the audience were dramatic, the most significant moment of the whole tour came in Chicago, when Laing was invited by a number of physicians to examine a young woman diagnosed as schizophrenic. Naked, incarcerated in a padded cell, she rocked back and forth, seemingly in a world of her own. Laing was asked for both diagnosis and prognosis. To their surprise, he took off all his own clothes and joined her, rolling back and forth *in her rhythm*. A little later, a half hour or so, she spoke for the first time in several months.

The proceeds from the tour, together with book royalties, eased Laing's financial straits. But 1973 was to be a traumatic year. Afflicted by something akin to writer's block, he felt unable to find any ideas inspiring enough for him to write about and, in any case, when he *did* come close, was unable to write them down. And Jutta was conducting an affair. It has been suggested[19] that she did so 'possibly in retaliation for Laing's many absences', yet this seems hardly just to *either* party. Laing's 'absences' were primarily concerned with the accumulation of money in order to maintain the lifestyle they both enjoyed. And would Jutta, the mother of Laing's children and deeply in love with him, betray him because he was not always home? Was that a sufficient reason? Whether or not he had given Jutta just cause for her betrayal, Laing nonetheless was profoundly hurt and emotionally and spiritually bereft.

Laing's response was, for a time, to drink to excess. He ruminated on the issues of trust and betrayal in relationships, and on the fact that the relationship he believed he enjoyed was not exactly as he thought. A photograph of him in *Rolling Stone* portrayed him as sad and unwell, out of condition, and not at all the stylish and elegant man that he undoubtedly was. These were difficult days. Susie, his daughter from his first family, appeared in a *Sunday Times* feature about the children of well-known individuals 'Heirs to a Name', and plaintively asserted that her father could 'solve everybody else's problems, but not ours'. Perhaps it was hardly surprising that Laing found solace in alcohol. None of us like to be reminded of our shortcomings, and few of us are perfect. In his biography of Laing, John Clay discusses both Laing's alleged shortcomings with his family and his use of alcohol. He suggests that Laing's reaction was 'to turn in on himself and start drinking in a self-destructive way', that he had failed to 'bring the insight he had gained in India to bear on the situation, any more than he used the understanding acquired as a psychoanalyst during the 1960s', and that it was 'an irony that he, the expert on families, should fail so lamentably to relate to his own first family'.[20] Let us carefully deconstruct his assertions. Laing was not drinking to destroy himself, but was seeking solace – some comfort in distress – and a means of expressing his anger in something approaching a socially-acceptable manner. As a physician Laing knew all too well how to destroy himself, should he have wished to do so. His love of both of his families would have made such a solution impossible. I suspect that Laing came to believe, to a considerable extent, that the so-called insights he had acquired during his own analysis amounted to little. He himself never practised in such a conventional manner such was his lack of belief in the efficacy of many of its principle techniques. As for the insights he gained from his Indian sojourn, what precisely was Laing expected to do on discovering that he had been betrayed by the woman he loved? Assume full Lotus, or show immediate compassion? Laing was a man of passion in addition to being an exponent of meditative and yogic practises. It does seem unjust that he is expected to behave, upon receiving devastating news, in a way of which few people would be capable. As a man of passion, and therefore seeking solace in the way he chose – he is damned. As superman, reacting calmly and logically, he is condemned as cold. Finally, that the 'expert' on families should fail 'so lamentably to relate to his own first family', is an accusation undeserving of its author. Clay's evidence is incomplete, one-sided and tied only to one particular period of time. I can recall spending a very pleasant evening with Laing and his daughter Fiona in his suite in a Glasgow hotel. We three sat, convivially cheering on the hopelessly defeated Scottish football team during a televised match. He and Fiona were relaxed and evidently both pleased to be in each other's company. He appeared to relate to her perfectly adequately. Laing did not claim to be an expert on anything. He merely wrote what he believed to be true about the patterns of communication that unfolded in particular families. Besides which, Laing was only one of the participants involved in the process. If there was a failure in communication, perhaps the members of his family could not or would not relate to him?

The Philadelphia Association, of which Laing was still Chairman, continued with its work and inevitably, within an organisation of its size and with members each of whom believed their own way was the best way, there were disagreements and factions. Laing had continued to develop his creative side which had begun with the writing of *Knots* and continued with his involvement in various projects, including the film *Birth* – showing a new-born baby in agony being circumcised without anaesthesia. There were also various theatrical and musical versions of some of his ideas, including *Life Before Death,* an album of some of his sonnets, spoken by Laing and produced and set to music by Ken Howard and Alan Blaikly. Some members of the Association believed that such activities and publicity were detrimental to the more clinically-oriented approach that they themselves favoured. Overall the Association's central activity, of providing asylum within supportive households, continued to operate. Indeed, over the decade beginning 1964, over four hundred people had received some form of sanctuary from one or other of the houses for a period exceeding seventy-two hours. Over one hundred and fifty of these people had already been hospitalised at some point in their illness. Less than forty people received conventional 'treatment' either during or after their stay. The Association's other activities also expanded, including the trainee psychotherapy programme, seminars and lectures, and yoga, meditation and other related activities. Within the lecture series there were conventional discussions on such items as Freud, psychoanalysis, existentialism, but also on *The Upanishads,* Zen and shamanism. While one faction within the Association favoured a more conventional approach, the other was more experimental and indeed *experiential* with an interest in groups and encounters. Laing appeared able to support and genuinely approve of both factions.

As 1973 came to an end, apparently so did Laing's and Jutta's differences. The following year, romantically on Valentine's Day, they married, nine years after they first met. In the same year they moved out of Belsize Park Gardens and to a new home, nearby in Eton Road. A former vicarage, it adjoined the church of an unorthodox vicar with five hundred exorcisms to his credit. To ensure that there would be no possibility of the house itself being haunted, Laing visited late one night and told any lingering spirits to 'fuck off'.

When they all moved in, Laing insisted that part of the garden be reserved for him. It was to be grown wild, a place where he would be able to be himself, scream and shout, and howl at the moon if he so wished. Indeed, as Laing accurately and distressingly remarked, 'where can you go in society and scream?'[21] Laing resumed the private practice he had closed prior to his Indian odyssey, and Eton Road became his surgery.

In the same year that Laing gained another son, Max, born on June 24th, 1975, he discovered that he was about to lose one of his daughters. Susie, a child of his first marriage to Anne, was suffering from a terminal illness, lymphatic leukaemia. She was only twenty one years of age, engaged to be married and, despite her comments in the *Sunday Times* article, extremely close to her father. The tragedy happened very suddenly – 'she was sailing along, absolutely fine and then, within a week or so, she wasn't well'.[22] Within months she was hospitalised in Glasgow. Laing subsequently became outraged at what he saw as the 'conspiracy' of silence enjoined by both his first family and the hospital staff, who decided to tell Susie that she was merely ill, and not that she was suffering from a condition from which it was impossible to recover.

> I almost had to fight my way to the nursing sister. I went up one Sunday afternoon and decided I was going to tell her. She was in this oxygen tent permanently, hardly able to lift her head off the apparatus that circulated the blood ... if you're disconnected from it you die in about three weeks maximum. The nursing sister said, 'Dr Laing, you're not going to tell her'. *Fuck off.* I told her. I just told her the facts, as I knew them, and she elected to be disconnected and taken back to her boyfriend's flat. Her boyfriend asked me if I would come and stay there when the end was in sight.[23]

Laing, quite correctly, felt obliged to tell his daughter that she was going to die so that she could prepare for her death. To do otherwise would have been the worst possible betrayal. Not only was it her inalienable right to know, he was also a firm believer in the non-Western tradition of the 'brave and conscious' death, death faced with full consciousness, not denied. Nevertheless Laing and his first wife Anne acrimoniously disagreed over the issue, although later they were partially reconciled.

He once told me a story about the twentieth century Zen master Taji, who died in 1953. As he approached death, his senior disciples assembled at his bedside. One of them, remembering the master was fond of a certain kind of cake, had spent half a day searching the pastry shops of Tokyo for this confection, which he now presented to him. With a wan smile the dying master accepted a piece of cake and slowly began munching it. As he grew weaker, his disciples inquired whether he had any final words for them. 'Yes', the master replied. The disciples leaned forward eagerly so as not to miss a word. 'Please tell us!' 'My, but this cake is delicious!' And with that he slipped away.

*

Earlier in the seventies Laing had begun to take an interest in issues surrounding pregnancy and childbirth and, in particular, the emotional and psychological consequences of *birth*. In 1972, he addressed the International Society of Psychosomatic Obstetrics and Gynaecology at the Royal Society of Medicine on the subject. He argued that the newly-born experienced as much pain as any adult, and that any painful memories of such pain would be stored up, to 'resonate in later life'.[24] Laing spoke of 'umbilical shock', the moment of cord-cutting, a situation whereby a 'few seconds can make a profound difference' to the remainder of a life. He claimed to remember the moment when his own umbilical cord was cut – 'a searing pain, a complete total organismic reflex' which, he claimed, took his breath away before he actually had got his breath and 'produced a triple red light, emotional, physical, and mental state of emergency and danger'. Laing concluded that 'being born was an experience I certainly wouldn't like to repeat'.[25]

There were, of course, intellectual precedents within the psychoanalytic tradition, especially Otto Rank who stressed the psychological consequences of the birth experience. He argued that in the process of physiological birth, each new arrival on the planet finds its first object, mother, only promptly to lose her again: 'the primal catastrophe'. For the tiny creature, this trauma (Greek: 'wound') is a loss beyond words and harbinger of life's incalculable suffering. As Rank puts it, 'even with the kindest of mothers and the least violent of births, the human being is born afraid, a shivering bundle of *angst* cast adrift in an uncaring world, a small island of pain floating on a vast ocean of indifference'. At the moment of birth, feeling neglected and misunderstood, the *infans* (Latin: 'not speaking') is 'expelled weeping from the paradisal womb, like Adam, leaving behind it an ineffable past'.[26] Rank argues that an individual's reluctance to accept the trauma of birth may lead to an unacceptable degree of reliance on the mother, or other first love object. Laing however, was more interested in the possibility of developing the work of such writers as Stanislav Grof and Arthur Janov. In particular he was interested in Janov who believed that no psychotherapeutic intervention would be successful which didn't uncover 'primal pains', hurtful and painful experiences undergone in the foetal and embryonic stages of life. Such primal pains, Janov argued, determined adult neuroses and to be dispelled had to be re-experienced through a process of painful catharsis. Although Laing was interested in such work, he believed that both Grof and Janov were inexperienced in working with seriously disturbed individuals, which was his initial aim. However, a more significant influence was the work of Elizabeth Fehr, a therapist he had encountered in New York while on his 1972 tour. Previously a psychotherapist, her own career changed when she was confronted by a man who had been diagnosed psychotic and who was facing a lobotomy. He told Fehr that for all his life he had felt *stuck*, as if in a manhole, and that he could neither get in nor get out. As he spoke about this belief he twisted and turned and it occurred to Fehr that he was in some sense trying to 'be born'. Though a novel, and somewhat bizarre technique, she attempted to re-enact his birth, performing the role of midwife for twenty minutes or so, until he was 'reborn'. Subsequently he felt less pained, less desperate and more calm.[27]

In her new career Fehr has continued to attempt to 'rebirth' over a hundred people, whereby she and her helpers form a human tunnel – a simulated womb – in an attempt to re-enact the birth process. With the helpers closing up this 'womb' the person fights free and re-experiences their birth. When Laing met Fehr he joined in one of her sessions. He himself would later explain the process as based on his belief that within each person's muscular system there were countless experiences and emotions of fear, pain, despair, all locked up, and that the re-birth would more than merely release these feelings, but also allow a 'physical realisation of one's existential impasse'.[28]

The following year Laing was orchestrating his own re-birthing sessions, with hundreds of participants, supported by Jutta and other colleagues. Many of those who struggled to emerge from the human tunnel that Laing built eventually emerged simulating the birth experience in all manner of ways – screaming, tearful, writhing and contorting. One such beneficiary, or survivor, of the process described her experience. Laing told her to relax and that she wasn't actually expected to do *anything*, just to lie in the foetal position and think of her own birth. She was allowed to choose her own helpers, which she did – those whom she knew and trusted – and who were to put pressure on her and help her through the experience. As far as she remembers, she simply moved around the floor with all the helpers around her until she 'came out of it'. She could not recall how long it lasted, though it seemed a relatively short time. Excited, she wished to share with Laing something that she felt in her legs as she finally emerged, something that seemed to her highly significant. Her father had suffered poliomyelitis and had been paralysed for two years previous to her birth. Though he eventually walked again, post-poliomyelitis syndrome had rendered him disabled in his later years and was, in turn, a source of anxiety for her throughout her life, caring for her father as she did. In a sense she had felt that she had been born feeling a need to respond to her father's disability. There had been for her, at the re-birthing session, something akin to a *release*, something extremely 'liberating about getting back to that moment'. It had also made her aware of the fact that the only recurring dream she had ever had was obviously her journey through the birth canal. That had never occurred to her before, the dream had merely frightened her. After the session it never frightened her again.[29]

There was a widespread belief that Laing had either run out of original ideas and was capitalising on someone else's, or was merely capitalising on a money-making exercise based on the 'workshop' idea that had been so successfully established in the USA through the various practitioners of the so-called Human Potential Movement. Or, alternatively, that Laing had simply mistakenly turned to something which he truly believed was interesting and beneficial. His own description of the procedure was of one which involved 'birth-like experiences, yelling, groaning, screaming, writhing, contorting, biting, contending', in which a lot of 'physical handling might ensue and a lot of energy' was released and redistributed, and that 'massage, bodily sculpture, improvised games' were all part of the process.[30]

In one sense Laing's new therapeutic endeavours were consistent with what he had developed over the previous decades. He had increasingly moved away from an obsession with the past as something to be endlessly discussed and dissected, to a focus increasingly situated in the *present*. At Kingsley Hall people were allowed and sometimes encouraged to regress, to 'go down', simply so that they may 'come up', to return to a more fruitful 'present'. Even though the procedure of re-birthing was to re-experience the *past,* it also enabled the effects of the past to be *immediately* diminished and therefore enable the participant to engage in the present more effectively. What *was* certainly consistent with all of Laing's previous ideas and therapeutic techniques was the centrality of the person's own perception of their *experience*, which through the re-birthing process was accepted as the only experience that was important. No interpretations were made, no analysis, but simple catharsis. There was, of course, perhaps the element of suggestibility, an almost hypnotic process whereby individuals felt that they *ought* to respond markedly to the procedure. Nevertheless, struggling to free oneself appeared to resonate elsewhere for many participants. The only differences, perhaps, between Laing's version and the versions of the other contenders in the marketplace, were the nuances that Laing brought to it, including setting and ambience. And, of course, Laing himself.

The theoretical ideas that he had developed both before and contemporaneously with his interest in re-birthing, were eventually published in 1976 in the book *The Facts of Life,* his first book in over six years. This relatively new departure into what Laing called *biopolitics*, codified with the publication of *The Facts of Life,* was not particularly well-received. In comparison to books such as *The Politics of Experience,* it was a commercial failure in the USA. However it did sell relatively well in Europe, especially in France and Germany. Some of the reviews were less than positive. For example, in *The Guardian,* the anthropologist Geoffrey Gorer wrote 'about as nasty a put-down review as his pen could find', Laing lamented. He adopted the view that Laing had been an *enfant terrible* of the 1960s and now after a lapse of several years had written *The Facts of Life,* which showed that in effect Laing 'was a played out and damp squib, and that there was nothing there in the first place'.[31] Psychiatrist Anthony Clare reluctantly described it as 'boring', yet erstwhile colleague Morris Carstairs found it stimulating, picking up on Laing's notion that many of the archetypal myths of mankind may legitimately be interpreted as a reliving of the fertilised ovum's journey down the fallopian tube, its 'coming to rest in a more or less unwelcoming endometrium, and its life within the womb ending within the experience of childbirth'.

Nevertheless many of the psychiatric and indeed the psychoanalytical profession believed that the book was the *final* nail in Laing's professional coffin, that it was proof positive that Laing was, at best, no longer to be taken seriously, at worst, that he had finally gone completely mad.

One of the accusations that Laing increasingly encountered from the mid-1970s, and from some quarters even earlier, was that his best work was behind him and that there would be no further contributions of value to come from him. Some commentators believed that after *The Divided Self* it had been a somewhat downward spiral, despite the subsequent books and innovations. It was as if in the 1970s he was already dead. In the same way that someone approached Fred Astaire at a party with the immortal words, 'did you used to be Fred Astaire?', Laing also felt that he was being increasingly perceived as someone who once was, but was no longer. One is reminded of the time the doctor-theologian-musician-philosopher Albert Schweitzer was asked, at age eighty six, who would replace him as head of his jungle hospital at Lambarene in Gabon. He remarked that he was always asked that question but that he still had much to do – 'I will never retire and am not yet dead. Please have a little reverence for *my* life'.[32]

The Facts of Life is a curious book in some respects, composed of seemingly unconnected essays on birth and pre-birth experiences and psychology, relentless critiques of conventional psychiatric practice, autobiographical memories and reflections, vignettes culled from his own clinical work and amusing observations on interpersonal communication as recalled from his own conversations and behaviour with others. In a formal sense the book does not appear particularly coherent, appearing as it does to have been assembled from disparate elements, yet it is still resplendent with unique and stimulating ideas and Laingian reflections on disturbed and disturbing patterns of communication. And at the centre is his consistent commitment to the primacy of a person's own explication of his or her own experience. There is the continued toying with those unanswerable questions that had provoked him since his teenage years, concerning life and death and the meaning of both. On opening the covers the reader is faced with Euripides – 'Who knows if life is not death, and death life?' Indeed, Laing asserts that the book is haunted by the question, 'what is the correct way to live?'[33] In the epilogue, Laing recalls how, in an attempt to resolve the riddle he posed the question to a reputed saint in Kashmir, alleged to be over one hundred years old – 'he looked like an ancient bird' – and was rewarded with the immediate response: 'Let your heart be like the sun. Shine alike on everyone'. Later in the same epilogue, Laing restates his belief that knowledge without love can never yield knowledge of love: of the Swiss theologian who accused him, in the company of all other Scottish theologians, of being a mere storyteller who did not theologise. Laing's defence is that 'parables, however, may be the only way, sometimes': and that he did not pretend that *The Facts of Life* was a guide to the perplexed, as he himself was perplexed. 'But I have tried, as best I can, to convey the nature of my perplexity'.[34]

As with Laing's other works, the central premise couched by the lyrical language of *The Facts of Life* is again that of trauma, memory of trauma and reaction to that memory of trauma. And again, Laing repeats the concept of the mother inflicting the first act of violence upon the child – but this time, prenatally. In the book, Laing raises the possibility of our being conscious from the moment of conception, and possibly before this. Further, that our experience of the odyssey of the egg, the blastocyst, into the womb, would reverberate throughout our bodies and minds for the rest of our life. The trauma suffered by the blastocyst on trying to embed itself into the endometrium – the womb's lining – would be re-enacted but in reverse during the trauma in birth. Therefore the rebirthing process would try to resolve the psychological injuries of implantation. As Laing explains, 'to put my proposition succinctly: birth is implantation in reverse and the reception one receives from the post-natal world generates a sympathetic resonance in us of our first adoption by our pre-natal world'.[35]

In order to elucidate his theory, he explains each of us as a mere collection of cells, all of which are the direct ancestors of the very first cells created in that body, and comprising the rapidly developing blasto-cyst. From the beginning, almost prior to fertilisation, these cells are sentient, sensitive to the environment, which is of course the uterine tube and the rich bloody lining of the womb. In fact, the blastocyst and the environment are in contact, transmitting and receiving messages. This of course is hardly science fiction. However, Laing next posits that the cells within the blastocyst, the pre-embryo, are not only sentient but capable of a kind of memory, long before the development of cells making up the neural tissue usually associated with the memory process. These first cells encode messages and store them as memories, which they then pass on to every other cell which develops in that living organism: 'what happens to the first one or two of me [meaning cells within the blastocyst] may reverberate throughout all subsequent genera-tions of our first cellular parents. That first one of us carries *all* my "genetic" memories'.[36]

So, if the cells receive and store information about the environment, and then pass the 'memory' onto every other cell, which will hold the memory all its life – what is the information? What are the memories? Laing: 'Our first experience of this universe occurs within the uterine tube of the female human body'. He explains that science is only just beginning to uncover the wealth of stimuli to which we might respond. Many are unknown, possibly un-dreamt of in our philosophy. Laing argues that the mother's body will create an environment that is either welcoming or un-welcoming, according to how she feels, consciously or not, about conceiving a child. Therefore the first message received by the pre-embryo, later to be the child and later to be the adult, are its mother's feelings about its existence. Either, 'I want you – you are welcome', or 'I don't want you – die'. According to Laing the majority of babies are unwanted – women may harbour conscious or unconscious thoughts of rejection, of miscarriage, or abortion. To be 'wanted' is not the statistical norm. The mother's emotional and consequently physiological response to the conception will influence the pre-embryo's next experience – the journey into the womb, and then the embedding process in the endometrium: 'A bed of crimson joy or a battlefield?'[37]

There is certainly physiological evidence to suggest that the journey and the implantation process are difficult: from conception the pre-embryo spends the first seven to eight days of its life travelling through the uterine tube, which is full of fluid that Laing suggests is oceanic, that is, capable of calm or storm. Once it reaches its destination, it can take several further days for the pre-embryo to become fully adopted and therefore protected by the womb. At least forty per cent of pregnancies are lost at this vital but early stage. As Laing points out, one simply cannot disprove and therefore one should accept the possibility that this most momentous journey of our lives might be both exhausting and traumatic, an experience which the cells within the embryo may well be capable of 'feeling', 'remembering' and 'communicating' to every cell within it, now and forever.

But what is the significance of this mystical process on behaviour and mental states? Laing sees that the trauma of the journey and implantation might manifest itself in later adult behaviour, all depending on the mother's emotional response to conception: either security or the insecurity rooted in a feeling that 'although I am, I live, my mother didn't-doesn't-want me'.

> Many people feel they have never been born
> Others feel they have never been implanted
> Others are *just* implanted, unreconciled, pining, mourning,
> crying for the moon, the ghost of themselves as
> blastula before burial in the womb.[38]

The cogency of this hypothesis is of course questionable, and one can imagine the reception it received within conventional psychiatric circles. However it is *at least* interesting, clear evidence of a man whose mind was not closed to possibilities un-dreamt of in his philosophy.

The germs of implantation trauma are of course grounded in biology and *prima facie* feasible. For example, the same cells which comprise the baby somehow separate to become placenta and umbilical cord. Therefore one can sympathise with Laing's argument that when the cord is cut, the baby might feel physical pain, in addition to the feeling that it is being severed from an integral part of its early life. Laing queried whether the child mourns its loss, and in later life is forever seeking to replace its first 'companion', the breast replacing placenta, relationships replacing the womb. Laing quotes his own experience of grief for the placenta and the cord. His parents had taken the eight-year-old Ronald to see a Ronald Colman movie, *Lost Horizon.* This appears to be similar to H. Rider Haggard's *She,* and a similar fate befalls its central female protagonist. As Colman and the Princess of Shangri-La cross the mountains, blizzard raging, she ages decades before his eyes and within seconds has crumbled and dissolved into an ancient crone and then into dust. Laing relates that, over his bowl of porridge, his eight-year old self caught a resonance of an earlier grief that pre-dated words or images – the grief of losing his placenta: 'One could remain in love with one's placenta the rest of one's life. Could I have registered the ageing and dying of my intra-uterine lover, and could that impress have been reverberated by a configurational resonance?'[39]

Obviously, that Laing believed the theory there appears to be no doubt. A great classics scholar, he translated the Greek myths into an intra-uterine journey, and drew comparisons between stories and feelings that arose during different patients' therapy sessions, all of which seemed to reflect reverberations of the intra-uterine experience.

The ideas of the book centring on the pre-birth period, from conception onwards, are those which some found difficult to comprehend, not least because of the difficulties of any empirical examination let alone falsification.

Another objection to Laing's theory is that an inhospitable intrauterine environment is by no means indicative of a mother's ambivalence or hostility towards her potential offspring. Even if a person could 'remember' an implantation trauma, there is no reason to presume that adverse circumstances occurring within the womb were the product of some antipathy on the mother's part.[40] Although I sympathise with the irrefutable logic of this argument, I cannot help but think it is irrelevant. If the blastocyst senses an inhospitable environment and its life from that point is adversely affected, what does it matter if the environment didn't reflect the mother's state of mind? Just as if a man is killed by a stray bullet –

the bullet will stop life, irrespective of the motives of the person pulling the trigger. And additionally, Laing emphasises that all environments are either for or against us, and that the body can react to things in the environment that we are only beginning to glimpse. Furthermore, Laing concludes that the statistical norm is for the foetus to be unwanted. Perhaps a woman who desperately wants a child will not produce a hostile uterine environment. And perhaps a woman who is either ambivalent or does not want a child cannot produce a welcoming uterine home: 'we have no way of putting a credible limit on the ways we may be influenced for weal or woe, without being aware that we are being thus influenced, perhaps without even dreaming we are thus influenced'.[41]

Around the same time that *The Facts of Life* was published, Laing was already completing his next project, a manuscript originally titled 'Why did the Peacock Scream?', later published in 1976 as *Do You Love Me?* Passages from the book were not only theatrically and amusingly read in private, but Laing and Jutta performed sections in public, at Ronnie Scott's jazz club. The collection was described as a series of verses and conversations, written in the tradition of music-hall and cabaret, with some of the themes inspired by and derived from jazz, popular songs and nursery rhymes. The reviews which emanated from the psychological and psychiatric world were less than favourable. His critics believed he should have reserved his pen and thoughts to those issues and concerns with which they were more familiar. Seen from a purely literary view, perhaps not all of the poems are of equal stature or merit. But how many published collections of poetry by psychiatrists are ever perfect? However, one can discern from even a cursory glance that this 1976 collection of poetry, conversation and other adages reflects the nuances of those themes which had always moved Laing sufficiently to write of them: primarily the mystifications and deceptions of interpersonal relationships, especially those of love.

> Jack and Jill are married and love each other
> Jack from time to time thinks Jill has affairs
> with Tom, Dick or Harry, but he is wrong

Jack's best friend is John
John's wife leaves him, and Jack invites John
to stay with him and Jill

While Jill is consoling John, John fucks Jill:
Jill thus discovers that Jack can't trust John

Enraged at John's betrayal of Jack,
she tells Jack he can't trust John, but not why
Jack feels Jill is jealous of John and him and is trying
to break up their friendship

Jack leaves Jill

Jack and John go off together.[42]

While others are merely amusing.

now
if not for ever
is
sometimes
better than never[43]

And in a number of them, one can recognise Laing's concerns with intra-uterine life. He was of course working on *The Facts of Life* at the same time as preparing *Do You Love Me?*

refugees from the sixth dimension
take care when you mention
what's past recollection

the womb
's a tomb
death
's our first breath[44]

Do You Love Me? was produced for BBC radio, with the music added and composed by Carl Davis. It was broadcast in a quite similar manner for both German and Swiss radio. Edward Petherbridge, who had produced *Knots* for the theatre, also adapted the text for the stage and arranged performances for 1977. Laing, however, was disappointed with the production. In true style he remarked that he thought Petherbridge should have 'let himself spend a bit more time with me'. Laing had foreseen the production as potentially a unitary event, but instead he considered it fragmentary. When it came to London's West End, following a regional try out, it flopped spectacularly. However, unlike London's rather provincial reception, *Do You Love Me?* met with greater success in perhaps the more philosophically advanced cities of Europe, and transferred successfully to Paris, Rome, Munich and Frankfurt, in some theatres running for several months. Laing intimated that had the production succeeded in London he might well have pursued 'the form' to a more significant extent, and would have attempted to develop it theatrically as a 'short story'. He was unsure whether he would have termed it a play or a ballet, and although he thought, unquestionably, he would use music, he knew that 'it wouldn't be an operetta'.[45]

The following year, and less than two years after the death of his daughter Susie, another of Laing's children suffered a setback. Fiona, his first child, was found weeping and distraught outside a place of worship in Glasgow. She was admitted to Gartnavel Hospital for examination and diagnosis. She was deemed to be suffering from 'mild schizophrenia', and was administered anti-psychotics. When told, Laing assured his family that he would move heaven and earth to ensure that she would not be given ECT. Later Laing arranged for her to visit a Philadelphia Association household in London, but after her visit, though she approved of what she saw, Fiona considered it too far away from Glasgow and the rest of her family.

Despite all the traumas that the children of Laing's first family had endured in relation to their father's relationships with their mother, they still enjoyed close relations with him. Adrian, the eldest son, spent some time with his father in London, on one occasion for a number of months. He has written amusingly of an evening he spent with his father, together at a performance of the musical *Jesus Christ, Superstar*, and about which Laing knew very little.

'Ah, next act must be the crucifixion – can't fail!' Ronnie muttered. While we waited with bated breath the curtain rose. To the tortuous sounds of blaring pop music the chorus launched into an appalling, wailing song of some description while Jesus appeared on a plastic cross, neon lights and all, rising from a trap door. Ronnie put his head in his hands and started wailing, 'What the fuck is this? I can't believe it, I can't believe it, no, no, no'. We sat it out to the end so that Ronnie could let them have it. Rising to the challenge he booed continually for what must have been a full ten minutes, interlaced with 'what a load of absolutely fucking rubbish'.[46]

Although Laing continued to produce work at a steady rate, apparently undaunted by the difficulties he had experienced writing *The Facts of Life*, publishers were less predisposed than they had once been. His American publisher was not enthused by *Do You Love Me?* and only published it through friendship and his belief that it was wise not to lose a well-known author. Neil Middleton at Penguin was equally not enthusiastic. As Laing awaited the 1978 publication of his slim book of poems and observations, *Conversations with Children,* a number of his writing projects failed to find a publisher. His proposed book on natural birth, tentatively titled *The Politics of Birth,* was surprisingly turned down by a number of publishing houses, perhaps due to the surfeit of similar books by such authors as Sheila Kitzinger, Michel Odent and, of course, that high priest of pain-free births, Frederick Leboyer.

On April 21st, 1978, at the exact time of Laing's birth, his father David died, aged eighty five, at the Levernhale Hospital, Glasgow. Laing travelled to Glasgow for the funeral, and he had vowed to be impeccably behaved, for his mother's benefit. Inside the crematorium the coffin reached its destination – 'an everlasting bonfire' – by a mechanical conveyor belt, the mourners seated in the adjoining chapel. Many years previously his father had requested that a recording of his favourite Italian song would be played. Amelia arranged the recording but made the whole event as short as possible. Laing recalls that he and his mother were looking straight ahead, and he turned to her and asked, 'Don't you find this somewhat moving?' And she replied, 'Ronald, think of something else'. That was the only remark, he claimed, he ever made to his mother about the death of his father.[47]

In a later diary entry, Laing noted the degree to which he had incorporated his father within himself, and that despite earlier feelings of fear and loathing toward him he had, over the years, and especially the previous decade, come to love and respect him. He expressed sadness for what his father had undergone, the pain and troubles he had suffered through his marriage to Amelia, and the dissatisfactions in life he had endured. Laing recalled that on a number of occasions his father expressed his hope that Amelia would predecease him, as he couldn't bear the idea of her living alone, without him. A sentiment which, Laing believed, was misplaced: 'little idea had he that' she 'was glad to have the house to herself', though 'I don't know whether it's fair to say she was glad to get rid of him'.[48]

After her husband's funeral, Amelia sent Laing a letter requesting that he never ever visit her again, either before or after her death, and moreover that he absent himself from *her* funeral. Written in pencil, it was unsigned. 'I promise', he replied, the words encircled by a heart. His relationship with his mother had never wavered from the bizarre and vindictive qualities which had been established since his birth. Laing relates a particularly sad example of his mother's eccentric, and at times crazy, behaviour towards him. His teenage daughter Susie had told him that Amelia had made a doll, which she had christened Ronald, and into which she was sticking pins in order to give the *real* Ronald, her son, a heart attack. Outraged, Laing decided to confront his mother over her witch-like behaviour to this quasi voodoo-doll, and chose the pretence of a Sunday afternoon visit for tea, on which he took all his five children along. The afternoon tea ritual was one in which everyone had to be impeccably behaved and to adhere to the conventions of the correct way to sit, to hold the tea-cup, to imbibe the liquid, and so on. One wonders if Laing deliberately chose this occasion simply for the amusing nature of the bizarre juxtaposition of practices: orthodox lower middle-class tea rituals mingled with black magic.

> Mummy was just starting the operation of getting the teacup up to her mouth. 'Susan tells me you've got a little doll called Ronald that you're sticking pins in in order to give me a heart attack'. She got the teacup almost up to her mouth and without any shred of anger turned around and said, 'Ronald, we don't talk about that sort of thing', and that was the end of that.[49]

By this time he was only too well aware that his mother harboured ambivalent and hostile feelings toward her only child, but he also realised

that the various states of mind she expressed and endured must have
been excruciatingly painful for her also. Was she mad? In Laing's view
her withdrawal from the world, from any contact with people other than
her husband with whom she had an ambivalent relationship, had started
before he himself was born. But not all his memories of her and home
were as devastatingly bleak as is sometimes believed. He saw his mother
as a woman with great energy and concern, and also one who lived a sad
existence, in which she dwelled in her own fantastic world.

Conversations with Children was published in 1978, receiving adverse
critical reviews and comments, both in Britain and America. The common criticism levelled against him was that he who had so extravagantly
exposed the family for the madness it caused was now living a bourgeois
lifestyle, producing books not on the terrifying interiors of family life,
but having the temerity to produce snippets of conversation with his own
children: it just wasn't fair, was it? Conversely, in Italy, a nation of child
lovers, the book was a best-seller and, while on a clinical-psychiatric visit,
he was introduced on Italian national television simply as the author of
Conversations.

The book comprises both diary entries which he had made over the
previous seven years concerning Adam and Natasha, what they'd said
and done, and what he thought of what they'd said and done, as well as
fragmentary reproductions of his children's conversations, with himself
and others. The collection is not as *slight* as many reviewers claimed.
Without sets of explanations and dependent clauses and other academic
techniques, Laing actually chronicles the cognitive and emotional development of his children, as seen through their changing language and
self-knowledge as well as interpersonal knowledge. He felt compelled to
write the text because, he asserts, he'd always enjoyed dialogue, repartee,
and interplay and reciprocity generally, both on a verbal and non-verbal
basis. However, he adds that he had spent a considerable part of his life
studying 'unenjoyable communication, miscommunication, and failure
to communicate, much of it in family contexts, and in depicting, describing and theorising about this domain of misery'. He had done so largely
because he attributed such importance to the way 'we get on or not, with
the people we live with. It affects everything; our intellectual, spiritual
and physical lives, as well as our emotional and social'. He described the
collective situations that he studied as 'this division of hell'. Conversely,

there was the other side of the story, the language of the happy dialogue of intelligent beings which, when it was not 'knotted, entangled or entangling then instead of this being a deadening suffocating zone, it is the free and open space between us, where we question and answer for the sheer heaven of it'. Laing adds that the conversations are sometimes fierce and dark, but 'hatred, spite, revenge, jealousy, malice and envy, and the other blights on life, are not seen here as triumphant'.[50]

On February 5th, 1973, Laing records a little moment between himself and his three-year old daughter, Natasha, who asks him – 'Daddy. Would you like Mummy to be your mummy?' One year later Laing asks his children the question, 'why did the peacock scream?' Adam replies, 'because he couldn't see himself', while Natasha, three years younger than her brother, replies 'because he wanted to hear himself'. In a real sense these could have been illustrations of Piagetian ideas concerning the development of cognition in children, with the older child already demonstrating more complex notions than the younger, and already beginning to consider his sense of 'self', of identity – slowly moving toward more symbolic modes of thought than his younger sister. What does not appear to be properly, if at all, appreciated is that Laing, fully conversant with the traditional mores of his profession, actually listened to people, to what they said or did not say. Likewise, amid the cacophony and chaos of domestic life he had an ear for the seemingly nonsensical chatter of his small children, and was capable of translating from it cognitive processes, developmental advances. Far from being a twee little collection of kiddies' chatter, *Conversations With Children* is an incisive, informative guide to the *qualitative* changes that take place in children's thought, which was so brilliantly yet densely documented by Piaget, and others.

In the winter of 1974, Laing records a particularly insightful conversation between himself and the four-year old Natasha.

Daddy	Natasha. I have to go away for a little while
Natasha	can I come with you?
Daddy	no I have to go away by myself for a little while
Natasha	and you're coming back in a little while?
Daddy	yes
Natasha	alright daddy (*reflective silence*) but daddy?
Daddy	yes Natasha

Natasha   do you love me daddy?
Daddy   yes I do love you Natasha
Natasha   well if you love me you have to let me be near you, you have
            to let me be near you if you love me[51]

In June 1976, Natasha asks a particularly interesting and potentially
illuminating question for a six year old child. *Natasha* – Can God kill
himself? *Mummy* – I don't know.

Among the inevitable round of what had come to be Laing's everyday
life, of publishing events, conferences and patients requiring attention,
there were a few notable events of 1979. At the conference held in
honour of E. F. Schumacher, Laing delivered a prophetic and passionate
lecture, titled 'Ecology of Mind'. Its dialectical motif was that 'disordered minds produce disordered environments and disordered
environments produce disordered minds'. There was also a change at
Eton Road, where his secretary was replaced by Marguerita Romayne-
Kendon, a woman who was to feature more prominently in Laing's life
somewhat later. She recalled that at first she had been immediately drawn
to this 'perfectly groomed, congenial man with a lovely Scottish burr,
who looked like an Oxford don, and who wore gold-rimmed half
glasses, over which he peered when making a point'. Another book of
poems, *Sonnets*, was also published in the same year. It was not widely
reviewed.

Sonnets they were not, in the strictly formulaic sense. They didn't
follow the convention of fourteen lines, nor did they all possess the
requisite ten syllables per line (as in the English style) nor did they always
follow either Petrarchan or Elizabethan rhyme schemes. Perhaps this was
Laing at his mischievous; perhaps he had found yet another way in which
to challenge convention, in which to turn established modes upside
down. Whatever, it is unlikely that he was genuinely trying to improve
on the accepted literary format of the sonnet. Nevertheless *Sonnets* is
interesting in that many of the poems reflect Laing's continued interest
in biopolitics and also, more significantly, the pain he felt over Jutta's
betrayal, and the hope that he felt toward their relationship. Indeed, he
had once remarked that his poetry was a result of extreme pain, 'crushed'
out of him. One 'sonnet' is actually titled 'For Jutta'.

> Will you reserve your next lifetime for me?
> I'll try to fix it so we're snuggled in
> A womb unfound by yet undreamt-of sin,
> Oblivious to what we do not see.[52]

Another lament follows.

> Love does not always find a way: but gives
> A promise that it cannot be destroyed.
> It's even killed and buried: yet it lives
> In every heart in which it's crucified.

A fifteen page conclusion, titled 'Adages', is a collection of Laing's conversations and ruminations following a traditional adage or maxim that he subsequently develops. Many are ruminations on Christianity and philosophical ideas, but some continue Laing's pre-occupations about love and betrayal.

> The satisfaction of desire may not be wrong, if it does not entail the betrayal of love; if neither takes advantage of the other; if no one is trespassing; if there is no deceit involved; no exploitation, no revenge, no callous, casual conception of a new being, already foredoomed to be killed.[53]

Another sonnet is centrally based on more theological ideas.

> No man is free.
> There are those who are neither the slaves of man,
> or woman, nor are they the slaves of God.
> They fancy themselves to be free men.
> They are the slaves of the devil.[54]

Buddhism was one of the two pillars of spirituality that Laing relied upon. Interestingly in Buddhism an essential, if not unique, aspect is that the messenger him or herself *is* the message. It is the Buddhist's own *way of being*, as it was the Buddha's himself, that is the necessary and true and visible manifestation of the system of belief and practice. Nothing less will do. Perhaps this is why Laing was so persuasive and powerful: his own presence and power exemplified his commitment and creativity as a healer of mental misery.

Spiritual questions had preoccupied Laing from the time he first began to read. When he systematically immersed himself in the great literature of the existentialists, and *The Bible,* and Eastern texts, the questions gained in intensity. When he began to experience the reality of misery first hand, not just his parents' misery, but the pain and anguish he encountered within the walls of the mental hospitals he stalked, he wondered aloud about the God who allowed such suffering to exist. Like all existentialists, the issue of death concerned him as did the theological questions surrounding the possibility of eternity. And Laing was socialised into an environment, especially at school, in which belief mattered: it could be a question of Heaven or Hell. Indeed, Laing participated in a BBC radio programme, titled 'Is there a future for religious belief?', broadcast in March 1970. He described his own background as 'lower-middle-class Lowland Presbyterian corroded by nineteenth-century materialism, scientific rationalism and humanism', and mentioned some of those thinkers who had contributed to his perspective, including Darwin and Voltaire. Without the benefit of conversion to a religious perspective he added, 'if one hasn't been brought up to take religious propositions seriously' one's relationship to them could be that of a 'naturalist comparing and classifying them as one would compare and classify plants, butterflies, ants and other species of animals'.[55]

As a schoolboy, Laing took religion as seriously as he did science, poetry and music. Yet he was sceptical, as were Kierkegaard, Nietzsche and Marx before him. He feared that believers were hypnotised. But he still said his prayers before he laid his head down to sleep at night. As a man, Laing was interested in ideas that were existentially relevant to his own life, so when he encountered Buddhism, with its emphasis on personal experience and practice, it appealed greatly to him. 'Be your own light – the Buddha is your own mind, but clarified'. It was a different mode of knowing than that of Christianity, say, in which one has to take the word of someone else – Jesus Christ.

Buddhism taught Laing the experience and wisdom of expanded consciousness, discipline, strength of mind and, perhaps more significantly, it reinforced his sense of compassion. It also affirmed, not that confirmation was necessary, the truth he had already discovered through existentialism and his own experience: *life was suffering.* Pain was inevitable as nothing was permanent – 'life is a bridge, therefore build no house on it' – and no satisfaction can last forever. Therefore, attachment to anything in the world would result in suffering. The Buddha did not suggest the 'abandonment of the world' as a solution to suffering, rather he proposed a 'middle-way', an eight-fold path of self-development, consisting of righteous behaviour and practise: *right* opinion, thought, speech, activity, means of existence, effort, attention, concentration. 'Cease to do evil, learn to do good, cleanse your own heart: this is the Teaching of the Buddha'. Buddhism teaches that both the mind *and* the heart have to be developed equally, for the path has to be trodden by the 'whole man', not merely the best of him. The Buddha was the All-Compassionate as well as the All-Enlightened One.

A Bodhisattva is someone who strives to be like the Buddha. This is not achieved through merely the acquisition of wisdom and mental concentration and mindfulness. The 'heart will not rest satisfied with the conclusions of the head', and the emotions cry out loud for expression – 'love is a force as great as wisdom, and he who strives for his own enlightenment is in peril of forgetting his neighbour and his neighbour's needs'. Indeed, the essential nature of all Bodhisattvas 'is a great loving heart (*Maha-karuna-citta*), and all sentient beings constitute the object of his *love*'.[56]

I cannot claim, no more than can anyone else, to be a party to the complex understanding at which Laing arrived in relation to his spiritual beliefs, and how his beliefs influenced his life and work (not that they were in any sense truly separate.) However, perhaps it is reasonable to suggest that from Buddhism he admired not only the challenge of mental self-development but also *karuna*, the compassion towards others that he attempted to practise throughout his life, sometimes more successfully than others. Unquestionably, he tried.

Although there is no impediment within Buddhism for a belief in God, that is not its concern. The Buddhist teaching on the existence of God – meaning, the sense of an ultimate Reality – is quite clear and logical. Whatever Reality may be, it is beyond the conception of the finite intellect. It follows, therefore, that attempts at description are misleading, unprofitable and a waste of time. For these good reasons the Buddha maintained about Reality a 'noble silence'. We cannot usefully discuss that which is beyond the comprehension of our finite consciousness. Laing, however, not surprisingly given his background and inquisitive nature was also interested in other traditions. At times he described himself as a 'negative theologian (*theologia negativa*)'. This appears, in a sense, to be the Christian equivalent of Buddhism. Negative (or apophatic) theology asserts that as God (Ultimate Reality) transcends all created conceptions, of which we and our language are, it is only possible to make statements about what God is *not* rather than what it is.

Laing was compassionate towards others; he *felt* for the suffering of those who sought his help in the relief of their pain; he was sceptical as to ultimate answers and explanations. But Christianity was not without its conscious influence on his life. Laing came to be deeply influenced by Christian writing on charity, or as it is more properly known, *love*. As Aldous Huxley has remarked, 'by a kind of philological accident', the word 'charity' has come to be synonymous with 'almsgiving', and in modern parlance is almost never used in its original sense, as signifying the highest and most divine form of love.

The first characteristic of *true charity* is that it is disinterested, seeking no reward, 'not allowing itself to be diminished by any return of evil for its good'.[57] As St Bernard of Clairvaux beautifully expresses it – 'Love seeks no cause beyond itself and no fruit; it is its own fruit, its own enjoyment. I love because I love; I love in order that I may love'. The second distinguishing mark of charity is that, unlike lower forms of love, it is not an emotion but a spiritual awareness, a tranquillity. St Teresa exclaims that 'the real love of God does not consist in tear-shedding, nor in that sweetness and tenderness for which usually we long, just because they console us, but in serving God in justice, fortitude of soul and humility'.[58] Humility, its third characteristic, is a necessary condition of this highest form of love – 'would you be a pilgrim on the road of Love? The first condition is that you make yourself humble as dust and ashes'.[59] In his *Confessions* St Augustine remarks that:

> Temperance is love surrendering itself wholly to Him who is its object; courage is love bearing all things gladly for the sake of Him who is its object; justice is love serving only Him who is its object, and therefore rightly ruling, prudence is love making wise distinctions between what hinders and what helps itself.[60]

Disinterestedness, tranquillity and humility. Where there is disinterestedness there is neither greed for personal advantage nor fear for personal loss or punishment; where there is tranquillity, there is neither craving nor aversion, but a steady will to conform to the Divine; and where there is humility there is no censoriousness and no glorification of the ego at the expense of others. From all of this it follows that charity is the root and substance of morality, and 'where there is little charity there will be much avoidable evil'.[61] All this has been summed up in Augustine's formula: 'Love, and do what you like'.

Go forth and live, with love in your heart.

*

My own experiences of religion and spirituality were close enough to Laing's for me to be able to understand some of the issues that concerned and disturbed him. As a young boy I used to clutch a small statue close to my chest as I fell to sleep. My slumber was not always the proverbial sleep of the innocent. I would often doze fitfully having previously heard and internalised the terrifying phrase, 'see God and die'. I was convinced, on those sleepless occasions, that He would indeed venture into my bedroom and I would be 'taken'. The statue was my friend, I relied on him to keep me alive. Not the 'transitional object' that Winnicott talked of; it never accompanied me out of doors and I never sought solace from it in unrelated moments of crisis. Just those uncertain times when I felt utterly alone and about to die.

The statue was chipped, not especially attractive in quality or design, and was of St Martin de Porres. This sixteenth-century Dominican lay brother devoted his life to helping the poor and needy, and died aged sixty after a violent bout of quartan fever. In 1962 he was canonised by Pope John XXII. I had encountered this Saint of the poor when I was taken by my parents to a monastery in Leicestershire. We were driven there by an eccentric uncle of mine whose idea of driving was to bounce off the side of other (terrified) motorists. By the time we had left the one dull county of Warwickshire and entered the adjoining one, we were all in need of spiritual edification. My only memory, as I recall it now, is of a small group of bald-headed men shuffling around a garden or selling statues and other memorabilia in a small monastery shop. For some reason I was attracted to St – or as he was then known, *Blessed* – Martin.

I do not think I have truly enjoyed a *spiritual* life, but simply (and somewhat sadly) a *religious* one. Raised a Catholic at a time when Latin was the preferred language of communication, I felt connected and moved by the ritual and the music. However I grew tired of the ritual, and when the exotic language was replaced by Standard English, laying the ritual even more bare, there was nothing left to move me further. I was fifteen years old. Perhaps the religion came too early, or my emotional crises too late: certainly I was not looking for any great answers and there were no questions that I needed to ask. Earlier there were questions – 'where are Heaven, hell, purgatory and limbo?', 'what is God like?' – and there were fears – 'please God don't let mum and dad die'. When I later *needed* some spiritual support it was at the time of my father's death. Weeping uncontrollably in the confessional, in preparation for subsequent communion the following day at the funeral, I asked God for help. I intoned, 'but I don't even believe!' The priest, a conveyor-belt Irishman, produced a $64,000 retort: 'but Robert, those who don't believe, believe most of all'. At the time it sounded stupid and trite. Later, I thought of it as some perceptive insight, some perennial wisdom. Now, I haven't a clue as to what he *really* and *honestly* meant.

My religio-spiritual development has been shaped by later life, especially through two influential teachers I met whilst making documentary films, in addition to a therapist I encountered by chance. In 1988, I had the privilege of taking the English-born Buddhist monk and scholar, the Venerable Sangharakshita, across India for Channel 4. He told me the story of the great Indian activist Dr B. R. Ambedkar, once an 'untouchable' and later (almost miraculously) the Law Minister in the Government of India. It was Ambedkar's belief that politics would not easily release his fellow untouchables from their miserable existence. The caste system was too entrenched for such a possibility to occur. Instead he believed that Buddhism provided a more realistic (and more beautiful) means of escape. Through *self-respect* the untouchable would be able to move onwards and upwards.

India in 1988 was a once-in-a-lifetime experience. Sagharakshita possessed an almost superhuman degree of patience and an equal amount of compassion. His intelligence was constantly in evidence. He chose his words so carefully on those rare occasions when he actually spoke. In the slums of Bombay and Pune, amongst destitute and sickly families, he said very little but serenely smiled and it was clear to see that in so doing he lifted hearts. At the meetings I filmed him speaking to thousands of Indian untouchables, and they gazed at this portly sixty five year old with love in their eyes. I never learned the meditation he practised, but I understood the tremendous gift of silence and of choosing words carefully. I also came to realise, again, that life was indeed about *suffering* (*dukkha*). Because nothing in the universe is permanent, no satisfaction or sense of happiness can last for ever, and its disappearance is painful. Message: do not become too *attached* to anything or anybody. Easier said than done. Since that time I have tried, unsuccessfully of course, to live by the principles, or should I say the suggestions of the Buddhist moral code, codified in the *Dhamaphadda*, a kind of Buddhist *Ten Commandments* – less 'thou shall not', more a 'if I were you ...'

En route to Pune we were forced to make an unscheduled stop. While the drivers preferred to save money and sleep in their cars we, the crew and the Buddhists, slept in an insect infested 'hotel'. Actually I only slept for one hour and then, on opening my eyes danced the dance of someone waking to see a cockroach sharing the pillow. There was no water and only *chai* for breakfast. Sangharakshita, of course, slept well. I told him about my unwelcome bedfellows and he just smiled – 'where should *they* sleep?' In Pune we had a one-week rest.

This city of some three million people came under the control of the British in 1817 and was used as the capital of the region during the monsoon season. There are still many Westerners walking Pune's streets, including the British. They are no longer there to rule, but rather for *karma cola*. Indeed, in this rest period I actually filmed at the famous Rajneesh Ashram. To cut a very long story short, Rajneesh – the proud owner of ninety nine Rolls Royce's courtesy of his Western followers – believed that 'there were enough religions for the poor', his was for the rich. The devotees who, laughingly, termed themselves *sannyasins* (ascetics), came from the West – Germany, the USA, Italy, the Netherlands, the UK, Greece, France, and so on. Rajneesh offered them his own meditation practices, guilt-free sex, and psychotherapy. It was a heady mixture that, taken in the middle of exotic spiritual India, seemed hard to refuse. After a brief Lufthansa flight, an AIDS test, a bit of meditation, a psychotherapy course, and the purchase of a maroon robe (for day wear) and a white robe (for evening wear), the devotee could receive a new name and become a *sannyasin*. In stark contrast Sangharakshita had fasted, had learned complex and painful meditative practices, read Sanskrit literature and, unusually perhaps, had walked the length of India with merely a begging bowl to his name. *Then* he became a monk.

To film in the Rajneesh ashram we, the crew, had to take AIDS tests. We climbed the stairs of a local clinic and were met with the sight of a dirty floor covered with syringes and cotton swabs. Reluctantly we tested. Three days later we were filming Rajneesh himself, even his arrival at Buddha Hall from his residence. He made the thirty-second journey in one of his Rolls Royce's, his residence being less than one hundred metres away. But the effect was startling. He was the consummate performer, milking the 'ascetics' for all his worth. His playful 'sermon' was one specially written for our benefit, in which he claimed the American government had poisoned him a couple of years earlier whilst he was being detained in an Oklahoma prison on immigration charges. After he left the stage, there was music – sitars and tablas playing Pink Floyd – followed by meditation.

Bhagwan Shree Rajneesh was as I expected. His followers, at least those whom we were encouraged to meet, were less predictable. They were arrogant, aggressive and as un-worldly and ascetic as Donald Trump. I told them about the distress I felt on seeing the sick families in the slums of Pune, and they laughed. What mattered to them was not the problems of others, but simply their own lives and their untapped potential as Buddhas. *Themselves.*

When I was again on the road with Sangharakshita – born Dennis Lingwood, in Tooting, 1925 – I mentioned that I had not spent the week idly. He passed no comment on my activities, though I am certain he disapproved. However, when I reported the *sannyasins'* prevailing comments, that it mattered not what happened to the poor and vulnerable individuals populating the streets of Pune, he was more animated – 'Any religion that does not feel and show compassion to the poor does not deserve the name of religion'. That was the gist of it. I was glad to be out of Pune, away from self-indulgence and back in the company of a compassionate, sensate and perceptive being. At Aurangabad, the gateway to Ellora and Ajanta, places of great religious history, we visited some of the hundreds of caves which are devoted to a variety of religions – essentially Buddhist, Hindu and Jain. Sangharakshita spent the time in meditation in one of the Buddhist caves. Sanity returned.

We left the State of Maharashtra with a visit to a nearby mosque, a sort of poor man's Taj Mahal, where Sangharakshita delivered an informal lecture against monotheistic religions, especially Islam. The local Muslims were not amused, especially when he delivered a diatribe about their lack of compassion and forgiveness. We packed away the equipment, said brief goodbyes and left. I will never forget Sangharakshita and what he stands for. Neither will I forget the next men of the cloth whom I met, both Muslims. I made a series on *Sufism*, sub-titled 'The Heart of Islam'. My initial contact was with a man as different as could be from Dennis Lingwood.

Shaykh Fadhlalla Haeri was an Iraqi-born Sufi master who had homes throughout the world, including England, and in particular an apartment in one of the more fashionable districts of London. Meeting him was the first time I had ever encountered the sublime ritualistic generosity which characterises Muslims like the Shaykh. Parted from my shoes, I would tip-toe into his lounge whereupon one of his wives would serve me rich and tasty sweets. The air was delicately and sweetly scented. Eventually the Shaykh would enter, constantly smiling. He always made me feel, momentarily at least, that it was *he* who was lucky in meeting me, rather than the reverse. His eyes sparkled. He teased me about my vegetarianism – 'men need strength' and, one of his favourites, 'man should partake of everything that God has created'. Shaykh Fadhlalla, as he liked to be called, was a man of certainty. He appeared to hold no doubts about anything, especially God (*Allah*).

If Sangharakshita had taught me that we should show compassion towards others, that we should try and humbly develop ourselves – our minds and our hearts – and that there is no God to guide us, simply the example set by the Buddha, the Shaykh asked me to surrender to God. Then all would be well, everything would fall into place, and I would no longer be plagued by self-doubts and questions which appeared to have no answers.

I travelled to Texas to film a small group of Shaykh Fadhlalla's followers, who had set up their head-quarters among the red-necks. About one hundred in total, they were a mixture of all races, both genders of course, and many children. I never worked out precisely how they earned the money necessary to survive, but they did so. Their leader was another Shaykh, an American who was an expert in the Turkish language. Like Laing, his presence alone was enough for someone to realise they were in the company of someone special. He was easy to be with, smiled often, possessed a voice which, had he been a different person, would have earned millions as a voice-over. When I filmed him I asked him what 'love' was, a theme central to Sufi writings. 'If you had never eaten an onion, how could I describe its taste to you? So imagine how difficult it is to talk of love'. He was very persuasive. When the men of the community would hold hands in a circle and chant 'Allah', he would act as ringmaster, urging them to greater intoxication. Once he encouraged me to join in: after a few moments I too felt myself surrendering to him (and perhaps to Him), so I removed myself.

I was sad when I left Texas. The Shaykh had almost convinced me that I should stay. 'Give me forty days and forty nights and I can help you'. I declined. He made me take his necklace of one hundred and eight beads, though I strenuously fought against accepting this beautiful and precious gift. 'Don't worry, we'll meet again – if you want to, you can return it to me then'. And surprisingly we did meet again. But the second time around, some of the magic had gone.

I never really understood what Sufism was all about, despite reading *The Koran*, a little Idries Shah, Annemarie Schimmel[62], Maulana Jalaluddin Rumi, Trevor Lings, and others. And despite interviewing at length numerous Shaykhs and followers. Perhaps that is the point? Somebody asked the tenth-century Sufi, Abu Hafs: 'Who is a Sufi?' He answered: 'A Sufi does not ask who a Sufi is.'

I remember sitting with Ronnie in Kitzbühel, in 1988, and discussing Sufism or, more precisely, my bewilderment at it all. Yes, of course he'd met Sufis, not the particular ones that I'd encountered, but yes many others. To him they were like all the other spiritual teachers. I pressed: 'how exactly?' He left the question unanswered.

I was lying on my bed in a Manhattan hotel flicking through the local cable channels, when I discovered a group of men discussing *The Tibetan Book of the Dead*. It was an extraordinary phenomenon: a channel *exclusively* devoted to the dissection and illumination of this text. Despite the annoyingly poor camera work and the unpredictable audio

I was glued to the box. Every now and then one of the participants would be captioned if they made a particularly lengthy intervention. So it was that I met Tim Williams, who intrigued me, for he was Welsh and spoke lyrically. His caption announced that he was a psychic healer and could be reached on the following number. I called him later and we met.

In his Greenwich Village apartment he spread out Tarot cards *et cetera* and performed the usual number but, interestingly, followed it up by simply talking with me. He told me that he felt uneasy about my return to England, particularly as he 'saw' pools of blood. As it happens on my return to England I was immediately involved in a road traffic accident and suffered deep cuts, bruises and a compressed fracture of the lower back. Yes, pools of blood. However, more significantly, he felt that I was spiritually 'blocked' and that I would benefit from '*classical* rebirthing' which, essentially, involved new ways of breathing. As I had little else to do the following day, I agreed that he would come to my hotel room and we would 'rebirth'. This procedure involved me lying on the carpet and breathing in a rhythm orchestrated by Tim. My eyes were closed and my mouth shut. Eventually, maybe a matter of twenty minutes or so, I felt completely weightless, as if my mind and body were totally separate entities. When I began to see a blue light at the end of a long tunnel, I grew afraid, and in a voice which must have sounded full of panic, told Tim what I could see. 'Praise God', he muttered. The light didn't go away, and my sense of weight and gravity didn't come back. The next thing I knew, I was calling out to Tim that I never wanted to return from this blessed state. It was truly a sublime sensation and convinced me, without any doubt, that my experience of the world was a limited one and that there were dimensions of consciousness I had not tapped into.

7

Swimming Mystics and Drowning Schizophrenics

I haven't got anything to write about. What do I know that others don't? I went into a field that was bankrupt from the start – philosophy had been dead for two hundred years. It was almost born a corpse. The riddle grows greater, not smaller, and there's absolutely no way to solve it. It's all hopeless.

Hertz Dovid Grein, in Isaac Bashevis Singer's
Shadows on the Hudson

In the beautiful twelfth-century monastery of Monasterio de Piedra, near Zaragoza, Spain, Laing was one of the principal speakers at a three-week conference in September 1980 titled 'The Psychotherapy of the Future'. In this monastery, which had been subsequently converted into a hotel, Jutta enjoyed sexual relations with someone who was not her husband. In this case, a youthful German translator. When Laing discovered the clandestine affair his spirit was broken. Perhaps he had never really known Jutta in the unique way in which he believed he had.

Among the other high-profile speakers at Zaragoza was Fritjof Capra, author of *The Tao of Physics* and a friend of Laing's. He believed that Laing's therapy was largely 'non-verbal', reaching far beyond mere technique, and that it had to be experienced to be truly appreciated and understood. Later, he participated in another seminar jointly with Laing, in San Francisco. During this seminar Laing explained that from his point of view, psychotherapy involved the communication of *experience*. He vividly demonstrated his argument by stating the obvious: that when someone came into his room and stood there, making absolutely no movement and saying nothing, he did not automatically assume that the person was a mute catatonic schizophrenic.

If I ask myself, 'Why is he not moving and not talking to me?' I don't need to enter into psychodynamic, speculative explanations. I see immediately that I've got a chap standing in front of me who is scared stiff! He's scared so stiff that he is frozen with terror. Why is he frozen with terror? Well, I don't know why. So, I'm going to make clear to this chap through the way I conduct myself that he does not have anything to be scared about with me.[1]

Capra wondered why Laing made psychotics feel at home, yet so-called normal people felt uncomfortable. Perhaps they frightened him? Laing replied, 'mystics and schizophrenics find themselves in the same ocean, but the mystics swim, whereas the schizophrenics drown'.[2] Capra recalls the last time he ever saw Laing, in 1988, when he visited him with his wife Elizabeth and daughter, Juliette. His lasting memory was of Laing seated on a sofa 'reading' a book with two-year old Juliette. He was explaining to her that the irregular white spots between the words were 'rivers running down the page'. Laing now had her full attention, turning page after page with her, teaching her how to squint her eyes so that she could better see the rivers.

The work which Laing discussed at Zaragoza formed the basis of his 1982 book *The Voice of Experience,* which he hoped and believed would re-establish his rightful position among European intellectuals. The book was a devastating critique of scientism and its spurious notion of objectivity, together with further forays into biopolitics. Laing states that the book considers examples of what happens in psychiatry, obstetrics and other fields, when 'scientific technology takes us over'.

He begins with the remark, 'every schoolboy and schoolgirl knows that appearances are deceptive'. Experience is not an objective fact; a scientific fact need not be experienced. 'Facts do not dream'. Laing asserts that our whole life cycle from conception to death is 'now scanned by the scientific look'. Scientific medicine is invested, in many parts of the world, 'with the power to determine how, when, where and by whom we are treated when we are born, give birth and die, or at any time when we cannot fend for ourselves, physically or socially'. Indeed, Laing extends the argument by quoting a contemporary scientist who asserts that 'we can no longer abide by complete adaption of the foetus to its pre-natal haven but must control that environment by every biologic means at our clinical command'. Are those the words of a 'scientist or a general?', asks Laing, adding 'Woman, who happens to be attached to that environment, her womb, in some scientifically unaccountable and irrelevant way has reason to quail before the present power of this scientific, clinical animus, enthused with intrepid, indefatigable missionary zeal'.[3]

Laing argues that natural science has rendered 'experience' outside its domain of investigative competence, and therefore of no value. Just a few other modes of existence outside the investigative competence of natural science, Laing adds, are

> ... love and hate, joy and sorrow, misery and happiness, pleasure and pain, right and wrong, purpose, meaning, hope, courage, despair, God, heaven and hell, grace, sin, salvation, damnation, enlightenment, wisdom, compassion, evil, envy, malice, generosity, camaraderie and everything, in fact, that makes life worth living. The natural scientist finds none of these things. Of course not! *You cannot buy a camel in a donkey market.*[4]

He argues that orthodox psychiatrists and psychoanalysts frequently testify that they cannot make any significant personal contact with some of the people whom they meet, and whom, they believe, render themselves 'inaccessible' to them, by their disordered thinking and confused emotions. However Laing argues that such individuals might just begin to make some sense, if 'we change around what they say, cutting it up, taking it apart, joining what is separate, turning it around, upside-down, inside-out, back-to-front'. A psychosis, he adds, 'like a dream, like a brain, is up for grabs, for rotation, reversal, reshuffling, slicing, apposing, juxtaposing and transposing'.[5]

In the sections of the book concerning biopolitics Laing compares experiential patterns he discerned with what he calls the 'biological story', as first delineated in *The Facts of Life,* from shortly after conception to implantation. Two examples are sufficient to illustrate his perspective.

A thirty-five-year-old man still has not 'made it', though he has made so many new starts. Each time he makes a new start he goes into a whirl, on a high. Then when he gets over that, and is ready to really get into it, and gives the signal, again, as always, 'something or someone pricks the balloon'. A woman has built herself up, as she herself puts it, on the principle of having 'no connections'. Connections lead to ties, and once you are tied you can get drawn in and that would 'suffocate her'. The price she has to pay, observes Laing, is to be cut off and out of circulation.

The Voice of Experience received mixed reviews, and did not sell well world-wide, with perhaps the sole exception of Germany, where it has been taken as a serious contribution to social theory. Like *The Facts of Life* before it, in Germany the book was considered proof that there was *no* decline in Laing's output or indeed his thinking.

In that year the decline in sales figures for his books was but one problem for Laing. Particularly disturbing, and deeply distressing and certainly disruptive, was the accusation made against him that during a visit to a Philadelphia Association household, he had slept with one of the residents. Another accusation was that he had assaulted some other residents in another household. Laing strenuously denied and contested the accusations. At the Association's annual general meeting later the same year, Laing was effectively removed as Chairman. The Association split, and those members enthusiastic about the more meditative and re-birthing type interventions left. Those who remained were more interested in re-positioning the Association as an analytical training centre. Laing also faced domestic upheavals. After both he and Jutta refused to leave their Eton Road home, the property was inelegantly partitioned.

Through arrangements made by his friend Theo Itten, in November 1982 Laing lectured at the world's most prestigious and well-known psychiatric hospital, the Burghölzi in Switzerland. Jung had worked there, as had Eugene Bleuler, who had coined the word schizophrenia, as well as Bleuler's son Manfred. Laing's talk was not open to junior psychiatric staff as he was considered to be a too 'controversial and dangerous figure'. To a hand-picked audience of white-coated senior psychiatrists, who were presumably considered safe from contamination by Laing, he lectured on schizophrenia. One week later he inadvertently met up with one of the audience, a senior biologist, who told Laing that a third of the audience had believed that he was either on drugs or was psychotic. When asked why he thought they had come to such a dramatic conclusion, the biologist remarked that it was Laing's endless movements at the lectern, with hand and facial gestures. This was not the practice in Switzerland. Laing's own reaction to this was to assert that that was simply the way he was – 'some people think I am crazy'. And that was something he didn't like. 'On the other hand, as long as they don't feel they can get hold of me and treat me accordingly, then I can live with that'.[6] On a Swiss radio interview, recorded around the same period as the Burghölzi lecture, Laing, ever the existentialist, in outlining his many current writing projects – none of which ever reached fruition – remarked that he might 'die at every moment, I might die the next moment. I am living in terms of not dying tomorrow but dying today, and if I had one minute to live I wouldn't be doing anything else than what I am doing now'.

Laing embarked on a less-frantic, less-headline inducing mini-world tour in early 1983, a trip which took in the American cities of Seattle and Los Angeles, in addition to selected cities in the Scandinavian countries Norway, Finland, Sweden and Denmark. While he spent time in New York he visited David Edgar's play *Mary Barnes*. He considered it to be too much Joseph Berke's notion of what Kingsley Hall was like, and not particularly as he himself saw it. He asked Edgar whether or not he had considered asking him, Laing, for his input into the play's writing, but Edgar said he had decided against it because he felt that it would have made the play too complicated. Edgar's actual phrase was that 'in researching the play, I decided not to meet Laing himself, fearful that – like kippers in the fridge – his presence would end up flavouring everything'.[7]

In 1983, Sue Sünkel re-entered Laing's life, having briefly met him some two years earlier at a conference. German-born, and a psychotherapist they had a lot in common. When they became intimate she recalls, somewhat amusingly, that – like teenagers – they would listen endlessly to one and only one CD, namely Bob Dylan's *Infidels*, a fellow poet of whom Laing approved and identified with. Someone else trying to make sense of a crazy world. They had a son together, Benjamin, but soon drifted apart. Sünkel remembers that she once lent Laing a book on love, a subject he was endlessly researching and writing about. It was Simone de Beauvoir's short story *A Woman Destroyed* which, she remembers, moved Laing profoundly. Written in diary form, it is a first-person first hand perspective of the gradual and painful unravelling of a woman's reality as she learns of her husband's affair.[8]

In the years of the decade left allocated to him, there would be many moments of what might be termed Laingian excess fuelled invariably by alcohol and often leading to almost surreal consequences. He was, for example, the main instigator and performer at the conference held in the Belgian city of Louvian, in 1981, the purpose of which was to establish the International Psychiatry Association. Before an assembled audience of over five hundred he successfully and emotionally performed songs and poems from the *Life Before Death* album, but then, later, became drunk and failed to chair the plenary session which was to bring the conference's formal business to discussion and action. At one point, Laing asked the delegates, that if they called themselves therapists and psychiatrists why were they unable to deal with him? Similarly Brett Kahr recalls the occasion when, together with a colleague, they escorted Laing from London to Oxford to ensure his attendance at the Oxford Psychoanalytical Forum at which he was to present a paper. In the back of the car Laing smoked some marijuana and drank some Calvados brandy. At the Forum, despite a warm and enthusiastic welcome, Laing was unable to concentrate and said very little, other than some of his true and less than favourable feelings and thoughts about Melanie Klein, the influential Freudian theorist whom he believed to be somewhat crazy. He then proceeded to pull at a tooth, dislodged it, and declared the session at an end.[9] But this was small fry compared to what was served up in California where Laing had been invited to a conference entitled 'Awakening the Dream: the Way of the Warrior'. Bored with the formal proceedings Laing visited a bar and began howling at the moon. The regulars in the bar believed he was making fun of them, a fight ensued and Laing received cuts and a black eye. The following day Laing claimed, in his terms quite accurately, that he was a high priest of the goddess Kali. An American shaman asked him to renounce Kali, beating him with a shovel as he did so. Laing's shoulder was dislocated but he bore no hard feelings toward the man. The *following* day he changed the text of his lecture, originally on the potential of healing, and instead talked about the notion of unconditional love.

In 1984, the artist Vicky Crowe was commissioned to paint Laing's portrait for the National Portrait Gallery of Scotland. He was impeccably behaved for the number of sittings Crowe required. Sometimes he would talk, other times he would meditate but with his eyes wide open never losing eye-to-eye contact with her. When they did talk the subject would often return to Christianity and religious faith. He told Crowe he regretted that no certain, true and sustaining theological position had come his way and, ruefully, he remarked that a Christian friend of his had told him that until his wrinkles on his forehead developed 'to form crosses' he would never be able to truly believe.[10]

After giving birth to Benjamin, Sue Sünkel decided to continue to work as a psychotherapist but was concerned about not being with her new-born son. She asked Laing's advice, in particular whether or not he thought it appropriate for her to take the small child into her sessions with patients. Laing considered it not only appropriate, but that his presence would probably do everyone some good. Besides, he added, Benjamin had already been participating in her sessions for nine months, the only difference now was that he was born.

Amidst the conviviality created by the birth of his ninth child, Laing had been arrested outside the London Rajneesh centre in Hampstead, after throwing a full bottle of wine through its window and calling out that Rajneesh's orange-clad followers were simply 'wankers'. He was taken to the police cells from which he called his son Adrian, by then a lawyer. After a conversation with a legal representative from the Rajneesh organisation they agreed to withdraw any charges, on condition that Laing pay for the damage. He agreed. However the police had found in Laing's possession some marijuana, and he had to await their deliberations over that small matter. And, indeed, some weeks later, he was charged with possession. The case came to court two months later, the indictment being that on September 17th 1984 he was found to be in possession of 6.98 grams of cannabis resin. Despite it being against his instinctual wishes and feelings, Laing agreed to submit a 'guilty plea', expensively and professionally represented through his son's connections. He was given a nominal sentence, a twelve month conditional discharge.

Burston decries Laing's behaviour in respect of the Rajneesh incident, arguing that Laing was envious of Rajneesh's ability to generate the adoration of many thousands of followers. Burston called it 'another sorry illustration of Laing's craving for fame and recognition'. Perhaps it had not occurred to Burston that Laing, having seen honest and pure *sannyasins* at first hand in Ceylon and India, having been profoundly moved by the teachings of the Buddha, and being a man who above all other things was a *thinker*, an advocate of *truth*, might simply have found the quasi-spiritual homiletics of Rajneesh somewhat unpalatable.

The Laing's marriage had effectively ended. He and Jutta had endured a few painful years sharing the same partitioned house but, of course, not the same bedroom. Laing was increasingly hurt and angry at her betrayal, more so than the fact of the adultery itself. The lying and the deceit were simply acts of behaviour he could not tolerate, and which pained him to the core. Towards the Christmas of 1984 he finally abandoned Eton Road and moved into Marguerita's apartment, a small and cramped loft, in Little Venice, London. From that moment, she became Laing's constant companion and love. She accompanied him on the many journeys he was subsequently to take. For example, they both became involved in the attempt to establish St Oran's Trust, a project intended to provide sanctuary for those people who had come to feel that their emotional and psychological lives had become a distress to themselves and to others. Unfortunately despite earnest attempts to find both a suitable geographical location and, more importantly, finance, neither of which materialised, the project sadly failed.

Throughout much of 1984 Laing had worked painstakingly on his memoir, *Wisdom, Madness and Folly*, which covered the first thirty years of his life. 'By the time this memoir ends I was thirty years old and had written my first book, *The Divided Self*. I knew what I wanted to address myself to for the foreseeable future in theory and in practice. I began to focus on this personal factor. You and me'.[11]

Five of the six chapters concern autobiography, from family life up until the time he left Glasgow for the more esoteric world of the Tavistock Clinic and the Institute of Psychoanalysis. Some of this auto-biographical material had surfaced elsewhere, especially within *The Facts of Life*. However, what makes the memoir so important is the chapter which basically constitutes a straightforward critique of orthodox psychiatry. Laing used the occasion as an opportunity to clarify what he *actually* believed, as opposed to what he was purported to believe, and the reputation which he had acquired, particularly the confusion which had arisen due to his work being erroneously conflated with that of David Cooper, the 'anti-psychiatrist'. Indeed, he asserts that he had 'never idealised mental suffering, or romanticised despair', that he had 'never said that parents or families or society "cause" mental illness', and that he had 'never denied the existence of patterns of mind and conduct that are excruciating'.[12]

Laing begins with an explanation that the word 'psychiatry' was coined to refer to a branch of medicine. However, etymologically the word means the psychological healing of the psyche, mind, soul, person. 'A mental healer may be a psychiatrist. A psychiatrist may or may not be a mental healer'. Psychiatry is dissimilar to other branches of medicine, although, of course, there are similarities too. Psychiatry is the only branch of medicine that treats people physically in the absence of any known physical pathology. 'It is the only branch of medicine that "treats" conduct, alone, in the absence of symptoms and signs of illness of the usual kind'. And it is the only branch of medicine that treats people against their will if it deems necessary, even to the extent of imprisoning them should it consider such an action appropriate. Laing reflects that in his early career, what he appeared to be asked to do, and indeed what he was attempting to do, was stop 'undesired states of mind and conduct', and to keep 'undesired people in such undesired states of mind and conduct' away from people who did not want them around. It is, of course, a societal problem. As Laing puts it, the need for the removal of such undesired people is not 'manufactured by psychiatrists', rather there is a 'consumer demand', and as long as there is, he adds, there will be some group appointed to meet it. And in modern technological societies it is the psychiatric profession that is deemed to be the appropriate enforcers.

> Mental hospitals and psychiatric units admit, routinely, every day of the week, people who are sent 'in' for non-criminal conduct, but for conduct which their nearest and dearest relatives, friends, colleagues and neighbours find insufferable. This is our society's only resolution to this unlivable impasse. If they refuse to go away, or can't or won't fend for themselves, it is our only way to keep people out of the company that can't stand them.[13]

As he reflects on his early career, Laing recalls the realisation that to truly begin to understand what was going on would need a major 'detective investigation', and not the brief, cursory patient 'history' he was expected to compile. Moreover the investigation would have to commence from the viewpoint that there *was* indeed something to uncover, a secret to behold. Laing comments that many psychiatric theorists argue that there is an 'unbridgeable gulf' between 'us' and 'them', the psychotic. Karl Jaspers called it an 'abyss of difference'. It was his belief that there was no 'greater difference' in the 'psychic life' of human beings than that between the normal person and the psychotic. Laing points out that Jaspers is referring to schizophrenics – one in ten of 'us'. In *Wisdom, Madness and Folly* there is none of the 'romantisisation' of schizophrenia that Laing is routinely accused of. While decrying the belief that no human bond could bridge the gap of 'difference', he added that he was in no doubt that there 'are enormous differences between states of mind, between different "realities" ', and that he would never gloss over such differences. Nevertheless, the question is: what sort of difference does this sort of difference make, to 'us', and what sort of difference do we take the difference between us and them to be?

One of the consequences of believing in such 'difference' is the perhaps logical assumption that this 'difference' results from genetic and constitutional factors. This doctrine of the abyss of difference between us and them, Laing argues, takes 'us' and 'them' to the brink of another sort of abyss. The question becomes: how do 'we' treat 'them'? 'The Nazi regime in Germany in the late thirties took this doctrine to its logical conclusion. They should not be allowed to breed, and there was no point, really, in keeping them alive. They started their cleaning and tidying up of Germany by killing 50,000 mental-hospital patients until they stopped under protest from the Churches and others'.[14]

Within two years of completing his psychiatric training, Laing had come to the painful realisation that he would not like to be treated the way his own patients had to be treated. Not only did he recoil from the thought of being locked away in a psychiatric ward, but he also came to doubt that the 'drugs, the comas, the electric shocks' he was expected to administer were the 'great recent advances in psychiatry' he had been trained to believe they were. In addition he was 'frightened' of the power invested in him by the law of the land, and of the manner in which he was expected to use it.

Even more worrying for Laing were the minds which had created orthodox psychiatric theory and practice. He cites as evidence a review of Kierkegaard's classic theological text, *The Concept of Dread,* written by a well-known American psychiatrist and published in 1944. The reviewer suggests that Kierkegaard's book was interesting as it 'inadvertently presents strong evidence that the writer is a psychiatric case himself', despite his reputation as a writer. Of course Laing was later to encounter the notion, especially in psychoanalytic circles, that genius is simply a masquerade for psychosis: Beckett, Strindberg, Joyce, Artaud, Van Gogh, Kafka, Nietzsche being such candidates. Indeed, Jock Sutherland, the Director of the Tavistock Clinic, remarked that Kierkegaard's *The Sickness unto Death* was a 'very good example of early nineteenth-century schizoid psychopathology'. Laing recalls that he increasingly 'dreaded much more than ever becoming like them' yet also 'felt an enormous relief and sense of gratitude that I was not one of them'.

In a most powerful passage, Laing describes the diagnostic interview between the psychiatrist and his patient as the most extreme case of dependence of one person on another.

> On the basis of possibly less than five minutes from the first laying on of eyes on a stranger, without that stranger perhaps even having moved or said anything (so: he is either malingering, or he is a mute catatonic schizophrenic), a psychiatrist can sign a printed form and make a phone call. This will be enough for that person to be taken away, imprisoned and observed indefinitely … in involuntary custody, and then drugged, regimented, reconditioned, brain given electrical lavages, bits possibly taken out by knife or laser, and anything else the psychiatrist decides to try out.[15]

Notwithstanding his withering attack Laing still notes that potentially a 'mental hospital may still offer hospitality and sanctuary from what can happen outside'. Indeed, when he lived in such hospitals he discovered a great deal of human warmth and camaraderie in them. But he quickly adds that this state of affairs is, however, unlikely, and that he was 'still more frightened by the fearless power in the eyes of my fellow psychiatrists than by the powerless fear in the eyes of the patients'. Laing ruefully adds that he dreaded the thought of *either* look appearing in his eyes.

Laing continues the discursive exploration of his psychiatric career by discussing his attempts, from Gartnavel in 1953 onwards, of treating people in the opposite way to which he had been trained. On both humanitarian and medical-psychiatric grounds he dreamt of an approach without 'exclusion, segregation, seclusion, observation, control, repression, regimentation, excommunication, invalidation, hospitalisation' and so on, an approach that belonged less to social power and more to medical therapeutics. He described the methods by which people could seek help, if they so desired, as in Gartnavel, Kingsley Hall and such like, in ways totally different from those they were accustomed to. But his ingenuity was greeted with demands of 'How could you?' He was seen as abdicating his medical responsibilities. Laing said that he was treated as if he proposed refusing insulin to a diabetic, as if by encouraging a schizophrenic to *talk,* he was committing a misdemeanour equal to encouraging a haemophiliac to bleed.[16]

Laing cites lines from James Fenton's poem 'Exempla' to describe the varied ways in which psychoapharmacological drugs may or may not be helpful to someone suffering mental distress.

> Psychopharmacological drugs
> which are claimed to be active in the clinic,
> whether anti-depressant like imipramine,
> or antipsychotic or neuroleptic
> like reserpine or chlorpromazine,
> have a very marked anti-mescaline activity
> in the mouse.[17]

Laing proceeds to list the potentially beneficial effects of various drugs: some of which may calm agitation, soften frantic feelings, tone down awful moods, regulate thoughts and the style and content of dreams and imagination, and so on. Then he discusses ECT which, he asserts, may well enable someone *not* to kill themselves by taking away, albeit possibly only on a temporary basis, suicidal feelings. In a conclusion that surprised many readers, Laing posits that if he were being driven 'frantic by mental and emotional torment that nothing I or anyone or any drug could stop I might beg for electric shocks'. However the critical issue is the politics of the matter – 'who has the power to do what to whom against whose will?'[18]

Laing concludes his ruminations on orthodox psychiatry by asserting that what the schizophrenic or psychotic patient requires above all, is *communion.* A real sense of communication without confusion or strife. In apocalyptic mode he argues that the greatest danger facing the human species is 'ourselves', for we are at war with ourselves and others, and not at peace. In the most profoundly moving passage Laing describes his experiences in psychiatric hospitals at the time of the Scottish New Year.

> In Gartnavel, in the so-called 'back wards', I have seen catatonic patients who hardly make a move, or utter a word, or seem to notice or care about anyone or anything around them year in and year out, smile, laugh, shake hands, wish someone 'A guid New Year' and even dance ... and then by the afternoon or evening or next morning revert to their listless apathy. If any drug had this effect, for a few hours, even minutes, it would be world famous, and would deserve to be celebrated as much as the Scottish New Year. The intoxicant here however is not a drug, not even alcoholic spirits, but the celebration of a spirit of fellowship.[19]

On a promotional tour for the book he also unveiled Victoria Crowe's portrait of him, hung in Edinburgh's National Portrait Gallery. Accompanied by his daughter Fiona and also his friend Johnny Duffy, the portrait was unveiled without any undue fuss or drama. At the same time, he gave a number of interviews at which he poured scorn on the diagnostic basis for orthodox psychiatry, *DSM III* (*Diagnostic and Statistical Manual*). Essentially he argued that within the pages of *DSM III* all manner of 'unusual' experiences, thoughts, feelings and actions were deemed undesirable and therefore in need of eradication, in order to improve 'our' culture. For example the *DSM III* cites the following list of sensory, emotional and interpersonal phenomena as 'unusual perceptual experiences', symptomatic of extreme mental disorder: 'others can feel my feelings'; 'I felt as if my dead mother were in the room with me'; inadequate rapport in face-to-face interaction; self-dramatisation, such as exaggerated expression of emotions; craving for activity and excitement; overreaction to minor events; irrational, angry outbursts or tantrums; egocentricity, self-indulgence; loss of interest in, or enjoyment of, sex, etc. Understandably Laing complained that the result of its excessively inclusive nature would be to culture-out all manner of 'ordinary manifestations of ordinary minds', and that when all speech and conduct had been 'corrected', we would be no more than 'homogenised creatures' that he could barely recognise as human.

He repeated the invective at a lecture he gave at Gartnavel Hospital, in which he claimed that the *DSM* was obsessed with the *classification* of human beings, the result of which deprived them of their humanity and treated them as *things*. Laing remarked that he was not going to offer a critique of it, but simply read some of its contents out – 'and if it's not obvious to you as I read it, then I can't help you'.[20]

Just as the *DSM* could easily result in distancing the psychiatrist from his patient, the one treating the 'other' as if an 'object' quite 'different' from 'him', Laing himself was just himself when, in late 1985, he was asked to interview a young schizophrenic woman in Phoenix, Arizona. The event was filmed live on the street and part of a conference, 'The Evolution of Psychotherapy'. The previous evening he had met this young woman who had been formally diagnosed and labelled a 'paranoid schizophrenic', and who suffered hallucinations and delusions. Laing showed great empathy with her and, when he left to return to the conference hall of one thousand delegates, she tagged along, much to Laing's pleasure and sat alongside him on the podium. He demonstrated a distinct rapport with her and when asked about Laing, she remarked that he had a wonderful ability to tap into her mind and was someone who did not try and find out anything, he just tried to be on the same level. Kierkegaard spoke of the 'two ways': one is to suffer, the other is to 'become a professor of the fact that another suffered'. Laing embraced both ways, through failing to escape his own pain and suffering and, at the same time, attempting to understand the pain and suffering of others.

Despite the triumph of promotional tours and the lingering value of the name 'R. D. Laing', *Wisdom, Madness and Folly* was not a great commercial success.

In 1985, Laing foolishly agreed to participate on the BBC Radio 4 programme, *In the Psychiatrist's Chair*. Its host, Anthony Clare, noted that when Laing arrived at the studio, 'drugs, drink and a significant degree of Celtic melancholia had taken their toll'. What precisely Clare meant by 'drugs' taking 'their toll', is anyone's guess. Did he mean that Laing was not seeing, speaking or hearing properly? And if not, then what? Significantly Clare, despite protestations to the contrary, has always misunderstood and misrepresented Laing. Indeed, he later wrote that Laing 'seemed' to suggest schizophrenia was no more than a social construct, that schizophrenics were 'possessed by some superior vision of reality and truth', and that psychiatry was nothing more than society's attempt to 'contain revolution'. Many parents of 'sufferers from schizophrenia', Clare adds, 'cannot forgive Laing either for adding the guilt of having "caused" the illnesses in the first place to their strains and stresses of having to be the main providers of support, the communities that truly cares for their sick offspring'.[21] *Well I cannot forgive Clare* for repeating damaging interpretations of Laing's work with the consequent effect on Laing's reputation.

Laing was open and frank with Clare. When asked whether he worried about losing his own sanity, he replied that despite having suffered a few 'spasms', it had never been a real fear. Laing then openly and honestly talked about his 'depression' and what he termed his 'so-called heavy drinking'. He claimed that he was himself a 'typical type of cryptopsychomotoretardation depressive', the type who would feel more tired on waking than when they went to sleep, and who would only feel a little better in mid-afternoon. He confessed that he had suffered from this condition periodically over the previous ten years, and that twenty years earlier he had worried he was 'going to run into a real Scottish involutional melancholia'. This 'downness', as Laing described it, evidently would appear, then, over time, disappear. He admitted that if he were desperate he would accept that Clare or someone similar could transport his body 'to some nursing home and if you had any drugs that you thought would get me into a brighter state of mind', he would accept them. Clare then asked Laing the question, 'what does the drinking do for you?' In response, Laing claimed that he was a 'seasoned drinker', that he was 'in two minds about drinking just now', and he emphasised the original Glaswegian cultural context of his drinking. Importantly, from his own point of view, Laing asserted that he'd never felt drinking had stopped him from doing anything he ever wanted to do, and that he did not feel 'mentally impaired'.[22] In subsequent years this seemingly irrelevant piece of radio, sincere and informative as it was in places, was to have further consequences for Laing.

On November 10th, 1986, while in New Hampshire, Laing was given the news of his mother's death. He wept, and declared that he wished he had hurt his mother more. He then chose a song from an old Victorian anthology, *Vocal Gems from Victorian Years*, to play as a piano duet with David Goldblatt. The chosen song, 'A Boy's Friend is His Mother', extolled a mother's legendary virtues: immutably good, inviolate and irreplaceable.

Then cherish her with care,
And smooth her silv'ry hair,
When gone you will never get another.
And wherever we may turn,
This lesson we shall learn,
A boy's best friend is his Mother.[23]

Laing reneged on his promise to his mother that he would not attend her funeral, and flew to Glasgow and did precisely that. In the presence of Amelia's coffin Laing wept uncontrollably.

By this time Laing had his own concerns about morbidity and indeed mortality. For almost two years he had been bleeding quite heavily from his rectum. He confided his situation to a couple of friends, and following the discussions, decided to do nothing about it. One must remember that Laing was a qualified doctor of medicine, qualified among other things, in surgery. He would have had his own reasons for non-intervention. Sitting opposite his friend, Johnny Duffy, he said 'I think I've got cancer'. Duffy asked him where, and Laing replied 'in the bowel'. Duffy asked him what he was intending to do about it, and Laing succinctly replied 'fuck all'. Duffy learned that it was progressively getting worse and that Marguerita had to change the sheets every morning, as the bed was soaking wet with blood.

*

1986 ended with Laing's divorce from Jutta. She was given custody of their children, and received a generous financial settlement. Laing was uncertain as to where his future lay, where his income would primarily be earned, and where he could lay his metaphorical hat, as he was now effectively homeless. But he did have the companionship and love of Marguerita, who remained by his side.

8

Theanthropic Mien

The unhappiest love is a happy love that has now become unhappy.
Gillian Rose *Love's Work*

You're irreplaceable. And because you are,
the life you gave me is condemned to loneliness.
Pier Paolo Pasolini *Prayer to My Mother*

Albert Camus wrote in *The Myth of Sisyphus* that there is but one 'truly philosophical problem and that is suicide'. Expressed slightly differently Camus asserts that 'judging whether life is or is not worth living amounts to answering the fundamental question of philosophy'. Steven Gans, a colleague and friend of Laing's, writes that he could imagine Laing as a university student in Glasgow 'reading this and thinking Camus is wrong – there is really only one philosophical question, for that matter one theological, psychological and sociological question, *the question of love*'.[1] Actually, Camus had also acknowledged, in *Notebooks 1935-42*, that he knew only of 'one duty, and that is to love'.

For Laing too, the question of love was at the core of his being. This was no mere philosophical or psychological question, but *the* existential and flesh-and-bones issue of his life. As he poignantly reflected in *The Facts of Life,* the 'main fact of life for me is love or its absence', and 'whether life is worth living depends for me on whether there is love in life'. Without a sense of it, or 'even the memory of an hallucination of it', he adds, 'I think I would lose heart completely'. In addition to seeking, finding and losing love, only to seek, find and lose again, and again, who knows how often, Laing also wrote about love continuously. Even in the somewhat dry tome *Interpersonal Perception* we are able to find the following: 'The most natural thing in the world is the desire to love and to be loved. Which is the greater misfortune, to love without being loved or to be loved without loving?'[2] In almost every book there are traces – some strong others barely visible – of this central concern and existential quest. Sometimes, as in *Sonnets* he is blackly humorous – 'You are making love. Are you making friends?' – and a similar kind of sensibility is at work in the pages of *Do You Love Me?*

he	what do you want?
she	make love to me
he	you are a
	placenta that sucks me dry and poisons me
	a womb that suffocates and crushes me
	an umbilical cord that stings and strangles me
	your vagina is the entry to hell
	not tonight Josephine
she	you would put anyone off
he	put out the light
she	you have put it out yourself[3]

Another 'sonnet' simply and movingly, expresses his hopes:

To desire and to love, and to be desired and to be loved in return, unreservedly, with no impediments of any kind, is, without doubt, one of the sweetest experiences of living.

In the same volume, there are continual reminders of the bitter-sweet pleasures of loving another person. He catalogues the pain caused by the many disappointments he endured in life. But without doubt, he still held out hope for the great healing power of love.

> If only you would tell me that you love
> Me still. Then I'd pretend I understood
> You have to do your thing. Somewhere above
> I'd find the strength to wish you your own good.

And another sonnet, more painful still.

> I just can't bring myself to contemplate
> That maybe you are not as you appear
> To me. I've even felt the pangs of doubt
> That if you had your chance to choose your mate
> I would not be the one that you'd hold dear.
> Don't speak. Forgive me. I must not find out.[4]

One of the final pieces of work that Laing engaged in, started at some uncertain point, was a book tentatively titled *The Lies of Love,* at other moments, *The Challenge of Love,* and never finished. It addressed one of the 'last frontiers not taken up in systematic fashion by psychology', namely the 'question of lies and deceit that come between man and woman or partners in love relationships'. He was concerned with emotional power: 'the capacity to affect the other person's mind, heart and soul, to the extent of joy, happiness, well-being or misery, despair, ontological insecurity'.[5] In workshops Laing had already shared some of the vignettes of infidelity, jealousy and deceit – 'bedrooms are the most dangerous places on earth, more than the streets of Los Angeles' – and chronicled these in preliminary studies to be contained in the book.

The Lies of Love was to offer rumination and illumination on the various aspects of lies, deception and betrayal, using classic sources – Ovid, Sappho, Spinoza, Sophocles, *Kama Sutra,* and others – in addition to relevant moments of his own life and those around him. As Laing explains, his book is not about 'other-worldly, spiritual niches in this world', not about 'Christ crucified in cathedrals between two candle sticks', it is about 'Love crucified between two thieves in our hearts'. It is about 'how we treat each other, in every way, in work and play, everyday, even in our love lives'.[6] The book has a recurring, central theme: the need to reconsider whether or not we really knew what we thought we knew, once we have discovered that a deception has been played on us or a lie told us: in other words, the need to reconsider our perception of reality once our mental equilibrium has been disturbed by the lies of love. Another section of the book was concerned with the fear of others – what Laing termed 'anthropophobia' – and in it Laing compares psychiatry and *DSM III* with the fifteenth-century witchcraft manual *Malleus Maleficarum.*

Laing enjoyed repeating a story told to him by a colleague, and which he himself used as a tool to ruminate on the possible subliminal influence of lies told in relation to infidelity. Laing speculates on the transpersonal effects of one person's thoughts on another person's body, and in so doing he returns to his earliest project, namely the notion of a possible science of neurophenomenology, the interaction of neurology and the mind. The story is basically this: his colleague has a patient, who has asked him whether or not it would be wise for him to commence an affair with a woman he met recently on a train. He wouldn't normally think twice, but this time he is hesitant because of a rather strange 'coincidence' that happened to this woman. His eyes had met the eyes of this woman in question, a complete stranger, just before they arrived at their destination. Without a single word passing between them they exchange telephone numbers, and then left. A few days later he received a call from her and she reported a rather bizarre event. At the *exact* moment that their eyes had met at precisely 3.32 p.m., her husband had suffered a heart attack.[7]

Much of *The Lies of Love* is stylistically and conceptually well-trodden ground. He attempts to understand deceptions of various kinds through an analysis of language. The ordinary grammar of human interaction, between the I, me, you, we, us, she, her, he, him and them, for the most part goes unnoticed, unconsidered and undiscussed. Yet much of the tangles, knots and confusions of our lives with one another centre around our lack of clarity, in regard to our use of these terms. For example, I may fail to realise that I am quite other than the 'you' that I am for you, and you are other than the 'you' I take you to be. Thus we treat each other like components of ourselves, instead of allowing each other 'otherness', instead of acknowledging and accepting and *respecting* that fact that you are *not* the 'you' that I perceive, because the 'you' that I perceive is actually nothing more than a figment of my imagination. But it is a figment that I say I love, and indeed feel that I do love. Inevitably, we will eventually fall into the emotional hypogeum that lies between the I that I am for me, and the you that I am for you. In a miasma of potentially mistaken identities, a betrayal may well be experienced as catastrophic and one or both partners may be shattered, reduced to a heap of broken images. It all falls apart – 'we' were a complete illusion.[8]

Thus Laing was searching for a formulaic manner in which he could systematically begin to examine the central question of his adult life: does real love exist, and is mutual love and reciprocity possible? Laing unquestionably had faith in love: 'To love one another, truly is to walk in the light, to live in truth, to be truly alive, and perfectly free. Otherwise we walk in darkness, live in the lie, are living lies, ignorant, blind, deaf, lame, crooked, diseased, mad, dead, in the body of death, in hell, on earth.'[9]

1987 was a terrible year for Laing. The General Medical Council had written to inform him they were investigating an allegation against him of 'serious professional misconduct', following a complaint from one of his previous patients who claimed that a drunken Laing had thrown him out of his session. The Council questioned Laing's fitness to practise as a psychiatrist, especially given his 'misuse of alcohol'. Soon afterwards the complainant dropped his allegations, but the Council decided to continue its action against Laing, citing his BBC Radio 4 interview with Anthony Clare as further proof of his unfitness. Finally they cited the malfeasant behaviour which had led to his court appearance following the Rajneesh debacle. Consequently, on February 26th, 1987, the Council wrote to Laing with the suggestion that if he withdrew from the medical registrar, no further action would be taken. Laing agreed, sending a hand-written note from Boulder, Colorado, confirming his decision.

This scandalous behaviour was hardly surprising. Laing had been a thorn in the side of conventional, orthodox psychiatry for over thirty years, and an act of revenge was perhaps inevitable. It is absolutely permissible for a psychiatrist to practice even if he barely has the time or interest to talk to, or develop any bonds with, his vulnerable patients; it is absolutely permissible for a psychiatrist to electrically shock a patient *despite* the limited knowledge of the procedure, including its efficacy and long-term effects; it is also absolutely permissible for a psychiatrist to categorise and label a patient *for life* after the most cursory and spurious of examinations. However, it is not permissible for a psychiatrist *qua* human being, to discuss publicly his own life and tribulations, *even if* such tribulations might lead to a greater empathetic understanding of the patients he treats. Indeed, the notion of the 'wounded healer' is integral to many healing and caring traditions. The phrase that always comes to mind is, 'never judge a man unless you've walked a mile in his moccasins'.[10] Laing's suffering was simply turned against him by conventional psychiatry determined to punish him.

The tenth and absolutely beautiful child of Laing's came into the world on January 6th, 1988, and was subsequently named Charles. He, like his father and mother, did not have a permanent home. Scotland would have been the favoured choice for Laing, but nothing materialised. As he expressed it, one side of him would have liked to have been Professor of Psychiatry at Glasgow University, but he also knew that it would be a 'hopeless quixotic fantasy', a duel-edged sword which would have prevented him from achieving those things which were really important to him. Laing's own views on the matter were heart-felt. He believed that though many of his ideas were innovative and challenging, the term 'radical' was applied to him as a means to invalidate him and subsequently to disbar him from potential roles. Indeed, he believed he was a 'conservative revolutionary', in that he wished to promote a revolution which re-introduced old values – traditional notions like establishing hospitals primarily as asylums, as places of sanctuary.

> I mean the term 'radical' is used to nullify, it is a term of abuse. They'll give me an honorary degree when I'm dead ... I hear about my death quite often, that I'm dead. They'll love that. Glasgow University has never invited me to give a fucking lecture in any department in the whole of my life. Well that's my home town. Well, fuck them.[11]

After Charles's birth Laing made a will, the provisions being that all earnings from his post-1980 writings would be for Marguerita and Charles, and the rest divided between all the other children, including Benjamin, and also his first wife, Anne. Jutta had already received a substantial divorce settlement and was excluded. In April 1988, and subsequent to making the will, Laing, Marguerita and Charles moved to Austria, courtesy of a German friend Knut Flughaupt, a wild and enthusiastic Laing devotee. They rented a small house in Going, near Kitzbühel, where Laing read and re-read, and continued working on *The Lies of Love*. He no longer drank and spent much of the time playing with baby Charles. Once every month he would travel to Vienna to supervise training psychiatrists. He would also occasionally travel to workshops and seminars, all bearing his name. He also spent time with me, both in Austria and elsewhere, as I continued my work on his biography. By this time I called him Ronnie, though somewhat reluctantly, as I did not wish to be considered his acolyte, or assistant. I was trying to find out as much as I could about how he himself saw his life, his work and the contributions of others, their personalities and *their* work. Already I had spoken with others who were telling me all too readily what they thought of *him*.

On August 22nd, 1989, Laing was on holiday in St Tropez, at the five-star Hotel La Pinède, as a guest of his American friend Robert Firestone, whom Laing was assisting with his book on child-rearing. Both men were enjoying the French sun. The entourage included, of course, Marguerita and Charles, and also two of Laing's other children, Natasha and Max. Adam was also expected to join them. Laing's condition had not improved, and his obviously deteriorating health was a constant concern for Marguerita. They had previously talked, sometimes humorously other times less so, about his eventual demise – who Marguerita was to call and in which order, 'what funeral arrangements to make; his cremation; in what order his different families were to arrive at the service etc.' Marguerita adds that, at that time, Laing began to 'cry disconsolately as he told me that he had never before, ever, had a companion with him in his life, until now'.[12] Two weeks before they travelled to St Tropez they had received a visit from one of Laing's friends, a woman recently widowed and who was still devastated by the death of her husband. Marguerita was so upset she took to her bed 'with the vapours'. After several hours, Laing came into the bedroom and sat by her side, 'peered over his glasses with that wonderful smile', and said to her – 'For God's sake, Marguerita, at least wait until I'm dead before you start to mourn me'.[13]

On August 23rd, Laing felt a little unwell. 'This may be the day', he remarked to Marguerita. Premonitions of his death, near-death experiences following a few minor heart attacks, experiences of other mental and bodily states through LSD and meditative states, were all features of Laing's life, especially in the later years. I personally doubt whether Laing wished to die, although playing tennis on a hot August afternoon when in poor health is unquestionably foolish. He had too many plans, too many projects and too much love for his children to have wanted to escape to the next phase so soon. But it is anyone's guess.

As he did with every other activity, Laing played tennis wholeheartedly and passionately that August afternoon, suffered a heart attack, refused medical assistance – 'doctor, what fucking doctor?' – and died cradled in the arms of his beloved daughter, Natatsha.

Marguerita later wrote:

> If only I could have lain with you again
> If only there had been three days and nights more

I would have bathed you with fragrant waters,
I could have anointed you with unguents
I could have clothed you in a cool white linen shroud for
this, your final journey …[14]

On August 23rd, 1989, I was still pacing the bedroom of a small hotel in Harrogate, angry after enduring an unpleasant call when the telephone again rang. I had just spoken with Shaykh Fadhlalla Haeri, the Sufi Shaykh whom I had filmed for my Channel 4 series, *Sufism: The Heart of Islam*, and to whom I had just sent a VHS copy of the films. He only liked two of the three of them and in no uncertain terms had told me so. I immediately became a child of eight and wished to cry. I presumed it was he on the line again, trying to put my fragile mind to rest. Instead I was given the news of Ronnie's death. It genuinely surprised me: of course I knew of his desire to die and his inquisitiveness about the next stage of existence, but I also knew of his love of life and of Marguerita and his family, both old and new, and I knew that he was fired-up with writing plans, media plans, performance plans. Besides, he just seemed to me indestructible. And, of course, I didn't want him to die: I was truly enjoying the book we were working on, enjoying his company and, perhaps most importantly, I thought 'to whom can I turn now?' As in life, so with death. Ronnie's unpredictability continued.

Sixty one years of age. So young.

The funeral service, held at Glasgow Cathedral, was a moving yet bizarre affair. Many of the congregation were visibly upset and angry, especially when from the pulpit the Reverend Donald Macdonald announced that on Iona, in 1986, Laing had returned to the Church of Scotland. Johnny Duffy, Laing's best-friend, recalled that he was sitting at the end of a pew and that when the coffin passed him, something died in him: 'That's my pal in there'. He almost burst into tears. 'To see him ignominiously being wheeled in a stupid fucking bogey, I just felt terribly sad. I loved Ronnie'.[15]

At the graveside David Goldblatt played *Basin Street Blues* on the trumpet, Mary Barnes threw earth on the coffin – 'such was the passing of a great man, a genius in mind, compassionate in soul' – and Leon Redler threw in a small bottle of whisky and a figure of the most pre-eminent Bodhisattva, Avalokitesvara. How appropriate. The Bodhisattva is of course the Buddha-to-be who postpones his final liberation to work tirelessly for the sake of other living beings. Avalokitesvara is *the* Bodhisattva of compassion. He is Lord of the Universe; the sun and moon come from his eyes, the earth comes from his feet, the wind comes from his mouth; he holds the world in his hand and each pore of his skin contains a system of the world. Avalokitesvara protects against all kinds of danger and denies no requests, not even the prayer to grant sterile women children. However, nothing could atone for the fact that the Laing family had had Ronnie *buried*. I, and others, can recall numerous conversations with Ronnie about his desire to be cremated in the Buddhist tradition. I hope he rests in peace.

The reception was held at Glasgow's Central Hotel. The mood was dark. Adrian Laing wished to fight Macdonald over his claim that his father had rejoined the Church of Scotland, and had to be forcibly restrained. Among the many people I encountered were those who certainly spoke in a language that I could not decipher. Francis Huxley was jolly. Leon Redler tearful. Mary Barnes saint-like. Marguerita and Charles, quiet and dignified. Jutta was – Jutta. I smelt violence in the air, and left.

The following January, 1990, a memorial and thanksgiving service was held at St James's, Piccadilly. Jutta Laing sang a Schubert *lied*. His sons spoke about their father. Other friends and colleagues paid their tributes. Leon Redler described Laing as an 'emissary from elsewhere', an 'incisive questioner, muse, warrior, Socratic gadfly, compassionate healer, one who embodied and lived the realisation that the art of medicine needs to be grounded in charity, care and love'. Other memorial services were held in New York, Los Angeles and elsewhere.

There were, of course, obituaries penned throughout the world. Richard Alpert, one-time LSD devotee and now renamed Ram Dass said, quite simply, that Laing knew too much and 'couldn't reconcile it philosophically and spiritually', that he had too much awareness of the pain of others. Francis Huxley described him as a 'deeply loving man, if often rough, and one who fought his way continually back to moral principles', while Morton Schatzman succinctly pointed to the importance of Laing's work – 'he always tried to see people's strange behaviour as a consequence of how other people had treated, and were continuing to treat, them'. The Buddhist Publication Society in Sri Lanka commented that in their opinion Laing had been 'a very devoted Buddhist' who must have collected 'much merit and should be happy throughout his journey in Samsara'.[16] Biographer Daniel Burston argues that there was a 'strong measure of convergence' among the many obituaries and tributes that followed Laing's death. Despite differences in emphasis, 'they all praise *The Divided Self* and 'lament the decline in creative power that seemed to follow on his increasing infatuation with fame'.[17] This was the mythology that began to take shape while Laing's corpse was still warm, and if not safely out of earshot, at least not able to answer back.

*

In 1978, my own father's death had already taken place, and represented yet another learning experience for which I had neither asked nor appreciated at the time. After almost forty years of industrial labour he retired, and his body never really recovered from the transition from labour to rest. Soon afterwards, instead of the idyll of gardening and peaceful sleep, he was in a hospital bed for what the doctor termed a 'twenty-four-hour job'. In fact this metamorphosed into an 'exploratory operation' soon followed, less than a day later, by an actual colostomy. I did not know then (and still do not now) what precisely was removed, but the end-result was the same: my father would be wearing a bag which would contain his excrement. In true Kafka-esque fashion the doctor, rather than admit some sadness and regret over the previous bizarre, devastating days which had left us all bewildered and terrified, simply asked if we would conceal from him that he had cancer. Of course we agreed.

When I first saw him in the ward he looked as if he were dead already, his skin yellow and his cheeks hollow. Apparently he had 'rejected' his colostomy, as he believed it to be totally disgusting. Inconceivable. Filthy. Smelly. When I sat beside him he tried to pull the bag off his sagging and paper-thin flesh. It was full at the time, full of excrement. My father was delirious and quite mad as a result of a morphine cocktail. He held a brief conversation with a group of invisible men who were hovering, he said, at the foot of his bed, wishing him well. But suddenly, as if he was collecting together the fragments of his mind, he asked me to pull the curtains around the bed and sit close to him. He wished to talk. All of our conversation was tear-stained. My father told me that he loved me more than he loved anything in his life. He implored me to look after mum after he'd gone. I reassured him that he wasn't going anywhere, but he knew better. 'Please look after her!' I told him that I would. He then, unexpectedly and with some venom in his voice, said that he had always felt that my mother had never thought him good enough for her. That she was a snob. That she had made him suffer all their life together. That she had given him so much pain.

I almost lost my balance as I left the ward. My father had, again, begun some more surreal conversations with Celtic Football Club players just as I left. I could not believe what I had just heard. Previous to these moments of revelation I had always believed that the one certainty in my life was that my parents were the happiest couple known to man. Yes, they didn't talk much, but they didn't argue. And they always looked out for each other.

Within a week he was on the mend. An old factory colleague had also suffered a colostomy, but he called in to my father to show him how he had learned to adjust to his fate. Yes, he was on the mend. The nursing sister shared her view that he was a resilient man and that she never failed to be surprised at the power of the human spirit. Two days later he was dead. *He knew* of course. He'd asked for a priest but was told 'not to be silly', that he was 'doing well' and was tucked in by the optimistic nurse. But he insisted and eventually they conceded and the priest was called. I was one hundred miles away, and my mother and sister arrived too late. According to the medics my father died 'peacefully', with the parish priest seated next to him, having administered the last rites. I doubt if his departure was 'peaceful'. He was anxious when meeting a stranger for the first time, so the prospect of eternity must have caused him great distress, with none of us there to hold his hand.

When I next saw my mother I wept. I had tried to put the conversation with my father behind me, but when I saw her it returned. I felt sorry for her, sorry for him, sorry for them both. And I couldn't believe he was dead and that I wouldn't see him again. I stroked and cuddled his watch, which my mother assured me he would have wanted me to have. It was engraved with his name and the number of years service he had completed at work.

The funeral seemed destined to get off to a bad start, then deteriorate. None of my father's relatives turned up, so my mother, in an attempt to avoid embarrassment, recruited some friends to make up the necessary numbers. The wreath didn't arrive. My response to my distraught mother was somewhat inappropriate: 'Dad wouldn't have minded, he would have thought it was a waste of money'. Inside the church the coffin seemed so small, for a man his size. Had he shrunk? Perhaps he had been crammed into the box? After a collective wail we went to my sister's for a small wake.

The house was mock Georgian, on a plot not yet finished. Because of the surrounding mud we were instructed to remove our shoes. I clung to my mother, limpet-like, and tried to feel as I imagined a 'head of the family' might feel. And then I tried to make my mother feel that that was who I truly was. We all talked about my father's qualities: his gentle and kind nature, his love of his family, and the sadness we all felt that he was not around to enjoy his retirement. My mother then turned to me, somewhat conspiratorially. 'Your father kept me back you know. If it wasn't for him I would still be in Scotland, not in this awful place. I had to clean floors to supplement his wages. No one had to put up with what I had to. He held me back'.

I was momentarily dumb struck. Then an uncharitable thought entered my head – should I tell her what *he* had told me about *her*? Wisely, I allowed the moment to pass. I, of course, realised that in such times of grief people are unguarded, vulnerable and perhaps honest. And that, as with my father, my mother was not thinking or talking about their *total* life together, merely reacting to the pain of recent events. Yet I felt I was a witness to a great and unnecessary tragedy. Had they both sacrificed all their personal and interpersonal hopes, ambitions and desires, because of their children? No wonder I carried around such guilt.

I returned home and slept uninterrupted for twenty six hours. No sweet dreams.

My mother lasted for one year after my father's death. She never again uttered a negative or critical remark about my father, and only spoke about him in terms of loss and admiration. She would sit in the same chair in which she had always sat, alongside my father's chair. She told me he 'visited' her. 'We have little conversations, you know'. I asked her when she saw him – did he visit her at particular times? 'Mostly the evenings, when I feel especially lonely'. I asked her if he *suddenly* appeared, or whether he slipped into her presence slowly and unannounced. 'He's here all the time'. Obviously, a suitable case for treatment.

*

Following the spate of spiteful or, at best, deeply ambivalent obituaries ensuing from Ronnie's death I came to see at first hand how reputations are tarnished and distorted, and how people are symbolically crucified in the knowledge that they are not in the position to fight back or contradict. After his death, I became more determined than ever to continue and complete the biography. A few years earlier I had approached Ronnie with my idea, which was *essentially* to show the continuing relevance of his work. We met at Eton Road, and congenially discussed the project and how we might work together to achieve it. He sat, slumped in a capacious chair, displaying those well-known characteristics: he rolled his eyes upwards, spoke haltingly but with considerable precision, and we ended by sharing some whisky.

Together we met Gillon Aitken the literary agent who had taken over the reins of Ronnie's authorial career, both past and present. We drew up an agreement that I would receive two thirds of any proceeds from the sales of the proposed biography and Ronnie one third, in return for his full co-operation. All three of us agreed that there would be a clause giving me full and final editorial control. I was quite prepared to forgo *any* financial rewards just for the opportunity to work with, and learn from, Ronnie. That is how it began and how it continued for two years. Ronnie allowed me access to all of his correspondence, diaries – in which he wrote almost daily – rough and incomplete drafts of books, and lists of contacts, together with a letter confirming his blessing for any interview about him that his contacts might grant me. I casually asked him for the names of those people he considered would be *especially* significant, and the following day he produced a list of some four hundred individuals with the caveat that there would be more, when he had had more time to consider the matter.

Some of the interviews were revealing, some disappointing. Two remain memorable, both of which were conducted with the pair of well-known revisionist psychoanalysts, John Bowlby and Charles Rycroft. I had previously encountered Dr Bowlby when I was the associate producer on a series I created for television, based on his work and provocatively titled *Are Mothers Really Necessary?* The series explored his unpopular ideas on the importance of consistent *maternal* love and its relation to mental health which, he argued, was as important as vitamins for physical well-being. Scornful feminists were interviewed, including Germaine Greer, in addition to proponents of his ideas. And, of course, centrally involved was Dr Bowlby himself. He was filmed at the Tavistock Clinic, at his Hampstead home, at his summer home on the Isle of Skye and in those surroundings which symbolised his argument that psychoanalytic thought would benefit from an integrative relation-ship with ethology – namely the Royal Zoological Society lecture theatre and London Zoo. Indeed, Dr Bowlby had so infuriated the film crew with his Victorian arrogance that when a chimpanzee evacuated both its bladder and bowel over him, the event was greeted with ironic cheers.

When I visited John Bowlby to record his recollections of Ronnie, he did not recognise me. I told him that I'd lost a considerable amount of weight, so perhaps it wasn't so surprising that I appeared different. He firmly suggested that I must have been extremely depressed to have allowed myself to get so overweight in the first place. I told him that, actually, the weight had dropped off simply because I had stopped drinking alcohol. 'Exactly so, that's why you drank, because you were depressed'. I did not argue because I knew it was pointless. Dr Bowlby believed that almost every activity, except life in a nuclear family with well-differentiated roles, was *deviant*. We sat down and I asked him for an evaluation of Laing's work. He provided me with two different answers, one that was tape recorded and the other given when the machine was switched off. The former consisted of comments amount-ing to a degree of grudging admiration, the latter consisting of his belief that Ronnie was 'of course' mad. He delightfully elaborated with in-stances of his unconventionality, which obviously as far as Dr Bowlby was concerned, amounted to the same thing. He concluded that he felt that 'Laing could have been somebody' but that, with Kingsley Hall and *The Politics of Experience and The Bird of Paradise,* he had 'blown it'.

Dr Rycroft was hardly loquacious, citing the various rules of confiden-tiality to which he claimed to adhere. I showed him a letter from Ronnie inviting him to speak with me openly. However, he was determined to be taciturn in his response to my questions, though later he was some-what less reticent with other biographers. Repeatedly, whatever the precise wording of the questions, he would mutter that Laing was 'interesting'. After some Chianti he was somewhat more forthcoming and expressed more strongly-held views. Essentially these amounted to the fact that it was difficult to support or approve of a man who had left his children and his 'lovely wife' – his first wife, that is.

During the time I spent with Ronnie in London, Glasgow and Kitzbühel I experienced the gamut of his expressive behaviour and emotions. From profound empathetic understanding, to rage and verbal violence at my ignorance, from compassion for me and others we met together, to bouts of terrifying aggression towards both friends and strangers, especially while in Glasgow. On one such occasion a young Scottish journalist came to interview him in connection with the biography the journalist was compiling on Alex Trocchi, the Glaswegian anarchist. As the interview proceeded it was clear that the young man had not done sufficient homework and was, to an extent, wasting Ronnie's time, who launched into a tirade of abuse causing the journalist to flee the room. Another time he insisted I fight with him: thankfully, after a few bruising minutes, *he* conceded that *I* genuinely had conceded. However, three things really stick in my memory, in addition to his wicked black humour. Firstly, his sheer intellectual ability, the breadth of knowledge, the wide reading – and his courage to tell the truth. As with his interpersonal, social relations, he never trotted out socially acceptable answers to unpleasant questions. Instead, he replied with what he believed to be the truth of the matter, and this was of course invariably unique. As he would say to me repeatedly, he thought that there were *at least* two sides to most things. He chastised me for writing my book on Bowlby. He read it, and then demanded to know whether or not I thought that single mothers had suffered enough; whether I might be contributing to that suffering by repeating Bowlby's arguments, ensuring that these women would feel guilty whenever they left their children with baby-sitters. And when I told him that I was struggling to keep off alcohol he launched into a vitriolic attack on all twelve-step therapies and programmes of alcohol abstinence. 'If you wanna give it up, give it up!' No more, no less. And he had memorised and could quote obscure passages from innumerable authors, from Kierkegaard to Marx, and beyond. Secondly there was his *presence* when faced with disturbed or disturbing or distressed people. The times when we were with such people, usually patients and ex-patients of his, he showed no fear or anxiety when confronted with what I considered to be uncontrollable aggression, but simply generated calmness and compassion. As he often would say, even during his schooldays other children had sought him out for advice or support. Ronnie possessed a *presence*, an almost theanthropic mien which allowed other people, particularly those in distress, to feel safe and cared for. Finally, I always felt that while he was alive there was at least one person in the world whom I could approach and from whom I could seek advice when in need. I had come to believe there was nothing he would not be able to deal with, no taboo, no fear.

In the winter of 1989, I received a letter from Adrian Laing, who had previously declined to be interviewed by me, stating that, as he was now writing a biography I was to return all correspondence, diaries, manuscripts and any other material I had been given by his deceased father. This I was very reluctant to do. I, of course, still wanted to write the book. Adrian however applied pressure, as lawyers do, and so I acquiesced returning all the material, with the exception of the tapes of my conversations with Ronnie. Many hundreds of hours worth.

When Adrian's own book appeared in 1994 I felt obliged to utilise the tape recordings, firstly to clear my own name, given the unfavourable light in which Adrian described my transactions with his father, and secondly due to the less than generous nature of his biography. It is perhaps understandable that Adrian might well write such an ungenerous account, to avenge himself on a father who deserted his mother and, therefore, himself. However, one should remember that there are *other* children of Ronald Laing who have chosen to remain silent and who, perhaps, have many other and possibly different memories. Also and not insignificantly, I objected strongly to many of the arguments expounded by Adrian in his book. Moreover, the tapes would represent Ronnie's point of view, not Adrian's or mine. Accordingly I transcribed some of the many tapes, edited them and prepared a book for publication *Mad to Be Normal: Conversations with R. D. Laing.*

When the books had been printed and bound, and the cover designed by Jutta Laing, the publishers and I received a solicitor's letter suggesting that if we tried to publish the book we would be sued. A meeting was held between myself, Gill Davies of Free Association Books, Adrian

Laing and another solicitor from Simons, Muirhead and Burton, at their Soho offices. It was the conversational equivalent to walking in treacle. The advice we had received from our solicitors was that the copyright lay with the person who supplied the mechanical device which recorded the conversations. In this instance, myself. We repeated this mantra-like but to no avail. They were singing another song. We left, after a couple of hours, with Adrian's parting words ringing in my ears – 'You'll publish that book over my dead body'. Two weeks later it was in the bookshops and nothing more was said.

I was neither pleased with winning the battle with Adrian Laing nor was I content to allow bad feelings to fester. I felt there was an opportunity to heal wounds by offering to help get *The Lies of Love* published. I received a curt reply to the effect that Adrian felt he could not work with me after the 'piracy' I had engaged in, and that I was never to write to him again.

*

In January 1999, almost a decade after his death, I was invited to speak at a one-day conference dedicated to Ronnie's work, and held under the auspices of the Royal College of Psychiatrists. Again, we were haunted by the ghost of controversy. It was indeed surprising that the Royal College had even agreed to host the event: but what was less surprising – and more revealing – was that the College had been unable to elicit the support of any sponsor. Obviously, no pharmaceutical company wished to have its good name tarnished by sleeping with Dr Laing. His reputation had, again, preceded him. Even dead for ten years, he was still considered dangerous.

However, his lingering influence cannot save his vision of the Philadelphia Association, which by the late 1990s had moved increasingly further away from his original conception of it. In February 1999, Leon Redler, the only person to hold the position of Chairman other than R. D. Laing himself, found himself so disappointed by the direction the Association is currently adopting that he felt he had no option but to resign. In his letter of resignation Redler complains that the inspirational work of 'our co-founder and first Chair R. D. Laing, has, in my opinion, been insufficiently taken on board within the PA in the last two decades'. Almost entirely gone from the Association, he adds, are artists, poets, musicians, anthropologists, practices of yoga, martial and healing arts, and meditative and other spiritual practices.[18]

Similarly, the literature that allegedly deals with mental suffering and mental distress is conspicuous by its absence. Despite Laing's books being still available on city shelves, the serious intent of his work has been displaced by the genre of pseudo-self-help. For instance, John Gray has dominated the popular psychology lists, as Laing once did, with his tomes explicating the previously unknown fact that men and women are different. Men, he claims, are (metaphorically) from Mars, women from Venus. Gray is everywhere. Type in 'Marsvenus' on the Internet and up he pops on his 'Official John Gray World Wide Web Site', where you can learn how to buy his merchandise: John Gray books, John Gray videos and John Gray CD-Roms. There is nothing wrong with society and culture: simply *us*. We just have to learn how to 'help ourselves' – which we are led to believe we cannot do without the help of the ubiquitous John Gray.

How can the R. D. Laing *oeuvre* survive, let alone flourish, in an environment of the fifteen-minute attention span, the commercialisation of art, and the shameful marketing and purchase of books as mere commodities, irrespective of their intrinsic value.

Ronnie's major themes remained consistent throughout the thirty years in which he put pen to paper. He focused unwaveringly on existential and ontological issues – questions about the formation and preservation of identity; autonomy and freedom, and the attempts to restrict them; and questions concerning alienation and the possibilities of authentic existence, conformity and normality. Centrally, he never ceased to find new ways to address the question of the purpose of our existence. Ronnie also wrote about violence. Violence that often masqueraded as 'love'. Violence that is perpetrated by parents on their children, siblings on each other, man against woman, woman against man, generation against generation, major nations against smaller ones, the haves against the have-nots. Violence that ranged from un-requested kisses, lies and deceit, electro-convulsive therapy, to nuclear weaponry.

Love was also one of his main concerns. Again, a love which, Medusa-like, could turn itself into violence. Never once was he diverted from charting the shark-infested waters of love and betrayal: from the love of the family which is inadvertently persecuting its child; the love of the child who loves but does not receive love in return; the love of the lover who does not betray but is betrayed and broken.

Despite the cacophony of derision that greeted Ronnie's *The Facts of Life*, the book was as consistent as any of his other publications, with its focus on a tightly-knit series of investigations. Although extremely complex, these investigations can be summarised in the following manner. Ronnie's work was concerned with the possibilities of existential life or death-in the pre-embryo, the foetus, the infant, the child, the adolescent, the mother, the father, the brother, the sister, *ad infinitum*. Consistently, he investigated the manner in which such an individual's experience of self and the world around him or her – be he or she a pre-embryo or a twenty-three-year-old adult – may be in danger of invalidation from a number of other agencies: the expectant mother and her feeling, often her gut feeling, toward her pregnancy; a family's collusion (often unconscious) against a particularly vulnerable family member; the power of conformity exercised by socialisation agents like the educational system which, as a result, affects an individual's possibilities for authentic existence, often irreparably, and often for the rest of the individual's life.

Ronnie was most concerned with the mental misery suffered by so many, and *their* experiences of invalidation. But he did not stop there: mental suffering is one thing, being labelled a schizophrenic, treated in a particular manner and possibly incarcerated is quite another. He ceaselessly described the way in which the psychotic's utterances were comprehensible were we prepared to truly *listen*. Consistently, he described in considerable detail the way in which a schizophrenic was attempting to live in an unliveable situation. Ronnie believed in 'natural healing', allowing someone to live through their madness in the company of others who cared, allowing someone to be given time and space to be themselves. But, of course, his ideas have continued to meet with resistance despite, for example, evidence such as the fact it is estimated that eighty per cent of all depressions *cure themselves without treatment* given sufficient time.[19]

Kingsley Hall is, as he argued, an ongoing experiment despite its actual closure. The *idea* still exists and is as salient as ever. Our streets – New York, London, Los Angeles, elsewhere – are littered with those individuals in desperate need of asylum, sanctuary and protection.

Instead, imprisoned not within the walls of psychiatric hospitals, they are locked into themselves through powerful drugs and locked out of society by the effect of those very same drugs.

Orthodox psychiatry remains unchanged. Even ardent exponents of the neurobiological explanation of psychosis concede that not even one variety of schizophrenic disturbance has been adequately defined and accounted for.[20] Yet the treatments remain. There is no pause in the action. Orthodox conventional biologically-based psychiatry should perhaps be renamed *pharmadox* psychiatry given its profound reliance on the psychopharmacological industry. Psychiatrists continue to sentence their patients to an internal life of imprisonment, locked in by powerfully acting drugs, with no parole; ECT continues to be used on individuals despite the evidence that all recipients sustain at least some 'permanent' memory loss. Maybe psychosurgery will carve out an innovative future by resurrecting surgical practices from its past, and the brain will be butchered by a laser beam, as opposed to an ice-pick. Who knows what might be around the corner?

Eugene Bleuler, sometimes referred to as the 'father of modern psychiatry', was a decent man. Working at the Burghölzi Hospital in Switzerland in the late 1890s, he was confronted by archaic conditions. Communication with the patients was extremely rare, and the chances of their personal, day to day requirements being met was absolutely non-existent. Bleuler would, however, spend hours talking with the patients and began to think of schizophrenia 'from the perspective of the patient's subjective state'. Against the prevailing orthodoxy he believed that all of his patients had 'feelings and thoughts'.[21] Ronnie took such a perspective into another sphere of understanding altogether. Almost alone.

Of course there are psychiatrists who routinely attempt to demonstrate care and understanding, compassion even. But there are plenty who fail in this basic yet elusive sensibility. And besides, it is difficult for a person to speak openly and honestly, to relax and not feel persecuted, when faced with a psychiatrist whom they know, or imagine, or faintly fear, could treat them against their will, or even incarcerate them, or even maim them. I asked Ronnie if he thought he'd influenced the biological psychiatrists, like Sir Martin Roth, in any significant degree:

You think I've cut into the conscience of everyone that Martin Roth teaches? My work has not made the slightest difference – *in fact it's only entrenched them.* A number of psychiatrists have made it clear that the main value of my work was to wake up psychiatrists so as to *refute it.* To that extent, by acting as a gadfly, I had done a service in leading them to do more research as to the biological causation of this sort of disorder. They always use the word causation or aetiology, as if the more they repeat the word the more they prove that it's true.[22]

Johnny Duffy believed that Ronnie was the 'most *tormented man*' he had seen in his life. He believed that Ronnie had seen 'so much suffering, and he did his best to alleviate the suffering, but I think he felt he was not doing well enough'.[23] He felt frustrated about not being able to do more. Of course he was a tormented man: he dived in to the depths of his and others' minds; explored his and others' dark sides; and for over thirty five years *listened* to an unimaginable degree of human misery, pain, torment and despair. *And he tried to help.* There is a Talmudic proverb, variously translated, but essentially saying that 'one who saves one soul, has saved the entire world'. Ronnie gave everything in the service of others, and will be properly rewarded.

Graham Greene has written that 'writing is a form of therapy; sometimes I wonder how all those who do not write, compose or paint can manage to escape the madness, the melancholia, the panic fear which is inherent in the human situation'.[24] Ronnie Laing wrote for *himself*, but also for *us – you and me.* He wrote for us in an accessible language that we could understand, and even enjoy if we had the sensibility, because he thought there were things it was important for us to know, for us to think about.

Art, Ezra Pound would have it, is news that *stays* news. The art, wisdom and compassion of Ronald David Laing will persist because of the two fundamental arguments he cogently expressed, both through his books and in his person. That there was more to mental distress than solely biological, chemical and genetic factors, that personal experience and interpersonal relationships played significant roles in the creation of such mental states. And, more significantly perhaps, that for psychiatry to become more effective and more ethically acceptable it would have to truly and sincerely see the patient always as a human being.

Epilogue

February 1999. St Mary's Hospital, Paddington.

I am sitting in a cubicle in the Accident and Emergency Department, waiting to see a doctor. I have been waiting two and a half hours already, and the end doesn't yet appear to be in sight.

A young Asian man is led into the cubicle opposite me and told to seat himself at the small, grubby looking table. On her way out, the nurse pulls the curtain across. The curtain is very short, so I can still see him from the shoulders down. I can hear his breathing, quick and shallow; nervous, I think. A large man wearing a violently orange jumper and holding a clipboard enters his cubicle, and introduces himself as the duty psychiatric nurse. He talks clearly, although not especially loudly – the fact that I can hear everything he says has more to do with the declining Welfare State than the volume of his voice. The young man is called Aravinda, and he speaks little English. In fact, he speaks little, full stop, but when he does, his voice is quiet and wavering – 'please, please, please help me', he says, 'I am so frightened'. I am embarrassed to be a party to what should be a private interview, and I look away and count the stains on the curtain pulled half way across the front of my cubicle to ensure *my* privacy. But I can still hear the interview: 'on a scale of one to ten, Aravinda, with one equalling suicide and ten equalling happiness, where would you say you are, at the present moment?' Silence. 'Aravinda, Aravinda. I can't help you if you won't talk to me ... (pause) ... Aravinda, is someone trying to steal your thoughts? Do you feel that you have a person inside your head who is taking your thoughts?' 'Yes. Sometimes. I think so. I just want to sleep. I can't sleep. I can't sleep and I feel so *bad*'. The nurse interrupts Aravinda's flow, which surprises me, as it is the most this young man, no more than a boy, has said throughout the interview.

'Is there a voice inside your head telling you what to think, or to do?'
Silence.
'Aravinda, do you think you will try to hurt yourself?'
Silence.
'Aravinda, do you think you might try to kill yourself?'
Silence.
'Aravinda, I think you need to see a psychiatrist ...'

I see the orange jumper as it passes me, on its way out. I can see the boy, his head appears to be slumped forward, and I can hear him talking – 'please help me. I am so frightened. I can't sleep, I just want to sleep. I feel so bad, I feel so ashamed. I am bad, I am bad ...'

It is the dead voice of an automaton, and indeed that is how he has just been treated. If the (initial brief, but important) diagnostic interview were to be likened to brain surgery, it had been performed with the precision of a knife and fork.

*

At around the same time as *Wisdom, Madness and Folly* was published in 1985, I voluntarily admitted myself to a psychiatric hospital. I simply had had enough.

Drinking voluminous amounts of alcohol over almost two decades had left me befuddled, out of touch with myself, anxious and depressed, fearless and irresponsible. Many of my hours were spent in the comfortable realms of fantasy. My alcoholism was not of the type that necessitated early morning drinks, nor did it ever lead to violence, penury or homelessness. My father rarely drank, and when he did his limit was quickly reached, at which point he would sentimentalise, romanticise and fall peacefully to sleep. Only on one occasion did I witness a bizarre reaction, when he foolishly accepted a drunken challenge to drink seven pints of beer and then run backwards around a cricket field. He was peculiar for several days afterwards, once, that is, he'd been successfully resuscitated and returned home. My mother was, understandably, none too pleased and threw him the kind of glance that had always reduced me to a state of chronic anxiety and painful guilt.

The culture I was exposed to as a youthful and impressionable boy undoubtedly contributed to my problem, and I imagine so did the psychological strength I appeared to lack. None of my family were especially *strong* in that department, although my mother possessed tremendous courage and energy, and my father had compassion in abundance. Despite all the good will and familial support that circulated, we were also accomplished at unwittingly making each other feel inadequate. I emerged with no strong sense of self or well-defined identity. But in the same way that some people can drink to excess and do no harm, so equally some people drink to overcome the consequences of a less-than-perfect childhood. Besides which, I share the view that the relentless, dogmatic search for 'causes' may often be Sisyphean. I share the view that many of our problems are more the result of what has been termed 'tragedy' – the fortuitous nature of life – than any more deliberate or coherent choice, pattern or plan.

Whatever the reason, I had spent too long wreaking emotional havoc and had had enough. Following a consultation with my general practitioner I was admitted late one evening to my local psychiatric hospital. On admission, so drunk that I could barely see despite being fully conscious, I remember being told that I would receive some vitamin B and something 'to help me'. The following day, after a disturbed sleep during which I believed I was being murdered by the police, I was informed that the medication I had received was the anti-psychotic drug, haloperidol. Apparently, unbeknown to me, I had been somewhat manic on admission. It can accurately be said that for the rest of the day I was dazed and confused. I continued to be medicated, ate lightly, avoided the other patients – all of us wearing the same pyjamas – and was told by the male nurse that I would be kept in for the night, for a rest. By the time it reached mid-evening a sadness descended upon me which made me weep for myself, that I had sunk so low. Another nurse spoke kindly to me, followed by the visiting cleric whose presence merely induced a further bout of self-loathing, which had the beneficial consequence of some more haloperidol, followed by a more satisfactory sleep.

Fear accompanied the sadness when I awoke the following morning, more aware of my surroundings. After a brief visit to the breakfast table I spent the morning, which seemed to last for an eternity, in the same way as everyone else: shuffling around aimlessly and silently in highly-starched striped pyjamas. At first the occasional scream terrified me, but I soon became accustomed to the sound and, perversely, awaited it. It punctuated the silence. Although bleak, I felt it to be a safe and secure environment. The psychiatrist told me that my drinking was damaging my liver and my mind. I concurred. That I was, in his opinion, depressed. Again I agreed. But when he said I could go home panic set in. Bizarrely perhaps, I had somehow hoped that the hospital would help me, not return me to *myself*. 'We'll send a letter to your doctor'.

Desperate men seek desperate measures. I banged my head on the wall enough times for the nurse, and his assistant, to restrain and sedate me. Later I heard the voice of my own doctor who was signing the papers for me to be detained for twenty eight days under the appropriate section of *The Mental Health Act*. When the medication wore off, I felt consumed with sadness and guilt, and no longer secure. But I was intelligent enough to realise that my actions were not the actions of a 'normal' person which, immediately, increased my sense of shame.

Twenty seven days to go and I felt more aware of my shortcomings, more certain that I could take more responsibility for myself than ever before, and *absolutely confident* that I could terminate my drinking. When I asked if I could leave, citing my awareness and determination, I was told that the previous day's events were proof enough that I needed to stay. My frustration at this response and the subsequent arguments that ensued led, I believe, to an increase in the dosage of my medication. I certainly slept longer and woke the following day more subdued. Like everyone else, I mindlessly fitted into the routines.

For another week I did what was expected of me: ate, shuffled, bathed, shuffled, ate, napped, shuffled, ate, slept. This daily routine was only interrupted by the visitors I received who spoke to me as if I was terminally ill, and the psychiatrist(s) who asked me how I was. I always replied 'fine', and they always smiled.

Twenty one days until discharge. I was so bored that I bathed six times a day. The medication made me restless, or so it appeared, and there was no one to talk to, nothing to do. The only thing I looked forward to was the evening medication which helped me sleep. I spent a lot of the time crying in the toilet. No one had the time or inclination to discuss my thoughts and feelings. Sadness once again descended.

When there was still two weeks left on the Section Order, I asked the nurse if he would *please* let me see the consultant who had the power to release me – I just wanted to return to myself, to walk around bookshops, along streets, hear the radio. We met and talked. I was frightened and agitated, he was confident and impassive. Through steely eyes, almost motionless, he told me that normal people did not damage their heads through banging them against the wall. 'But I feel better now, it won't happen again'. 'I think you'll be better off here until you feel better'. 'But I *do* feel better'. Silence. I asked him what was wrong with me, what made him so certain that I was so abnormal and needed continued hospitalisation. Reluctantly he muttered the words 'borderline personality disorder'. I was then casually escorted from his office and returned to the ward.

Thirteen days until release. The following day I was visited by the registrar who informed me that my medication was being changed. I asked why, and what it was? 'Don't worry, it'll help'. I was too tired and too disheartened to quarrel. Whatever it was, it appeared to act quickly. Within hours I began to feel heavy in my body and when I walked, from the bed to the toilet and back again, I felt as if my feet were extra large and as if I were walking in a glue-like substance. I became terrified that I was losing my mind. At the same time I felt frightened, it appeared to me as if everyone else were laughing at me. Thankfully I slept soon afterwards and the following day I simply became acclimatised to what I knew then were simply the effects of a new drug.

The registrar called on me again. He was somewhat more talkative, and spent at least ten minutes with me, over which time I told him about my mother and my fears about what she had herself had endured, namely ECT. 'It won't happen to me, will it?' He was neither able to give me a straight answer nor was he able to look me in the eye. 'I'll make a note of it', was all he could muster.

For almost two more frustrating and pointless weeks I took my medicine, lived in fear of being given ECT and then left with barely a goodbye. I never had *one* conversation with anyone, nurse or psychiatrist, about the reasons why I had arrived there in the first place, or my own feelings about why I drank and felt so awful, so sad, guilty, and full of shame.

Daylight almost blinded me. On my return to University my colleagues treated me with either sympathy which, inevitably, made me feel sadder, or with caution as if I were capable of dangerous and unpredictable behaviour. I continued to drink. When my own doctor read the psychiatric report he laughed out aloud.

Less than one year later, I felt even worse. My self-loathing reached new heights, though I successfully concealed this emotion from others. One afternoon, I once again decided I had had enough. I felt that death itself was too good for me, but suicide was what I deserved. Such was my muddled thinking. Dvorak's *Cello Concerto* increased my sadness, but photographs of my children ensured that I couldn't take my own life. They were far more important than the triviality of my pain. I drank and drove. But where to go? I knew the hospital would provide no sanctuary and besides, with my record, they might be harder on me the second time around. These were my thoughts.

Quite by chance, driving aimlessly with tears and mucous streaming down my face, beer in my belly, I arrived at a convent. With drink-sodden bravado I knocked on the door, and entered. Inside was silence. And cleanliness. Eventually, a small woman, a nun in her forties perhaps, sat the other side of a grille, somewhat like a confessional. I poured my heart and conscience out to her, told her of my lack of belief *in anything,* and of my utter self-hatred. Three hours of this and I was a little calmer. 'But how could *you* understand', I provoked her. She then told me that *she* was receiving counselling after a breakdown, precipitated by her belief that she had fallen in love with a fellow sister.

On arrival at my own doctor's surgery I burst into tears. 'I have to give in drinking'. He held me and gently stroked my back. By pure chance, if such things exist, he knew the *only* clinical psychologist in the region who worked psychotherapeutically on the National Health Service. While I awaited my first appointment I stopped drinking. After a week or so of feeling physically unwell, I began to experience terrible states of mind between sleeping and waking. Invariably these experiences involved large terrifying animals creeping up the bed from the bottom making their way to my face. To consume me.

My therapist had an angelic face. She was actually a Buddhist. She made it absolutely clear from the beginning that she was 'on my side'. She had no interest in trying to 'figure anything out', she simply allowed me to talk, offered comments and insights from time to time, and tried to reassure me that I would be all-right. She was my friend, or at least she enabled me to think she was. I don't know if she had that metamorphic, chameleon-like ability to be all things to all men, but she provided me with what I needed at that time; someone who was immutably on my side, who would not judge, who could let me talk, ramble, gibber if necessary, until I had expunged, expurgated and exorcised my torment. With her, I had true communication – communion even. After a year, no dramas, no moments of enlightenment or conversion, she suddenly said – 'I don't think we can go any further. The next step is a spiritual one'. I left. She eventually, with the courage of her convictions, left her chosen profession and became ordained at an isolated Buddhist monastery where she remains.

I still experience unusual states of mind. I know that I am slightly paranoid. I overwhelm myself and others with my jealous feelings. I can occasionally fall into the clutches of hopelessness but, thankfully, it lasts merely a short time. I can wake up unbelievably sad. Tired beyond belief. But as long as there is *human warmth* in the world, in *my* world, it will be all-right.

*

I am more an 'alarmist' than a hypochondriac, though I am that too. It is not that I think I am always ill, rather that when I *am* ill, I fear the worse: a headache is a brain tumour, a stiff neck meningitis, a cold, the flu. Since my days of alcohol I have suffered a mild form of aphasia, or word blindness. This is not, I have been persuaded, a terminal illness, rather an unpleasant and at times inconvenient psychological befuddlement. It started at King's Cross railway station when I could 'see' the list of destinations posted on the board, but could not 'speak' the words which were their names. I could not pronounce their names either publicly or silently to myself. Within a few moments this confusion left me and I was able to continue life as before. I have suffered the same sensation on several occasions since then, sometimes with a period of years between episodes, but each experience has been more painful than the last. Once I literally went blank and could not remember my name, could not attach words to the objects around me, and felt increasingly that I was losing my mind. A friendly doctor reassured me that I was neither suffering a stroke, given my relatively youthful age and general good health, nor did I have a brain tumour or anything like it. An electroencephalograph confirmed that neurologically I was basically sound, so it was a case of shrugged shoulders. Only once since the early days of this malaise have I seen another physician who, again reassuringly, told me that it was almost certainly anxiety and that I was not to worry.

If they are right, and I can only hope that they are, the experience verifies, for me at least, the stupendous power of the mind, of psychological processes and of the perniciousness of anxiety. If Ronnie were alive I would tell him about my symptoms. He would smile, stare at me over the top of his reading glasses, and in that quiet, reassuring voice tell me that I almost certainly have a brain tumour, most likely inoperable and probably fast-growing. And then he would laugh aloud and say, 'Oh, for fuck's sake!'

Notes

Chapter One

1. Clay(1996), p.12. Although I disagree with many of their interpretations and arguments, I have found the biographies of Laing by John Clay, Daniel Burston and Adrian Laing invaluable.
2. Burston (1996), p.12.
3. Laing (1986), p.35.
4. Laing (1967), pp.143-44.
5. Laing (1967), pp.146-47.
6. Artaud (1948), p.46.
7. Vincent (1997), p.65.

Chapter Two

1. Laing (1986), p.87.
2. See Robert Youngson and Ian Schott's *Medical Blunders*.
3. Burston (1996), pp.30-31.
4. Laing (1994), p.47.
5. Clay (1996), p.44.
6. Laing (1986), p.98.
7. Laing (1986), p.96.
8. Quoted in Vincent (1997), p.84.
9. Vincent (1997), pp.79-82.
10. Vincent (1997), p.87.
11. Duffy (1997), p.99.

Chapter Three

1. Barrett (1967), p.3.
2. Macquarrie (1972), p.13.
3. Lomas (1968), p.119.
4. Quoted in Macquarrie (1972), p.15.
5. Macquarrie (1972), p.21.
6. Laing, in Mullan (1995), p.314.
7. Laing, in Mullan (1995), p.149.
8. See Mullan (1987), p.33.
9. Laing, in Mullan (1995), p.347.
10. An opinion expressed by all Laing's biographers, Burston, Clay and Adrian Laing.

11. Clay (1996), p.68.
12. Quoted in Burston (1996), p.51.
13. Laing (1965), p.17.
14. Laing (1965), p.38.
15. Lomas (1968), p.121.
16. Laing (1965), p.192.
17. Laing (1965), p.200.
18. Laing (1965), p.200.
19. Laing (1965), p.189.
20. Laing (1965), p.205.
21. Laing (1965), p.202.
22. Huxley (1977: orig 1954), p.111.
23. Semyon (1997), p.189.
24. Clay (1996), p.115.
25. Laing, Phillipson and Lee (1996), p.3.
26. Bateson, Jackson, Haley and Weakland (1956), p.762.
27. Clay (1996), p.89.
28. Laing and Esterson (1964), p.13.
29. Laing and Esterson (1964), p.120.
30. Laing and Esterson (1964), p.124.
31. Laing and Esterson (1964), p.124.
32. Laing and Esterson (1964), p.128.
33. Laing and Esterson (1964), p.128.
34. Laing and Esterson (1964), p.129.
35. Laing and Esterson (1964), p.130.
36. Clay (1996), p.106.
37. Laing, in Mullan (1995), p.281.
38. Laing and Esterson (1990), p.x.
39. Clay (1996), p.95.
40. Laing and Cooper (1964), p.6.
41. See Laing (1967).
42. See Clay (1996), p101.
43. Russell (1992), p.176.
44. Burston (1996), p.75 and Clay (1996), p.119.
45. Laing (1965), p.12.

Chapter Four

1. Mosher (1997), p.2.
2. See Ciompi (1997).
3. Jensen (1997), p.295.
4. See Burston (1996).
5. Personal communication, Leon Redler.
6. Laing (1986), p.26.
7. Laing, in Mullan (1995), p.188.
8. Goldblatt (1997), p.273.
9. See the account by Thompson (1997), pp.333-37.

10. Laing (1967a), p.16.
11. Laing (1967a), p.19.

Chapter Five

1. Laing, in Mullan (1995), p.271.
2. This certainly is Burston's view.
3. Laing (1967), p.11.
4. Laing (1967), pp.22-3.
5. Laing (1967), p.23.
6. Laing (1967), p.24.
7. Laing (1967), p.26.
8. Laing (1967), p.87.
9. Laing (1967), p.91.
10. Laing (1967), p.93.
11. Laing (1967), p.95.
12. Laing (1967), p.101.
13. Laing (1967), p.101.
14. Laing (1967), p.110.
15. Laing (1967), p.112.
16. Laing (1967), p.124.
17. Laing (1967), p.136.
18. Laing (1967), p.137.
19. Laing (1994), p.132.
20. Laing (1967), p.147.
21. Laing (1967), p.155.
22. Styron (1991), p.66.
23. Laing, in Mullan (1995), p.317.
24. Laing, in Mullan (1995), p.324.
25. Laing, in Mullan (1995), p.318.
26. Laing, in Mullan (1995), p.319.
27. Laing, in Mullan (1995), p.322.
28. Laing, in Mullan (1995), p.329.
29. Laing, in Mullan (1995), p.329.
30. I have learned much about this and other matters, from my friend Leon Redler.
31. Laing, in Mullan (1995), p.331.
32. See Acutt's beautifully written account – Acutt (1997).

Chapter Six

1. Laing (1971), p.20.
2. Laing (1971). Also published as *Intervention in Social Situations*, CBC: p.9.
3. *Intervention in Social Situations*, p.16.
4. Reproduced in Laing (1976a), *Do You Love Me?*
5. Laing (1970), p.i.
6. Laing (1970), p.4.
7. Laing (1970), p.23.

8. Burston (1996), p.113.
9. Laing, in Mullan (1995), p.350.
10. Esslin (1997), p.17.
11. Burston (1996), p.95.
12. Burston (1996), p.109.
13. Laing, in Mullan (1995), p.237.
14. Laing, in Mullan (1995), p.242.
15. Laing, in Mullan (1995), p.243.
16. Laing, in Mullan (1995), p.249.
17. Laing (1994), p.157.
18. Laing, in Mullan (1995), p.299.
19. Burston (1996), p.123.
20. Clay (1996), p.172.
21. Durden-Smith (1989), p.209.
22. Laing, in Mullan (1995), p.77.
23. Laing, in Mullan (1995), p.78.
24. Clay (1996), p.163.
25. Laing (1994), p.166.
26. See the many works of Rank, especially *The Trauma of Birth*.
27. Clay (1996), p.168.
28. Laing (1994), p.210.
29. See de Villeneuve (1997), pp.111-15.
30. Laing (1994), p.180.
31. Laing, in Mullan (1995), p.356.
32. Quoted in Puner (1978), p.270.
33. Laing (1976), p.151.
34. Laing (1976), p.150.
35. Laing (1976), p.42.
36. Laing (1976), p.24.
37. Laing (1976), p.41.
38. Laing (1976), p.49.
39. Laing (1976), p.57.
40. This is one of Burston's (1996) *many* criticisms of *The Facts of Life*.
41. Laing (1976), p.26.
42. Laing (1976a), p.12.
43. Laing (1976a), p.15.
44. Laing (1976a), p.49.
45. Laing, in Mullan (1995), p.301.
46. Laing (1994), p.192.
47. Laing, in Mullan (1995), p.56.
48. Laing, in Mullan (1995), p.58.
49. Laing, in Mullan (1995), p.47.
50. Laing (1978), p.2.
51. Laing (1978), p.10.
52. Laing (1979).
53. Laing (1979).
54. Laing (1979).

55. Annemarie Schimmel's *Mystical Dimensions of Islam*, is the nearest a *reader* can get to understanding Sufism.

56. Laing (1994), pp.153-54.

57. Humphreys (1951), p.159.

58. Huxley (1994: orig 1946), p.98.

59. Huxley (1994), p.100.

60. Huxley (1994), p.104.

61. Huxley (1994), p.107.

62. Huxley (1994), p.108.

Chapter Seven

1. Laing, quoted in Capra (1997), p.289.

2. Clay (1996), p.199.

3. Laing (1982), p.25.

4. Laing (1982), p.27.

5. Laing (1982), p.49.

6. Laing, in Mullan (1995), p.344.

7. Edgar (1997), p.28.

8. See Sünkel (1997).

9. Kahr (1994).

10. Crowe (1997), p.123.

11. Laing (1986), p.146.

12. Laing (1986), p.8.

13. Laing (1986), p.5.

14. Laing (1986), p.7.

15. Laing (1986), p.14.

16. Laing (1986), p.19.

17. See James Fenton (1983) *The Memory Of War*, Penguin, p.75.

18. Laing (1986), p.23.

19. Laing (1986), p.29.

20. Clay (1996), p.229.

21. Clare (1997), p.3.

22. Clare (1992), p.37.

23. Words by Henry Miller and music, Joseph Skelly. See also *The Parlour Song Book*, edited Michael Turner, Michael Joseph:London, 1972.

Chapter Eight

1. Steven Gans, unpublished paper, 'Awakening to Love: Ronnie Laing's Phenomenological Therapy', 1999.

2. Laing, Phillipson and Lee (1966), p.34.

3. Laing (1976a), p.23.

4. Laing (1979).

5. *The Challenge of Love*, also known as *The Lies of Love*, remains unpublished. Laing (1989), p.7.

6. Laing (1989), p.9.

7. See Gans (1999).
8. Gans (1999), p.22.
9. Laing (1999), no page number.
10. Beecher-Moore (1996), p.248.
11. Laing, in Mullan (1995), p.342.
12. Marguerita *Laing* (1997), p.142. This is how *she* describes herself.
13. Marguerita Laing (1997), p.142.
14. Marguerita Laing (1997), p.143.
15. Duffy (1997), p.102.
16. Laing (1994), p.15.
17. Burston (1996), p.145.
18. Personal communication, Leon Redler.
19. Wolpert (1999).
20. See Muselam (1990), in Burston (1996).
21. Cromwell (1993), p.3.
22. Laing, in Mullan (1995), p.378.
23. Duffy (1997), p.102.
24. Graham Greene (1981) *Ways if Escape,* Penguin: London, p.211.

Bibliography

Acutt, Michael (1997), pp.181-83, in Mullan ed.(1997).

Barnes, Mary (1997), pp.417-18, in Mullan ed.(1997).

Barrett, William (1967) *Irrational Man*, Heinemann: London.

Bateson, Gregory, Jackson, Don D., Haley, Jay and Weakland, John (1956) 'Toward A Theory Of Schizophrenia', *Behavioral Science*, Volume 1(4), pp.251-64.

Beecher-Moore, Nan (1996) 'Psychosynthesis', pp.241-58, in Mullan, Bob ed.(1996) *Therapists on Therapy*, Free Association Books: London.

Burston, Daniel (1996) *The Wing of Madness*, Harvard University Press: Cambridge, Massachusetts.

Capra, Fritjof (1997), pp.278-90, in Mullan ed.(1997).

Ciompi, Luc (1997) 'The Soteria Concept', Lecture given at the 93rd Annual Meeting of the Japanese Society of Psychiatry and Neurology, Tokyo, 29-31 May 1997.

Clare, Anthony (1992) *In the Psychiatrist's Chair*, Heinemann: London.

Clare, Anthony (1997), pp.1-3, in Mullan ed.(1997).

Clay, John (1996) *R. D. Laing: A Divided Self*, Hodder: London.

Cooper, David ed. (1968) *The Dialectics of Liberation*, Penguin: London.

Cromwell, Rue L. (1993) 'Heritage of the Schizophrenic Concept', pp.3-13, in Cromwell, Rue L. and Snyder, C. R. eds. (1993) *Schizophrenia*, Oxford University Press:London.

Crowe, Victoria (1997), pp.116-25, in Mullan ed.(1997).

Duffy, John (1997), pp.97-110, in Mullan ed. (1997).

Durden-Smith, Jo (1989), in Green, Jonathan (1989) *Days in the Life*, Minerva:London.

Edgar, David (1997), pp.26-29, in Mullan ed. (1997).

Esslin, Martin (1997), pp.15-19, in Mullan ed.(1997).

Goldblatt, David (1997), pp.270-75, in Mullan ed.(1997).

Humpreys, Christmas (1951) *Buddhism*, Penguin: London.

Huxley, Aldous (1977: orig 1954) *The Doors of Perception* and *Heaven and Hell*, Grafton: London.

Huxley, Aldous (1994: orig 1946) *The Perennial Philosophy*, Flamingo: London.

Jansen, Elly (1997), pp.295-303, in Mullan ed. (1997).

Kahr, B. (1994) 'R. D. Laing's Missing Tooth', *Journal of the Society for Existential Analysis*, Volume 5.

Laing, Adrian (1994) *R. D. Laing*, Peter Owen: London.

Laing, Marguerita (1997), pp.132-43, in Mullan ed.(1997).

Laing, R. D. (1965) *The Divided Self*, Penguin: London.

Laing, R. D. (1967) *The Politics of Experience and The Bird of Paradise*, Penguin: London.

Laing, R. D. (1968) 'The Obvious', pp.13-33, in Cooper, ed. (1968).

Laing, R. D. (1970) *Knots*, Penguin: London.

Laing, R. D. (1971) *The Politics of the Family*, Tavistock Publications: London.

Laing, R. D. (1976) *The Facts of Life*, Pantheon: New York.

Laing, R. D. (1976a) *Do You Love Me?*, Penguin: London.

Laing, R. D. (1978) *Conversations with Children*, Penguin: London.

Laing, R. D. (1979) *Sonnets*, Michael Joseph: London.

Laing, R. D. (1982) *The Voice of Experience*, Pantheon: New York.

Laing, R. D. (1986) *Wisdom, Madness and Folly*, Macmillan: London.

Laing, R. D. and Esterson, A. (1964: 2nd ed.1990) *Sanity, Madness and the Family*, Penguin: London.

Laing, R. D. and Cooper, David (1964) *Reason and Violence: A Decade of Sartre's Philosophy, 1950-1960*, Pantheon: New York.

Laing, R. D., Phillipson, H., and Lee, R. (1966) *Interpersonal Perception: A Theory of Method and Research*, Tavistock Publications: London.

Lomas, Peter (1968) 'Psychoanalysis – Freudian or Existential', pp.116-45, in Rycroft ed.(1968).

Macquarrie, John (1972) *Existentialism*, Penguin: London.

Mosher, Loren (1997) 'R. D. Laing and Alternatives to Mental Hospital', paper delivered at the conference *In the Wake of R. D. Laing*, London, May 11 1997.

Mullan, Bob (1987) *Are Mothers Really Necessary?*, Weidenfeld: New York.

Mullan, Bob (1995) *Mad to be Normal: Conversations with R. D. Laing*, Free Association Books: London.

Mullan, Bob (1996) *Therapists on Therapy*, Free Association Books: London.

Mullan, Bob ed. (1997) *R. D. Laing*, Cassell: London.

Russell, Roberta (1992) *R. D. Laing and Me: Lessons in Love*, Hillgarth Press: Lake Placid.

Rycroft, Charles (1968) 'Introduction: Causes and Meaning', pp.7-22, in Rycroft ed. (1968).

Rycroft, Charles ed. (1968) *Psychoanalysis Observed*, Penguin: London.

Schimmel, Annemarie (1975) *Mystical Dimensions of Islam*, University of North Carolina Press: Chapel Hill.

Semyon, Mina (1997), pp.184-209, in Mullan ed.(1997).

Styron, William (1991) *Darkness Visible*, Jonathan Cape: London.

Sünkel, Sue (1997), pp.211-213, in Mullan ed. (1997).

Thompson, Michael (1997), pp.325-39, in Mullan ed.(1997).

Villeneuve, Jan de (1997), pp.111-15, in Mullan ed.(1997).

Vincent, Marcelle (1997), pp.65-88, in Mullan ed.(1997).

Wolpert, Lewis (1999) *Malignant Sadness: the Anatomy of Depression*, Faber: London.

Index